# THE RECIPE

# WRITER'S

# HANDBOOK

Revised and Expanded

# The Recipe Writer's Handbook

Revised and Expanded

Barbara Gibbs Ostmann
and Jane L. Baker

Foreword by Antonia Allegra

WILEY

JOHN WILEY & SONS, INC.

Copyright © 2001 by Barbara Gibbs Ostmann and Jane L. Baker. All rights reserved
Published by John Wiley & Sons, Inc.

Published simultaneously in Canada

*Library of Congress Cataloging-in-Publication Data*

ISBN-13: 978-0-471-40545-0
ISBN-10: 0-471-40545-0

*Book design & photography by Richard Oriolo*

PRINTED IN THE UNITED STATES OF AMERICA.
11

To the memory of my mentors in the kitchen—my mother, Ernestine Kelly Lietwiler, and my grandmother, Eva Sue Lietwiler—whose culinary skills continue to inspire me.

—JLB

To the memory of my grandmother, Sophronia Armilda Conner Gibbs, who baked the best biscuits in the world by adding ingredients to the flour in her blue graniteware biscuit bowl until the mixture looked and felt just right. To my mother, Virginia Dell Oliver Gibbs, whose coconut cream pie can't be beat. And to the memory of my beloved father, Rex Gibbs, who enjoyed fly fishing, squirrel hunting, vegetable gardening, and cooking.

—BGO

# Contents

**Chapter Five:** Cooking Terminology       135

**Chapter Six:** Preferred Spelling of Commonly Used Food Words       165

**Chapter Seven:** Generic Terms for Brand Names and Trademarks       181

**Chapter Eight:** Metrics       191

**Chapter Nine:** Nutrition Analysis of Recipes       203

**Chapter Ten:** Copyright, Plagiarism, and the Ethics of Recipe Writing       211

**Chapter Eleven:** Recipes for Radio, Television, and the Internet       215

**Chapter Twelve:** Purchasing Information       231

THE FIRST TIME I WAS asked to write a foreword to Barbara
Ostmann and Jane Baker's *Recipe Writer's Handbook,* I was delighted to
do so. The book was a much-needed guide for food professionals: magazine and newspaper writers, food editors, cookbook authors, recipe
testers . . . anyone who needed help translating the act of cooking food
into words on a page in a cogent and intelligent fashion. For my colleagues and myself, the book has remained a constant source of information, and it has provided an ideal wealth of recipe-writing details for
beginning food writers as well.

With this new edition, Baker and Ostmann have expanded on the
original material to make *The Recipe Writer's Handbook* even more help-

ful than it was before. All the essential material is here—enlarged and modernized—to make life easier for the professional and more helpful to the reader: an understanding of the art of recipe writing, codified instructions for the various parts of a recipe, resources, style rules, definitions of terms, measurements, equipment, even ethics.

Included in this new edition are instructions and metric measures for all English-language recipes, thus making this the global guide for recipe writers above and down under the equator. There is also attention to detail in the expanded style sheet, which has added sample recipes for children's and food service/large-quantity recipes. Writing for television, radio, or the Internet? You will learn innovative directions for all those specialties within that updated, greatly enlarged chapter.

For those who hold that the heart of fine recipe writing is recipe testing, put on your apron and run, don't walk, to Chapter Four for insights on such key issues as judging target audience, doubling recipes on paper and in reality, how to deal with testing/writing about ethnic ingredients, as well as measuring foods with variable volumes such as some fruits and vegetables and pastas. There is no question that by observing the recipe-testing and writing instructions, you will create recipes crystalline in style, leading toward successfully prepared and cooked foods.

Cookbooks sprawl along the walls of my kitchen and home, silently speaking of my passion for the written word when it comes to eating, cooking, and learning about the people of the world through food. But when it comes to writing about that passionate interest, I turn to the small square bookshelf beside my computer. Four books stand like ready sentinels in that collection: a dictionary, a synonym finder, a collection of stories by food/life essayist M.F.K. Fisher, and *The Recipe Writer's Handbook*. My wish is that this definitive work brings clarity and insight to you and imparts the true pleasure of writing recipes to a food-loving audience.

—Antonia Allegra, past President, International Association of Culinary Professionals, and Director, Symposium for Professional Food Writers

One certainly cannot learn the technical details of cookery
entirely from books, but if the cooks of the past had believed
that written recipes were unnecessary, we should now be
in a sad plight indeed.

—Elizabeth David

WHAT IS THE SOUL OF a written recipe? There is a basic creativity
about recipe writing that balances the traditional verbal passage of
a culinary procedure with the scientific accuracy of a laboratory formula. Ideally, a recipe captures the essence of the food in question, as well
as the very culture of the dish and the personal interests of the recipe
writer.

Is there a magic to popular recipes? It seems to me that a good recipe
resembles a good joke. If you can quickly grasp the food concept and
repeat the method with relative ease, chances are the recipe will find a
niche in the culinary repertoire of cooks, be they experienced or novice.

As a result, some recipes, just like great one-liners, pass from generation to generation.

Behind the success of such recipes lies a detailed formula. In this book, Jane Baker and Barbara Ostmann present a complete range of recipe formulae. As a result of the authors' extensive research, this text turns the tables on most recipe experiences in order to teach the intimate elements of the recipe-writing art. In fact, the standard use of a recipe moves from the sourcebook—generally a cookbook—to the finished presentation at table. The pace here is reversed: Written recipes result from analysis and understanding of the food. By harnessing the names of a basketful of ingredients, listing amounts for culinary preparation, and describing cooking methods in brief detail, the recipe writer can best understand and describe the process of cooking.

In a sense, the aims of a perfectly written recipe closely resemble the aspirations of a well-balanced life. Consider the key goals: order, clarity, accuracy, and style. One possible outcome of such goals achieved, whether related to life or to recipes, is longevity—given well-chosen input and a good measure of luck.

—Antonia Allegra
St. Helena, California

A RECIPE IS A CREATIVE VENTURE from start to finish. First, there is the innovative process of developing the recipe, then comes the process of writing the recipe in such a way that it can be successfully reproduced by others. This book is designed to help you take the recipe from the kitchen to the printed page. Within these pages, we share an accumulation of knowledge that spans more than 30 years.

We came by our knowledge through hands-on experience. In the mid-1970s, we became food editors at major metropolitan dailies with large weekly food sections. Our jobs involved combining stories, photos, and recipes into interesting sections for newspaper readers to use and enjoy.

Jane, with a degree in commercial foods and prior experience in the food industry, suddenly was immersed in the world of commas, colons, and typefaces. Barbara, with bachelor's and master's degrees in journalism, was cast as a food expert without ever having taken a foods class. The backbones of the newspaper business, *The Associated Press Stylebook* and the copy desk, were of little help to us in editing food copy, especially recipes.

Our desks were constantly flooded with recipes from food industry representatives, chefs, readers, freelance writers, cookbook authors, cooking school teachers, and various other food experts. A surprising number of these recipes were flawed—some too wordy, some too brief, and others just plain inaccurate. More than once we suspected a recipe had never been kitchen tested.

One thing that food editors learn quickly is that a mistake in a printed recipe is unacceptable. Readers let you know immediately if something is wrong. Printing a correction does little to placate the cook who wasted time and ingredients. The recipe has to be right the first time.

Using a reporter's common sense and an editor's approach to facts and accuracy, we painstakingly forged a style for what became award-winning food sections.

In the early 1980s, we began editing a series of cookbooks featuring food editors' and writers' favorite recipes. The task involved merging the diverse writing styles of more than 60 contributors per book into a consistent format that readers could easily understand and use, while retaining the personality of each contributor.

As the books evolved, we discovered that food writers often have trouble putting on paper the recipes they create at home. We could scarcely believe the condition of some of the recipes: ingredients out of order or missing, no can or pan sizes, no yields, vague instructions, no oven temperatures or baking times.

In addition, each book presented a unique set of style decisions. A cookbook on soups, for example, called for different ingredients and used different wordings from a book on cookies. Each new batch of recipes resulted in long lists of preferred spellings, common package sizes, and suggested wordings for frequently used techniques. We scribbled our ideas for a consistent style on scraps of paper and jotted notes in the margins of proofs.

Over time, we developed a distinct recipe-writing style, although much of the formula for the style was in our heads, not on paper. Our hallmarks became accuracy, consistency, and ease of understanding.

For many years, it seemed as though we were alone in the quest for well-written recipes. When we accepted the publisher's challenge to put our expertise into words, we discovered that other food professionals shared our frustration about the imperfect state of recipe writing.

As part of the research for this book, we asked food professionals to share their thoughts on what is a good recipe. What we received from the food community was an outpouring that mirrored our own frustration and highlighted the lack of easy-to-use recipe style manuals.

Our goal is to make this book a one-stop source of information that can be used by anyone who tests, writes, or edits recipes or plans to do so in the future. We hope it will come in handy whether you're working at your computer or in the kitchen.

With practice, you will develop your own style of recipe writing, which will vary from project to project. Whatever your style, be guided by two principles: accuracy and consistency.

Recipe writing is not a speculative venture; recipes are based on facts. You must be accurate about the ingredients used and the procedures necessary to prepare a recipe.

No matter what wording or what punctuation you use, or how you identify ingredients or utensils, be consistent. Use the same style for all the recipes that appear together, whether in a cookbook, newspaper column, brochure, or other publication.

Nothing that we share with you in these pages is as important as the principles of accuracy and consistency.

In this revised and expanded edition, you'll find even more of what you liked and used in the first edition. There are more entries in the style sheet, more sample recipes, a completely revamped chapter on recipe testing, greatly expanded purchasing information, and many more resource listings, including many international sources and a list of food writing courses and seminars.

Although the focus of this book is writing recipes for home cooks, we've added information on testing and writing large-quantity or professional recipes. Look in the recipe testing, sample recipes, pan sizes, and purchasing information sections.

You'll also notice a new focus on other English-speaking countries. We recognize that American English is not necessarily the same as

British English! Look for an added international element in the style sheet, metrics, resources, and the comments by food authorities throughout the book. We've also beefed up the chapter on recipes for electronic media with comments from experts in radio, television, and the Internet.

Recipe writing is a new art form. Our grandparents seldom used written recipes because recipes were passed down from parents to children by word of mouth. The last 25 years have seen a proliferation of written recipes. This is a trend that will undoubtedly continue as more and more people struggle to prepare food without the hands-on instructions or advice of parents and grandparents.

Our own grandmothers were classic examples of a bygone era. Marvelous cooks, they prepared delicious cakes and breads by adding a pinch of this and a dash of that. As a young child, Jane once watched her grandmother prepare the batter for one of her specialties—a homemade white cake with lemon filling and coconut frosting. "How much flour do you add?" asked Jane. "Until it looks just right," was her grandmother's reply.

We hope that the following pages "look just right" and give you the recipe for recipe writing.

## Note to Readers

As you use this book, you will undoubtedly come up with words, terms, and style questions that we didn't mention. If you think of items we should have included but didn't, or if you have suggestions for future editions, please send your ideas and comments to:

Recipes, Ink.
4467 Big Creek Road
Gerald, MO 63037 USA
573-764-4481
Fax: 573-764-2732
E-mail: barbostmann@yahoo.com
Web site: www.recipewritershandbook.com

The authors are available to teach workshops on the principles discussed in this book and can be reached at this address.

Acknowledgments

THE GROUNDSWELL OF SUPPORT FROM food professionals around the country as we worked on this book was overwhelming. Individuals, small businesses, and major corporations opened their files and shared their expertise with the future readers of this book. A heartfelt thanks to each of you:

- All those who contributed their thoughts on what makes a good recipe: Antonia Allegra, Elizabeth Alston, Elizabeth Baird, Melanie Barnard, Harriet Bell, Rose Levy Beranbaum, Sally Bernstein, Andrea Bidwell, Nancy Byal, Anne Byrn, Irena

Chalmers, Jennifer Darling, Sue Dawson, Susan Derecskey, Pip Duncan, Nathalie Dupree, Tui Flower, Betty Fussell, Allyson Gofton, Barbara Haber, Carol Haddix, Karen Haram, Joanne L. Hayes, Kate Heyhoe, Lauraine Jacobs, Madeleine Kamman, Lynne Rosetto Kasper, Susan Manlin Katzman, Aglaia Kremezi, Cecile Lamalle, Bonnie Tandy Leblang R.D., Elizabeth Luard, Robyn Martin, Ferdinand E. Metz, Fran McCullough, Carolyn O'Neil, Greg Patent, Susan Purdy, Rick Rodgers, Marie Simmons, Marlene Sorosky, Harvey Steiman, Bonnie Stern, Tina Ujlacki, Jeanne Voltz, Karen Weisberg, Loukie Werle, Chuck Williams, Kasey Wilson, and Diane Yanney.

- The companies and organizations that generously shared their style guidelines and other information: the American Egg Board, Better Homes and Gardens, California Tree Fruit Agreement, Canadian Living, Chicago Tribune, Chronicle Books, Country Home, Duyff Associates, Food & Wine, Kraft General Foods, General Mills, H. J. Heinz Company, Jerome Foods Inc., National Cattlemen's Beef Association, National Live Stock and Meat Board Test Kitchens, National Pork Producers Council, The Pillsbury Company, Restaurant Hospitality, Simon & Schuster, S. J. Thoms and Associates, Inc., Southern Living, University of Missouri College of Agriculture, Food and Natural Resources, Weldon Owen Inc. (for Williams-Sonoma Kitchen Library and Collins Publishers), The Wheat Foods Council, The Wimmer Companies, and Woman's Day.

- The many friends, colleagues, and family members who offered advice, encouragement, moral support, technical assistance, or other help: Darina Allen, Rosemary Barron, Marlys Bielunski, Carol Boker, Linda M. Braun, Roberta Duyff, Teresa Farney, Barbara Pool Fenzl, Patricia Driscoll Godfrey, Wendely Harvey, Beverly Hawkins, Natalie Haughton, Martha Holmberg, Sue Huffman, Marlene Johnson, Lynn Kinney, Robin Kline, George Laur, William LeBlond, Karen K. Marshall, Janet Myers, Marilyn Mook, Eleanor Ostman, Susan Lamb Parenti, Warren Picower, Suzanne Pingree, Ruth Pretty, Sue Rakes, Don Ranly, Linda Kay Rebstock, Susan Reynolds, Martha Hollis Robinson, Donna Segal, Rosemary Stanton, William Stringer, B. Mary Taylor, Sara Jean

Thoms, Lois Tlusty, Barbara Tropp, Sue Wakelin, Barbara Willenberg, Cici Williamson, Glenn Wimmer, and Irene Yeh.

- Julia Child and Judith Jones, senior editor at Alfred A. Knopf, who gave us sound guidance and practical advice at the beginning of this project.

- Maria Pallante, for her outstanding legal knowledge and skills.

- Alexandra Nickerson, for a useful index.

- Ralph Reese at Dial Publishing, who gave us the freedom to hone our editing skills on the nine cookbooks we have edited for him since 1987. We were subconsciously preparing for this book all along the way.

- Gretchen van Houten at Iowa State University Press, for her belief in this project, and Judi Brown, also at Iowa State, for her recognition of the importance of food journalism and for her patience.

- Pamela Chirls, Susan Wyler, Maria Colletti, and Tia Prakash of John Wiley & Sons, and Claire Thompson for sharing our vision for this book.

- Wil Ostmann and Leland Allen De Priest, whose love, patience, and support made this book possible.

- Last, but not least, the readers of our newspaper food sections, without whom we would never have learned the skills we attempt to share in this book. It is, ultimately, for them—and for readers of recipes everywhere—that this book has been written.

THIS BOOK IS INTENDED TO be an easy-to-read, easy-to-use manual. We expect most food professionals to use it while they are working, either at their computers or in the kitchen.

To simplify your search for information, items are listed in alphabetical order under several different headings, and there are many cross-references. The chapter introduction explains what is contained in that chapter and where to look for additional information.

We recommend that you begin by reading Chapter One, "The Philosophy of Recipe Writing," Chapter Two, "Recipe Writing Style," Chapter Four, "Recipe Testing," and Chapter Ten, "Copyright, Plagiarism, and the Ethics of Recipe Writing." This will give you a good overview of the many aspects of recipe development, testing, writing, and editing. It also will help you develop a mind-set for the many details necessary in every recipe. Then thumb though the other chapters to get an idea of the type of information each contains.

The more you use this book, the more easily you will be able to find information. If what you're looking for is not in one list, try another probable heading. For example, you can make a quick spelling check by consulting Chapter Six, "Preferred Spelling," get a detailed definition in Chapter Five, "Cooking Terminology," or see how to use the term in a recipe in Chapter Three, "The Style Sheet." We know the system works because we have used it in developing, testing, writing, and editing recipes.

Our goal is to make this book a one-stop source of recipe writing, editing, and testing information. We don't pretend to replace dictionaries, encyclopedias, and other reference books, however. If what you need isn't included here, check Chapter Fourteen, "Resources," for the names of food organizations, government agencies, and professional associations, and a list of suggested reference books.

# THE RECIPE

# WRITER'S

# HANDBOOK

Revised and Expanded

# Elizabeth Baird, Canada

Food editor, *Canadian Living* magazine, and television cook, *Canadian Living Television* on Life Network and *Canadian Living Cooks* on Canadian Food Network

I like to think of a recipe as your mother or grandmother at your elbow, leading you through a new experience. Practical by nature, mothers and grandmothers pass on time-honored tips about using leftovers and make-ahead stages. But what your mother and grandmother offer goes beyond times, amounts, and how-tos. They put all your senses into play: The nuts toast until they tempt your nose, the marmalade boils noisily, with popping sounds as it reaches setting point, biscuit dough looks ragged and shaggy just before you gather it into a ball, you feel the silkiness of a properly kneaded yeast dough. These are the points that make the cook really learn how to cook and not just watch the clock. Make the dish sound so irresistible, the story behind it so fascinating, that I will actually get up and head to the kitchen. Just as if my mother or grandmother had invited me there.

# Chapter One

# The Philosophy of Recipe Writing

JUST AS KITCHEN TESTING IS the key to a successfully prepared recipe, editorial testing is the key to a well-written recipe. Editorial testing? That's just a fancy way of saying you should literally think your way through a recipe, asking the same questions you would ask if you were in the kitchen.

Think about what you're writing. Does it make sense? Is it logical? Do the steps flow chronologically? Should the sauce, which is listed last, actually be prepared first so that it can simmer while the cook is completing the rest of the dish? Are all the ingredients accounted for in the directions? Is the condition of the ingredients clearly stated—at room temperature, chopped, cooked, thawed, drained?

It sounds almost too simple, but it works. And it's based on experience.

When one of the authors started her job as food editor for a major metropolitan newspaper in 1975, she was fresh out of college and had never taken a home economics course. She soon realized that in some ways her lack of a culinary background was a blessing.

In writing a recipe that was clear enough for herself to follow, she also was writing one that would be clear for any reader. Should the bread crumbs be dried or fresh? Should the pan be covered or uncovered? Are the canned beans drained or undrained?

By asking dozens of questions of her recipe testers, she was able to write clear, concise, complete recipes that provided all the information necessary for successful results without getting bogged down in the specifics of food chemistry or sophisticated terminology. With a reporter's common sense and an editor's approach to detail, she developed a recipe-writing style based on thinking her way through a recipe. You can do the same.

Many of the questions you need to ask when editorially testing a recipe are covered in Chapter Four, "Recipe Testing." Read that chapter carefully to develop a mind-set for the things you should include in a recipe, whether working in the kitchen or at the computer.

The recipe writer-editor needs the same information that can—and should—be gathered during the recipe-testing process. If you do not do the testing yourself, you should have the phone number of the recipe tester so you can call to resolve any questions.

## Never Assume Anything

Sometimes, such as when you're editing a wire story, there is no source to call. You can make many editorial corrections based on standard information (such as basic can and pan sizes) or by comparing the recipe in question with similar recipes to estimate approximate yields. But if certain aspects of a recipe are unclear and you have unanswered questions, don't pass them on and expect the readers to figure out what to do. They'll be on the phone asking those very questions—or, worse, in their kitchens, angry at your publication because they're having trouble with the recipe.

If a recipe is not clear and questions remain, use a different recipe. *Never assume anything,* in regard to either the ingredients and directions, or the reader's level of ability.

## Know Your Audience

Know your reader. How you write a recipe depends on the cooking experience of your target audience. Recipes for children or beginning cooks require more explanation than recipes for basic home cooks, and recipes for professional chefs need yet another approach.

An experienced reporter who was assigned to work on a newspaper food section did not know the difference in recipe writing between a lowercase t and an uppercase T (teaspoon and tablespoon, respectively). Needless to say, he didn't last long on the food beat. The point is that this reporter's level of knowledge may be typical of the people reading your recipes. Never assume knowledge on their part.

Phone calls we've received from readers illustrate this point. For example, a woman called to say she had a new oven. She wanted to know whether it was preheated. Another person complained that her cake had turned out gritty. Had we had that problem? In going over the ingredient list with the caller, we discovered that she had used whole eggs— shell and all.

Another caller had driven all over town looking for powdered sherry. She was furious that we had listed an ingredient that wasn't available. The recipe had called for dry sherry.

Other calls we've received include questions about how far to drop drop cookies, how to tell whether a pan is 9 inches, where to get a soup can of water, and whether the recipe would fit in the caller's yellow bowl.

Even before food safety became a critical issue, there were alarming calls. One cook had left a turkey on the kitchen counter for several days and wanted to know whether it was still OK to serve. "How could you miss a 20-pound turkey?" we asked. "I just didn't see it," she replied.

Most food professionals who answer consumer calls can tell similar stories. The point is that you must know your audience. Always keep foremost in your mind your audience's level of knowledge and sophistication, its access to ingredients, time constraints, food budget, and other key considerations.

## Accuracy and Consistency

Regardless of the audience, accuracy is paramount. Mistakes cost readers time and money and consequently can cost your publication a loss of goodwill. Food writers and editors put a great deal of effort into building a reputation for sound, accurate, reliable, workable recipes. One mistake can destroy reader confidence, wiping out years of hard work.

Consistency is a close second to accuracy in importance for the recipe writer. Once you decide how to specify an ingredient or spell a cooking term, be consistent. If you specify green onions in one recipe, don't call for scallions in the next. Style decisions such as these can vary from project to project, depending on the audience and the employer, but be sure that your nomenclature and style are consistent throughout the recipes in a particular project, be it a brochure, an article, or a book.

Clarity and conciseness go hand in hand with accuracy and consistency. Make each recipe as clear and easy to follow as possible. Don't get bogged down in elaborate explanations. If you're mired in a hopelessly complicated sentence, break it into several short sentences. The passage will be easier to read, understand, and follow. Although you want your recipes to be concise, you also need them to be complete. Don't sacrifice completeness for conciseness.

In some cases, style matters will be dictated by recipe-writing guidelines developed by a publisher or food company. By all means, follow your employer's preferred style. Always ask for a style sheet before beginning any major project—this will prevent your having to rewrite or adjust your recipes later.

If you have serious reservations about certain style decisions, discuss them prior to beginning the project. If you explain your reasons for handling matters of style in a particular way, the company might well accept your suggestions. In researching this book, we learned that many major publications don't even have written style guidelines. Such companies might welcome your input.

## Culinary Illiteracy

Several recent studies by national food companies have shown that an overwhelming number of today's recipe users are cooking illiterates—that is, they haven't learned to cook alongside their mothers or grandmothers, and they lack knowledge of what many food professionals consider basic food terminology and skills. These young adults, aged 25 to 30 years, are often called the "lost generation" in the kitchen.

A national food literacy survey, conducted in late 1990 by National Family Opinion Research, Inc., on behalf of the National Pork Producers Council, revealed some startling results. Although 90 percent of the 735 adults (aged 25 to 54) surveyed considered themselves good to excellent cooks, almost three-fourths of them flunked a basic 20-point cooking quiz. Only one person out of the 735 people surveyed received a perfect score on the multiple-choice, true-false test, which included such questions as:

- How many ounces are in one measuring cup?
- One stick of margarine or butter is equal to (a) 1 cup, (b) ½ cup, (c) ⅓ cup, (d) ¼ cup, (e) don't know.

A staggering 45 percent of respondents didn't know how many teaspoons are in one tablespoon. Most of the respondents expressed a desire to cook, but they cited lack of time and lack of basic cooking knowledge as the main reasons they didn't. However, 51 percent said they try a new recipe at least once a month, and 30 percent said they try a new recipe at least two to three times a month. When looking for recipes and cooking information, one-third of the respondents reach for a cookbook; one-third reach for the telephone to call a friend or family member; and about one-fifth take cooking classes.

Keep in mind that many people just like those responding to this survey are in your audience.

## Put It in Plain English

A mong the many frequently misunderstood cooking terms are *fold, sauté, braise, cream, dice, roast, deglaze, cube, blend,* and *pan-broil.* Instead of using these terms, describe the technique in simple words that are readily understandable to both novice and experienced cooks. For example, instead of saying "braise," say "simmer, covered." Many cooks frequently braise meat—they just do not use this term.

In Chapter Five, "Cooking Terminology," and Chapter Three, "The Style Sheet," we suggest terms to avoid and offer substitute wording. Like many of the guidelines in this book, these are not hard-and-fast rules. Often, there is no one right way. For example, although *ketchup* is the preferred spelling, if you want to spell it *catsup,* that's fine—just be consistent.

## Personalized Style Sheet

Y ou might find it useful to create a style sheet for each project or a personal style sheet of problem words. A style sheet can be as simple as scribbled notes on a sheet of notebook paper or as well organized as a photocopied form with spaces labeled alphabetically.

For example, if working on an assortment of beverage recipes, you might jot down can and bottle sizes of frequently used ingredients. For a collection of grilling recipes, make notes on food safety, marinades, and grilling times.

Decide on your preferred wordings or terminology for common procedures and list these phrases and terms. Note your decisions on spelling, capitalization, and hyphenation, and refer frequently to these notes to maintain consistency. During work in progress, a quick glance at the style sheet can clarify a fuzzy editorial memory. Another advantage is that should you need to turn a project over to another person, the style sheet will ensure that the project continues smoothly.

If you save these various style sheets in a folder, you will soon have the makings of a style manual, customized for the type of projects you frequently do.

## Recipe Format Study

Although some recipe-writing rules are considered universal, such as listing the ingredients in the order in which they are used, even such basics are open to dicussion.

A qualitative research study on recipe format, conducted in November/December 1992 for the Test Kitchens of the National Live Stock and Meat Board (now called the National Cattlemen's Beef Association) by Gatten & Company, produced results that challenge conventional wisdom. Although we do not endorse all of the results in our writing guidelines, they do provide interesting food for thought.

Eight focus groups in four cities across the country produced several general findings, including the observation that consumers lack confidence in their ability to cook. This lack of confidence limits their ability to make decisions regarding alternatives and substitutions, so all or most of the decision making should be taken out of recipe preparation. For example, if a recipe calls for a medium onion, consumers want to know that a medium onion is about 3 inches in diameter.

The study showed the following consumer preferences.

## Format/Recipe Style

- **Straightforward recipe name.** Consumers prefer names that clearly describe the finished dish rather than names that are fun and creative.

- **Ingredient breakout style.** The ingredient list is grouped according to recipe parts, such as filling, topping, sauce. The recipe is easier to read, is perceived as shorter and simpler, and shows the dish as a whole.

- **Numbered or bulleted preparation steps.** The recipe is easier to follow and appears simpler.

- **Easy-to-read large print with adequate spacing.** When a recipe is easy to read, it appears simpler and easier to prepare.

- **Photograph of finished dish.** Consumers have difficulty visualizing a recipe, so a photograph helps.

## Ingredient Listing

- **Meat listed as first ingredient.** Because meat (or fish, seafood, or poultry) is usually the main component and most expensive ingredient, it is an important factor in meal planning and grocery shopping.

- **All ingredients listed before the method.** The ingredient list provides consumers with a quick, easy-to-read pantry checklist and/or shopping list.

- **Readily available ingredients and/or ingredient substitutions.** The use of available ingredients encourages consumers to try a recipe. Substitution information decreases confusion and guesswork, thus ensuring consumer confidence in cooking and offering an opportunity to adapt the recipe to personal tastes.

- **Multiple measures for ingredients.** Giving more than one way to measure an ingredient (such as 1 small apple, about ½ cup chopped) decreases guesswork, thus ensuring confidence. It also provides clarification.

- Avoidance of abbreviated measurements. Spelling out units of measurement prevents confusion, improves readability, and encourages accuracy in measuring.

- Elimination of "divided" for multiple-use ingredients and "each" for repeat measurements of different ingredients. This decreases confusion, encourages accuracy, and helps prevent errors. The preferred form is to list each ingredient measurement separately.

## Preparation Directions

- Concise, but sufficiently detailed directions. A recipe should appear simple and easy to prepare. It should not confuse the reader, require guesswork, or offer inadequate guidance. Consumers want to be told what *not* to do, as well as what to do.

- Equipment specification. Specifying the exact equipment decreases the need for guesswork and helps to ensure consumer confidence.

- Preheating directions. Giving directions provides clarification and helps to prevent consumer frustration.

## Recipe Features

- Preparation time, cooking time, and/or marinating time specified at top of recipe. This information helps consumers decide whether to make the recipe and permits better planning of meal preparation.

- Nutrition information (particularly calories, cholesterol, fat, and sodium). There is an increased interest in this type of information among consumers.

- Number of servings per recipe and size of each serving. This information permits better meal planning.

## Greg Patent, USA

Author of *New Cooking from the Old West* and other books

The [recipe] headnote is like a beautifully wrapped gift—attractive and enticing, creating a sense of anticipation. A headnote can evoke a mood, a scene, a taste, or even a smell. It doesn't have to be long-winded, but it ought to stimulate the imagination and the taste buds. A headnote should have the power to transform. Armchair cooks know the effects of well-written headnotes. They transport the reader to places all over the world.

## Personal Style

Although we can provide some do's and don'ts for writing recipes, what we can't do is provide a universal formula that works in every case for every recipe. Nor would we want to. The charm of cookbooks and other recipe collections is the unique voice that comes through in each.

As Judith Jones, one of the country's most respected cookbook editors, told us when we prepared the first edition of this book, "I hope you're going to say to write recipes with some real feeling, not with a formula. There should be real writing—the readers should know there's a person there. You should observe what you're doing [as you prepare the dish], then let the readers know you've cooked it and you've been there. Tell them how the food is supposed to look and what is going to happen."

Harvey Steiman, cookbook author, radio show host, and magazine editor, agrees. "One of my pet peeves is recipes that lapse into instruction-ese," he says. "Except for model airplane builders, who enjoys following tedious instructions?"

The convoluted sentence structure and lack of articles that constitute what is often referred to as "recipe shorthand" put a barrier between the writer and the cook, he argues. Such stilted language, Steiman says, "implies that recipes are just a set of instructions instead of a creative process."

Recipes are indeed a creative process, for both the writer and the user. Many people read recipes and cookbooks for enjoyment, so writing style is almost as important as cooking reliability. Although certain basic information should be included in every recipe, the way you word this information can reflect your personal style and entice the reader. The headnotes on recipes provide an especially good place for the author's voice to shine through.

## Lauraine Jacobs, New Zealand

Contributing food editor, *Cuisine* magazine

Many's the time I've cooked inspirational creative food that has been enjoyed and eagerly devoured by those sitting around my kitchen table. "Write it down, Mum!" cries my son, but it's rare that I do, and the exact recipe is lost. I try to re-create the dish, and there's always a slight difference, whether it's a change of an ingredient, a different measurement, or just not the same creativity and attention. Rarely, without careful recording, can I repeat the dish. Recipe writing is a skilled task, and there's nothing more rewarding than the thought that something you have written is being devoured and enjoyed by others, in the spirit that you wrote it.

Chapter Two

# Recipe Writing Style

ACCORDING TO AN EDITOR AT Time-Life Books, "Recipe style is a quagmire." The purpose of this manual is to help you chart a course through this treacherous terrain. We begin with guidelines for the standard components of a well-written recipe; Chapter Three then presents the details in an alphabetical style sheet.

As will be evident, every rule has an exception. We note the varying schools of thought on major issues. Often, we indicate our preference and then give options that are equally acceptable. Armed with this knowledge, you can make your own decisions based on what works for the target audience of any given project.

These guidelines are constantly evolving. When we look at recipes we edited 10 or 15 years ago, we find that we can revise them, tighten them, and improve them. Don't let yourself get stuck using a format just because a recipe came to you in that form—put it into your own style of clear, concise wording.

Theoretically, a cook reads a recipe through before beginning to prepare it and, therefore, notes any secondary recipes, steps to do ahead, special equipment needed, and so forth. In reality, however, cooks often begin without thoroughly reading the recipe and discover halfway through the preparation that they don't have a necessary ingredient or pan or that they should have marinated the meat two hours earlier.

It is the recipe writer's responsibility to do much of the preliminary work for the cook. By anticipating difficulties and incorporating preparation tips and how-to advice, you can help the cook obtain a good result. Figure the appropriate measurements, plan the most logical and efficient order of preparation, suggest accompaniments, and give tips on substitutions and sources of unusual ingredients. Remember that nothing is too basic. Above all, never assume anything.

## Standard Components

The standard components of a recipe are the headnote or introduction, the title or name, the ingredient list, the method or directions, the yield, notes and/or variations, and nutrition information.

### The Headnote

The headnote, or introduction to the recipe, is what draws a reader into a recipe and gives a collection of recipes a personality. Not every recipe needs a headnote, but most successful cookbooks include headnotes to add interest.

A headnote can alert the reader to peculiarities in the recipe, mention special techniques or ingredients, give tips on presentation or preparation, acknowledge a source, or just tell a bit of the recipe's history or origin.

## Bonnie Stern, Canada

Owner, Bonnie Stern School of Cooking, and author of many cookbooks

My favorite recipes are user-friendly, casual ones that people really cook. I also enjoy reading exotic recipes that take forever to make and to find all the ingredients for, but they are another genre.

## The Title

The recipe title or name should be descriptive as well as interesting. It should attract the attention of the reader while providing information about the recipe. Avoid the use of brand names and flowery or cute words.

Keep in mind the future indexing of the recipe. A descriptive title will help the reader find the desired recipe.

Avoid using proper names in recipe titles. Instead, include any attribution in the headnote or in an acknowledgments section. Alternately, give the contributor's name below the title or at the end of the recipe.

## The Ingredient List

The ingredient list should state, clearly, the ingredients that are called for and the form they should be in.

- Spell out every term—tablespoons, teaspoons, pounds, ounces, and so on.

- Break up the ingredient list with subheads, such as "Crust," "Filling," and "Topping," to help simplify a lengthy recipe. In the method, use corresponding subheads, such as "For crust" or "For filling," to help the reader.

- List the ingredients in the order of use. Don't place the main ingredient at the top of the ingredient list unless it is the first ingredient used. (This is sometimes done in advertisements or on package labels by food companies to highlight their product, but it is seldom done in standard recipes. The recipe format study described in Chapter One showed a consumer preference for listing the main ingredient first, but this finding conflicts with established practice. Perhaps further studies are needed.)

- When the order of use makes no difference or when a number of ingredients are used at the same time, here are some suggested ways to list them:

  (a) In descending order according to volume, with dry ingredients first, followed by moist or liquid ingredients.

  (b) Light-colored ingredients before dark-colored items (so the same measuring spoon or cup can be used).

  (c) Ingredients needing similar preparation, such as chopping or slicing.

  (d) In order of preparation. For example, list citrus peel before citrus juice because you need to grate the peel before juicing the fruit.

  (e) By time factor. For example, if an ingredient needs time to thaw, drain, or soak, list that ingredient first.

- List each ingredient separately.

  1 teaspoon salt

  1 teaspoon white pepper

  1 teaspoon paprika

  NOT: 1 teaspoon each salt, white pepper, and paprika

- When listing the number and size of packages, cans, or bottles, do not use two numerals together, as in "1 6-ounce can"; this can lead to typographical errors and reader confusion. Instead, use parentheses to set off one of the measures. Decide whether you are going to put the size before or after the word "can" (or "package," etc.), then be consistent.

  1 (6-ounce) can tuna

  1 can (6 ounces) tuna

  2 (16-ounce) cartons yogurt

  2 cartons (16 ounces each) yogurt

**½ (8-ounce) can tomato sauce**

**½ of an 8-ounce can tomato sauce**

Do not say "½ can (8 ounces) tomato sauce," because this wording is unclear as to whether the can is 8 ounces or ½ of the can is 8 ounces (i.e., a 16-ounce can).

- Include in the ingredient list any garnish or accompanying food that is integral to the recipe (such as hot cooked rice or noodles). Garnish items that are optional can be listed in the ingredient list, followed by "(optional)" or ", if desired" or can be mentioned in the method.

- When an ingredient listing begins with a word rather than a number, capitalize the first word. Beginning with a lowercase letter makes it appear that the entry is a continuation of the preceding line or that something is missing:

  **Salt and black pepper, to taste**

- Do not put a period at the end of the final item in the ingredient list.

- Equipment and utensils are not ingredients and should not be included in the ingredient list. If you want to specify equipment, do so under a separate heading, in the margin notes, or in the first paragraph of the recipe method.

## Preparation of Ingredients

- Call for each ingredient as it is commonly purchased from the grocery or market, then add simple preparation techniques.

  **4 large peaches, pitted and quartered**

  **10 pitted dried plums, quartered**

  **2 eggs, beaten**

  **4 ounces Cheddar cheese, grated (about 1 cup)**

- If the preparation of an item is complex or lengthy, you might choose to include it in the method rather than in the ingredient list.

  **INGREDIENT LIST: 1 whole chicken breast (about ¾ pound), skinned, boned, and halved lengthwise**

or

> INGREDIENT LIST: 1 whole chicken breast (about ¾ pound)
>
> METHOD: Skin and bone the chicken breast; halve lengthwise.

- If an ingredient has to be thawed, soaked, softened, or otherwise prepared ahead of time, indicate that in the ingredient list so the cook can plan accordingly.

  > 1 (10-ounce) package frozen spinach, thawed and drained
  >
  > 1 (3-ounce) package cream cheese, softened
  >
  > 1 (9-inch) pie shell, partly baked
  >
  > 2 tablespoons butter, melted

- Describe the preparation of ingredients in the appropriate place. For most foods, chopping, slicing, or other preparation is done prior to measuring. List, for example, "½ cup chopped celery," not "½ cup celery, chopped." The cook must chop the celery in order to measure it.

  Sometimes, however, preparation does indeed come after measuring, as in "1 cup cake flour, sifted." There is a quantitative difference between 1 cup sifted cake flour and 1 cup cake flour, sifted, or between ½ cup whipped cream and ½ cup heavy cream, whipped.

  For melted butter or margarine, give the measure and then follow it with ", melted." Although 2 tablespoons melted butter is the same as 2 tablespoons butter, melted, the implications for the cook are different. Some cooks might melt a large amount of butter and then measure the amount called for, when it is much easier to measure the amount of butter and then melt it.

  The same reasoning applies to directions for toasting nuts or coconut, as in "1 cup chopped almonds, toasted." The cook should measure the amount called for, then toast that amount, rather than toast a large amount and then measure the amount needed.

  If you get a recipe from a tester that has the preparation listed after an ingredient, don't automatically change it to precede the ingredient; check with the tester to verify exactly which measurement is intended.

- Sometimes the wording of the preparation is difficult to put prior to the ingredient. You can list it after the ingredient but without a comma:

  1 cup carrot cut into julienne strips

  Another solution is to qualify the preparation in parentheses following the ingredient:

  1 cup cut green beans (1-inch pieces)

  1 cup cubed potatoes ($\frac{1}{2}$-inch cubes)

- If an ingredient calls for a simple cooking procedure, such as toasting, include the directions in a note at the end of the recipe.

  1 cup shredded coconut, toasted

  NOTE: To toast coconut, spread coconut in an ungreased pan. Bake in a preheated 350-degree oven 5 to 7 minutes, stirring occasionally, or until golden brown.

## Ingredient Measurements

- Be specific regarding ingredient amounts; give size, weight, volume, and/or number of units. It is helpful to provide two different measurements, when possible.

  6 medium potatoes (about 2 pounds), peeled and quartered

  1 green bell pepper, chopped (about $\frac{1}{2}$ cup)

  $\frac{1}{2}$ pound fresh mushrooms, sliced (about 2 cups)

- Make notes during recipe testing and/or check Chapter Twelve, "Purchasing Information," regarding the quantity of items in a can, package, or other container. When possible, give two different measurements.

  1 (2-ounce) can anchovies (10 to 12 anchovies)

  1 (28-ounce) can whole tomatoes, drained (about 2 cups)

  1 cup egg yolks (about 14)

- When possible, specify the amount needed rather than calling for "one recipe" of something. This enables the reader to use an equivalent item, perhaps substituting a refrigerated pie shell for a homemade single-crust 9-inch pie shell or canned broth for 2 cups homemade broth.

- Do not use "of" after "dash," "pinch," or "few drops." Generally, "dash" is used with dry powdered ingredients or liquid ingredients that are shaken out of a bottle. "Dash" or "pinch" can be used for dried herbs. "Dash" or "few drops" can be used for less than ⅛ teaspoon of liquid ingredients, such as food color or extracts.

  **Dash salt**

### Divided Ingredients

- When an ingredient is used at different times in a recipe, list the total amount in one place in the ingredient list, then add, ", divided." This alerts the reader to the fact that part of the ingredient will be used at that point and part will be added later in the recipe. In the method, indicate the amount of the ingredient used at each point.

  | | |
  |---|---|
  | INGREDIENT LIST: | ³⁄₄ cup all-purpose flour, divided |
  | FIRST USAGE: | Add ¹⁄₂ cup of the flour, . . . |
  | SECOND USAGE: | Stir in remaining ¹⁄₄ cup flour. |

- Some stylebooks recommend listing the amount of an ingredient each time it is called for, rather than listing a divided usage. If you prefer this system, be sure to indicate in the method both the amount and the ingredient each time it is used.

  | | |
  |---|---|
  | INGREDIENT LIST: | ¹⁄₂ cup all-purpose flour |
  | | ¹⁄₄ cup all-purpose flour |
  | FIRST USAGE: | Add ¹⁄₂ cup flour, . . . |
  | SECOND USAGE: | Stir in ¹⁄₄ cup flour. |

- In a recipe with a subdivided ingredient list, such as for a filling and a topping, list each ingredient amount under the appropriate subhead, regardless of whether a different amount of the ingredient has been called for in another part of the recipe. It is

## Loukie Werle, Australia

Food editor of *Cosmopolitan Australia* and *SHE Australia,* and author of *Saffron* and other cookbooks

Don't assume the reader knows how to make a crepe or poach an egg. In a book, there may be a section at the back where such basics are covered. In a magazine, maybe this kind of "recipe within a recipe" could follow the main recipe. Recently one of the people in my cooking classes asked if, when you boil potatoes, they should be put into cold or boiling water. We take these things for granted, but for a beginner these can be real obstacles.

not necessary to repeat the amount of the ingredient in the method; it will be clear that the cook is to use the sugar for the filling or the sugar for the topping.

### Secondary Recipe

- When a secondary recipe is listed with the ingredients, it can be listed first with a cross-reference—"1 cup Herb Sauce (see recipe)"—and the first paragraph of the directions can state, "Prepare the herb sauce." Or the secondary recipe can be listed with the ingredients in the order of use. The latter approach assumes that the cook will read the recipe through before beginning and will note the preparation of the secondary recipe—a risky assumption.

## The Recipe Method

Keep your audience in mind when writing directions. Be complete, clear, and concise. Use simple, standard preparation techniques that are easily understood. Describe new or less familiar techniques.

- Write the directions in the tested order of preparation.
- Repeat each ingredient as it is used in the directions. This provides a double-check for both the copy editor and the cook. Make sure divided-use and reserved ingredients are completely used.
- Do not repeat preparation steps that have already been given in

the ingredient list. If the ingredient list calls for "2 carrots, grated," in the method, do not say, "Grate the carrots."

- If advance preparation is needed for a later step, mention this early in the directions. For example, tell the cook ahead of time to bring the water to boiling for the pasta or to arrange the oven rack and preheat the oven. The proper timing and sequence for such steps should be noted during recipe testing.

### Numbering Steps

Whether to number the steps is a style decision that should be made for each project, depending on the audience, the format of the printed material, and the realities of the workplace.

Readers tend to prefer numbered steps because the numbers make it easy to keep track of where they are in the recipe. Numbers also make the recipe appear simpler and more orderly. Numbered steps can be used by the recipe writer to simplify instructions in recipe variations, as in, "Prepare the recipe through step 3."

However, the realities of page makeup and on-deadline editing can make numbered steps impractical in some cases. For example, a newspaper editor will have to renumber all the steps if space restrictions call for combining some paragraphs to save a few lines of type.

Whether or not numbers are used, be sure to put each step in a separate paragraph. Avoid creating long blocks of type, which are daunting to the reader and make it difficult to find one's place.

T I P S    F R O M    T H E    E X P E R T S

## Rose Levy Beranbaum, USA

Author of *The Cake Bible* and other books

A good recipe is one that begins with a headnote that not only whets your appetite but also gives you an accurate description of the taste, texture, ease of preparation, and how the recipe is unique. . . . A good recipe ultimately makes you feel as though its author is a friend, standing by your side, cheering you on, and sharing in the joy of its creation.

## Useful Information

Provide helpful information throughout the method to give the cook confidence.

- Describe how a mixture should look or feel at a certain stage: "The batter will be quite thin."

- Give amounts if they are in a different form from the measurements given in the ingredient list: "Cut the bread into 1-inch cubes; you should have about 2 cups."

- Provide visual descriptions of doneness tests: "Cook and stir about 10 minutes, or until onions are soft and translucent."

- Give the reason for doing something: "Stir in sour cream at the end of cooking to prevent curdling" or "Rinse bean sprouts to remove salty, canned taste."

## Referring to Ingredients

- If an ingredient is listed more than once in more than one form, it is helpful to specify the form when calling for the ingredient in the method. For example, say, "Add chopped onion to meat mixture," and later in the method, "Arrange sliced onion on top of casserole."

- When referring to a mixture in the method, identify it by its primary ingredient. Instead of saying "dry ingredients" or "moist ingredients," which sometimes can apply to more than one set of ingredients within a recipe, identify the dry ingredients as "the flour mixture" or "the sugar mixture" (or other appropriate wording) and the moist ingredients as "the egg mixture" or "the milk mixture" (or other appropriate wording).

  **Stir in the remaining tomato mixture.**

  **Stir flour mixture into egg mixture; mix well.**

- Remind the cook to remove and discard any inedible items (such as bay leaf, bouquet garni, cinnamon sticks, wooden picks, kitchen string) before serving the dish.

## The Yield

Include a yield for every recipe. When possible, give the yield in both number and size of servings. For some foods, a volume measure is more useful than a number of servings.

The yield is usually placed either at the beginning, under the recipe name, or at the end, usually on its own line. The yield can be indicated by "Yield: 4 servings," "Makes 4 servings," "4 servings," or other such wording.

Be consistent in both wording and placement of yield information throughout a project.

## Notes

Use a note at the end of a recipe to provide additional information that doesn't fit elsewhere in the recipe. Tips on alternative ingredients, equipment, or techniques; simple preparation tips or techniques; tips on storage or reheating; serving suggestions; explanation of an unusual ingredient or where to find it; suggestions for using leftovers; wine suggestions; or other helpful advice can be put in the note. Limit a note to one or two items.

## Variations

Indicate a variation at the end of a recipe, if desired. If a variation constitutes a substantially different recipe, you might want to give it a name.

> VARIATION: One pound ground turkey can be substituted for the ground beef.
>
> VARIATION: For an old-fashioned boiled dinner, add 2 sliced carrots and 1 cubed potato to the cabbage mixture. Proceed as directed.
>
> VARIATION: Chicken Fajitas. Instead of beef, use 2 pounds skinned, boned chicken breasts. Marinate as directed. Drain. Grill 8 to 10 minutes per side, or until light brown and cooked through. Slice cooked chicken into strips. Assemble fajitas as directed.

## Nutrition Information

Many recipes include nutrition information, especially when the recipe is part of a collection that makes some sort of health or nutrition claim, such as being low fat, low calorie, or appropriate for diabetics.

The amount of nutrition information included and the format in which it is presented vary. The nutrition information can be as simple as a sentence at the end of a recipe that gives the calorie and/or fat content or as detailed as a chart that lists numerous nutrients, diabetic dietary exchanges, and percentages of types of fats.

The decision about information to include and how to present it will vary according to the publication, the purpose of the recipe, the audience, the page design, and the graphic capabilities.

For information on how to select a software program for nutrition analysis, see Chapter Nine, "Nutrition Analysis of Recipes."

## Grammar and Punctuation

This manual is not intended to replace a handbook on grammar and punctuation. For a more detailed discussion of punctuation, see *The Associated Press Stylebook,* a reference that you should have on your desk. A dictionary and a copy of *The Elements of Style,* by William Strunk Jr. and E. B. White, also should be at your side when you are writing and editing. See Chapter Fourteen, "Resources," for other reference books.

Some peculiarities of recipe writing, however, are discussed here. See the alphabetical style sheet in Chapter Three for treatment of specific words or phrases.

### Sentence Structure

Some recipe stylebooks instruct the writer to begin each direction by naming the utensil to be used ("In a bowl, mix . . ."). In some cases, this is useful in alerting the reader to the needed equipment. All too often, however, it leads to awkward, stilted language and inverted sentence structure that is confusing to readers who are not familiar with "recipe shorthand."

Straightforward, descriptive sentences are best. Begin with a verb, when appropriate, and use the verb that best describes the action. Strive for short, declarative sentences.

> AWKWARD: In a 12-inch skillet, over medium heat, place butter and onion; heat, stirring, about 5 minutes, or until tender.

BETTER: Melt butter in a 12-inch skillet over medium heat. Add onion; cook and stir about 5 minutes, or until onion is tender.

- A suggested sentence structure is: verb–subject–equipment–treament–technique–time–doneness test.

    Heat milk in a small saucepan over low heat, stirring frequently, 8 to 10 minutes, or until hot and bubbly.

- If a sentence becomes too long and wordy, with too many prepositional phrases or clauses, break it into two or more short sentences. Do not use more than one semicolon per sentence.

- Avoid using nouns as verbs.

    Season to taste with salt and pepper.

    NOT: Salt and pepper the meat.

    Ladle the sauce over the pasta.

    NOT: Sauce the pasta.

- Be constantly on the lookout for dangling modifiers.

- Edit yourself for unnecessary or redundant words. Tight writing applies to recipes just as it does to any other writing.

## Articles

The use of articles ("a," "an," "the") in recipes is a major point of debate. There are two main schools of thought. One says to avoid articles except when necessary for clarity. The other says to always use articles, except when it is necessary to omit them because of space restrictions. The middle-of-the-road approach is to use articles with equipment and utensils but not with ingredients. Decide your style and be consistent.

## Adjectives

- Adjectives preceding a noun should be used in logical sequence or in order of preparation, with the adjective closest to the noun being the main modifier.

    1 teaspoon grated fresh ginger

    1/4 cup finely chopped fresh parsley

    2 cups shredded cooked chicken

- The logical order of preparation should be used when the adjectives follow the noun.

  **2 chicken breasts, skinned, boned, and halved**

  **1 cucumber, peeled, seeded, and grated**

- Compound adjectives are usually hyphenated when they precede the noun they modify, but not when they follow the noun.

  **German-style potato salad**

  **all-purpose flour**

  **sweet-and-sour vegetables**

  **old-fashioned cake**

  **the recipe is old fashioned**

  **a seafood stew, Spanish style**

- Compound words that form a single concept that modifies a noun do not require a hyphen.

  **ice cream cone**

  **whole wheat flour**

  **white wine vinegar**

  **graham cracker crust**

- Compound adjectives that include adverbs that end with -ly do not take a hyphen.

  **finely chopped parsley**

  **lightly sweetened cereal**

## Prepositions

Many uses of prepositions are idiomatic, but they are not necessarily right or wrong. Some words typically require a particular preposition in certain idiomatic uses, such as "blend with," "coat with," "cut in half," "cut into pieces," "dip into," "dredge in," "drizzle over," "drop onto," "insert in," "invert on or onto," "place in," "plunge into," "put in or into," "spoon into, onto, or over," "spread in, on, over, or with."

## Capitalization

Capitalization is one of the thorniest issues in recipe writing. Before beginning a project, check with the editor about the preferred style. An "up style" indicates a liberal use of capitals. A "down style" indicates a limited use of capitals. Within these broad categories, the rules are numerous and varied.

The *AP Stylebook* and a good food dictionary can be your best resources, along with our lists in Chapter Six, "Preferred Spelling," Chapter Seven, "Generic Terms," and Chapter Three, "The Style Sheet."

The most important rule is to be consistent. Once you have decided on a capitalization style, stick with it throughout the project.

## Commas

As a general rule, commas are used to separate each element in a simple series of three or more items, including a comma before the conjunction. Most newspapers and periodicals do not use a comma before the conjunction, but most publishing houses do. Even publications that do not use a comma before the conjunction in a simple series do use it when necessary for clarity. Verify the style of your publication or company before beginning a project.

> WITH: **Butter, sugar, and flour**

> WITHOUT: **Butter, sugar and flour**

Use a comma to separate the cooking time from the test for doneness, as in "Bake 45 minutes, or until a knife inserted near the center comes out clean."

## A Final Check

Before giving final approval to a recipe, either in the test kitchen or at the computer, read it two more times.

Read it through once just for logic and common sense, making sure it doesn't call for something obviously wrong, such as "2 cups salt," or that it doesn't contain an easy-to-miss typo such as "cook cookies on wire rack" instead of "cool cookies on wire rack." Make sure the recipe title is appropriate and that the recipe fits the project—for instance, is it quick and easy or low in fat? Does the preparation flow logically, or should the method be rewritten?

Then read the recipe one final time while running a mental checklist. Are all the ingredients listed in the order used, and is each one called for in the recipe directions? Check divided-use and reserved ingredients—is the entire amount used? Are the ingredients properly described and measured, and will the reader understand exactly what is meant? Is simple preparation noted, such as drained, toasted, or chopped? Is the type of equipment specified? Should the pan be covered or uncovered, greased or ungreased? Are the oven temperature and baking time specified? Do all cooking times include a test for doneness? Is the yield indicated?

Now the recipe is ready to send to the next stage of production.

## Elizabeth Luard, Wales

Author of *The Old World Kitchen* and other cookbooks and novels

A good recipe is one that first encourages the reader to cook, and then delivers what it promises. A well-written recipe takes you by the hand and says, don't worry, it'll all be okay, this is what you're looking for, this is what happens when you chop or slice or apply heat, and if it goes wrong, this is how to fix it. And when you've finished, this is what it should look and taste like, this is what to eat it with. But above all, take joy in what you do.

# Chapter Three

# The Style Sheet

THIS CHAPTER'S ALPHABETICAL LIST OF common factors in recipe writing is designed to be a quick, user-friendly way to look things up. It might at first seem confusing to have a variety of items—ranging from how to dissolve gelatin to how to word a test for doneness—listed together, but you'll soon find the style sheet is quick and easy to use in on-deadline writing and editing.

If what you're looking for isn't listed under one term, try a similar term. If it isn't in this list, check the alphabetical list of preferred spellings in Chapter Six or the alphabetical list in Chapter Five, which includes definitions of common cooking terms and suggested alternative wordings, as well as comprehensive lists of types of ingredients.

## Harriet Bell, USA

Vice president and editorial director, HarperCollins

A good recipe is one that is clearly written, that contains ingredients I have on hand (I don't care how many), and that makes me want to run into the kitchen and immediately prepare it.

If you need a generic term for a trademarked word or a brand name, check the alphabetical list in Chapter Seven. Are you looking for a pan size? Consult the chart in Chapter Thirteen. For can and package sizes and equivalents, see Chapter Twelve.

You might find it helpful to make notations in the margins for ingredients or wordings that appear frequently in your work.

If you can't find what you need in this book, consult Chapter Fourteen for suggested reference books and lists of food promotion organizations or government agencies that provide food and cooking information.

(Note: References to temperature are in degrees Fahrenheit, except when specifically marked Celsius.)

## Style Sheet

**A**

**abbreviations** As a rule, avoid abbreviations. In some instances, however, abbreviations might be required or necessary. Abbreviations of units of measure are the same for both singular and plural. Following are some standard abbreviations and symbols:

| degree | ° | ounce | oz. |
| dessertspoon | dsp. | package | pkg. |
| dozen | doz. | pound | lb. |
| feet | ft. | quart | qt. |
| gallon | gal. | second | sec. |
| hour | hr. | tablespoon | tbsp. |
| inch | in. | teaspoon | tsp. |
| minute | min. | | |

See Chapter Eight for abbreviations of metric terms.

**about/approximately** Can be used interchangeably. Decide your style and be consistent.

**accent marks** If your computer software includes diacritical marks (accents, cedilla, circumflex, diaeresis, tilde, umlaut, etc.) for foreign words, use them, but be sure to use them correctly. Consult French-English, Spanish-English, and similar dictionaries for correct spellings and usage. Do not use accent marks with capital letters.

**add** Adding an ingredient doesn't indicate mixing or stirring. Do not use "add" if another verb ("stir," "mix," "beat," etc.) is more specific. Or use "add" and then qualify it, as in:

*Add onion; cook and stir until light brown.*

**alcoholic beverages** For wine, beer, liquor, or liqueurs, specify standard household measures (cup, tablespoon; not jiggers) if using less than a whole bottle. For wine, liquor, or liqueurs, specify metric measure if using a whole bottle. For beer, specify ounce weight if using a whole can or bottle.

**all ingredients** In general, avoid this terminology. Instead, name each item in the directions as it is used. This provides a double-check for both the copy editor and the cook.

If the recipe is short and simple and all the ingredients are used at once, you can say "mix all ingredients . . ." if necessary. Be consistent in style throughout a publication.

**all-purpose flour** See FLOUR in Chapter Five, "Cooking Terminology."

**almond extract/almond flavoring** Specify which is to be used.

**almonds** Indicate "blanched" or "unblanched" when the use of only one is preferred.

**alternately/alternatively** Use "alternately" when you mean first one and then the other. Use "alternatively" when you mean one instead of the other.

**alternative ingredients** Include an alternative ingredient in the ingredient list when something unfamiliar is called for or when an ingredient is difficult to find or expensive. If the wording for the alternative ingredient is too lengthy for the ingredient list, put it at the end of the recipe as a variation or a note. Sometimes alternative ingredients can be described in the headnote.

There is no need to refer to an alternative ingredient in the recipe method unless it requires a different preparation. If so, put the alternative technique in parentheses or indicate its use in the proper place by saying, "If using . . . , stir into mixture at this point."

*1 tablespoon chopped fresh parsley, or 1 teaspoon dried*

*¼ cup chopped fresh parsley or chervil*

**alternative techniques** When giving a choice of techniques in a recipe, put the second technique in parentheses.

*Rinse beans. Put beans in a large kettle and add enough water to cover beans. Cover and soak 6 to 8 hours, or overnight. (Or, bring beans and water to boiling. . . .)*

**aluminum foil** Use both words in first reference, then use "foil" in subsequent references. Specify heavy-duty aluminum foil when essential to the recipe.

**among** Use this term when distributing among three or more things. See BETWEEN.

**ampersand (&)** Avoid using an ampersand in recipe title, recipe instructions, or text.

**angel food cake pan or angel cake pan** The preferred term is "tube pan."

**anise** Specify form:
Extract: *⅛ teaspoon anise extract*

Oil: *2 drops anise oil (available in drugstores)*
Seed: *½ teaspoon aniseed (or anise seeds)*

**arrange** Use to indicate a more specific action than "place."

*Arrange bell peppers in rings, alternating colors.*

**bacon** Use the term "bacon slices," not "bacon strips."

*3 slices bacon, crisply cooked and crumbled*

**bacon drippings** Use this term to refer to the fat left after bacon is cooked. Also called "bacon fat."

**bake** Indicate whether the pan is covered or uncovered.

*Cover and bake in a preheated 325-degree oven 25 to 30 minutes, or until light brown.*

*Bake, uncovered, in a preheated 350-degree oven about 20 minutes, or until hot and bubbly.*

**baking blind** Indicates baking a pie shell without a filling. Prick the shell all over with a fork to prevent blistering and rising. Some cooks line the pastry shell with aluminum foil or parchment paper and fill it with dried beans, uncooked rice, or pie weights (small metal or ceramic pellets). Be sure to remove the foil and weights a few minutes before the end of baking time to allow the crust to brown. See PIES.

**baking dish, baking pan** See COOKING AND BAKING UTENSILS.

**baking powder** Repeat both words in recipe directions. Be sure to check the expiration date on the can. To check to see if the baking powder is still potent, stir 1 teaspoon baking powder into ⅓ cup hot water; if it bubbles actively, it is good.

**baking soda** Repeat both words in recipe directions. (Do not just say "soda"—some people might think of soda pop or soda water.)

**barbecue** This term has many meanings as both a noun and a verb. As a noun, it refers to a brazier or grill; to meat, poultry, or fish cooked on a brazier or grill; and to the informal outdoor entertaining at which such meat is served. As a verb, it refers to a method of slowly cooking meat, poultry, or other food in a covered pit or on a spit, using charcoal or hardwood for heat. Barbecued food is usually basted with a seasoned sauce. In most recipes, the correct cooking term is "grill," rather than "barbecue." See GRILL.

**bars** Use this term (instead of "cookies") in the names and yields of bar cookie recipes. Indicate the yield in exact numbers, rather than in dozens. See COOKIES, SQUARES.

> *Cut into 3 × 2-inch bars.*
>
> *Yield: 24 bars.*

**beater** See MIXER.

**Belgian endive** See ENDIVE.

**bell pepper** Use "green bell pepper" ("red bell pepper," "yellow bell pepper," etc.) in the ingredient list. Use "bell pepper" in the directions, unless it is necessary to indicate the color.

**benne seed** A term used in the American South for sesame seed. Use this term when appropriate. Include toasting directions if the recipe calls for toasted benne seed.

> *¼ cup benne (sesame) seeds, toasted*
>
> To toast benne (sesame) seeds: *Spread seeds in ungreased pan and bake in preheated 375-degree oven 10 to 12 minutes, stirring occasionally, or until golden brown.*

**between** Use this term when distributing between two things. See AMONG.

**bite-size** Not "bite-sized."

> *Break toffee into bite-size pieces.*

**bitters** The preferred term is "aromatic bitters." Angostura bitters is a brand name.

**blend** Avoid using this term except when indicating the use of an electric blender or food processor. Use a more specific verb: "mix," "stir," "beat," etc.

**blender** Usage example:

*Place tomatoes, peppers, and cucumbers in container of electric blender. Cover and blend on high speed about 20 seconds, or until finely chopped. Stop blender occasionally to scrape sides.*

Include the food processor option when appropriate:

*Place tomatoes, peppers, and cucumbers in container of electric blender or bowl of food processor. Cover and blend or process about 20 seconds, or until finely chopped.*

**blue cheese** Not bleu cheese or Roquefort (unless you really mean Roquefort). Use crumbled (instead of grated or shredded) to describe blue cheese.

*3 tablespoons crumbled blue cheese*

**boil/boiling** Usage examples:

*Bring/heat to boiling.*

*Bring/heat to a boil.*

*Boil gently, uncovered, about 5 minutes, or until of desired consistency.*

*Bring to a full rolling boil.*

*Return to boiling.*

*1 cup boiling water*

**bottled** Do not use this term when calling for commercially prepared ingredients unless necessary for clarity (for example, if most of the other ingredients are homemade).

*1 cup barbecue sauce*

*½ cup mayonnaise*

**bouillon** Specify form:

Cubes: *3 beef bouillon cubes*
Granules: *1 teaspoon chicken bouillon granules*
NOT: *1 teaspoon instant chicken bouillon*

**bouquet garni** Explain what herbs to use, in parentheses. Depending on the audience, it might be necessary to give simple directions.

*Bouquet garni (parsley, bay leaf, thyme)*

*Bouquet garni (parsley, bay leaf, and thyme tied together, or tied in a cheesecloth bag)*

**bowl** If the size of the bowl doesn't affect the outcome of the recipe, you do not need to say "in a bowl." If the size of the bowl is of importance, indicate small, medium, or large bowl.

Examples of when the bowl size is of importance: if using a small bowl results in better volume; when the ingredient being beaten will increase in volume (such as whipping cream or egg whites); when large amounts of additional ingredients will be added to a small amount in the bowl.

*Beat eggs in a small bowl until thick and pale.*

*Pour whipping cream into a large bowl. Beat on high speed with an electric mixer until soft peaks form.*

*Beat sugar and margarine in a large bowl until light and fluffy. Beat in eggs. Add bananas, milk, and vanilla; mix well. Add flour mixture; stir just until dry ingredients are moistened.*

See MIXER/MIXING BOWLS.

**braise** Avoid using this term unless your recipe audience is likely to be familiar with it. Say, "cover and simmer" or "simmer, covered."

**brand name** A product name that carries a registered or unregistered trademark. Do not use brand names in recipe titles. Do not use brand names in the ingredient list or in the recipe method unless it is necessary for clarification. Substitute a package size and generic term for the brand name.

For example, the generic term for Milnot is "dairy soya blend." Most cooks don't have a clue what that is. You could say:

*1 (12-ounce) can dairy soya blend (such as Milnot)*

See Chapter Seven, "Generic Terms."

Exception: Writers working for food manufacturers will use the company's brand names in recipes.

**bread crumbs** Not "breadcrumbs." Repeat both words in recipe directions. Be sure to specify dry, soft (fresh), or seasoned. Indicate fine or coarse if important to recipe results.

*1 cup soft bread crumbs (about 1½ slices bread)*

*¼ cup dry bread crumbs*

*¼ cup seasoned dry bread crumbs*

**bread cubes** Not "breadcubes." Repeat both words in recipe directions. Be sure to specify dry or soft (fresh). Indicate size of cubes if important to results.

*3 cups soft bread cubes (about 5 slices bread)*

*3 cups dry bread cubes (about 4 slices bread)*

**bread machine** When writing recipes for use in a bread machine, emphasize the order in which ingredients should be placed in the container and emphasize accurate measuring of ingredients. Indicate the weight of the resulting loaf, because various brands of machine accommodate different size loaves. Be aware that the terminology, as well as the size, varies from manufacturer to manufacturer.

**British culinary terms** Some commonly used British cooking terms and their American equivalents:

| | |
|---|---|
| aluminium foil | aluminum foil |
| aubergine | eggplant |
| bacon rasher | similar to Canadian bacon |
| bangers | sausages |
| beetroot | beet |
| biscuit | cookie or cracker |
| blind pie case | pastry shell baked without a filling |
| blood heat | lukewarm |
| bottling | canning |
| cake tin | cake or baking pan |
| cane sugar | granulated sugar |
| caster / castor sugar | superfine granulated sugar |
| chilli / chilli powder | chili / chili powder |
| chilli(es) | chile(s) |
| chips | french fries |
| coriander | cilantro, Chinese parsley |
| cornflour | cornstarch |
| courgette | zucchini |
| demerara sugar | brown sugar |
| dessertspoon | 2 teaspoons |
| essence | extract |
| filbert | hazelnut |
| fish fingers | fish sticks |

| | |
|---|---|
| flour | all-purpose flour |
| frying pan | skillet |
| gammon | ham |
| gelatin jelly | Jell-O |
| gingernut | gingersnap |
| girdle | griddle |
| golden syrup | light corn syrup |
| green prawns | raw prawns or shrimp |
| grill | broil |
| hard-boiled egg | hard-cooked egg |
| icing sugar | confectioners' sugar |
| maize | corn |
| maize flour | cornmeal |
| marrow | very large zucchini |
| mash | mashed potatoes |
| minced meat/mince | ground meat |
| neeps | turnips |
| off-cuts | scraps |
| oven slide | baking sheet or pan |
| palette knife | spatula |
| pastry case/pie case | pie shell |
| pawpaw | papaya |
| pips | seeds |
| potato crisps | potato chips |
| rocket | arugula |
| rockmelon | cantaloupe |
| scone | biscuit |
| seed/stone | pit |
| self-raising flour | self-rising flour |
| sieve | strain |
| silverbeet | Swiss chard |
| sippets | croutons |
| speciality | specialty |
| sponge fingers | ladyfingers |
| sponge-roll tin/Swiss roll tin | jelly-roll pan |
| spring onion | green onion |
| sultanas | golden raisins |
| swede | rutabaga |

| | |
|---|---|
| sweet dry rusk | zwieback |
| sweet pepper (capsicum) | bell pepper |
| tattie | potato |
| tin | can |
| tomato sauce | ketchup |
| tomato puree | tomato sauce |
| treacle | molasses |
| tunny | tuna |
| vegetable mill | food mill |
| white sugar | granulated sugar |
| wholemeal/graham flour | whole wheat flour |
| yoghurt | yogurt |

In addition, British spellings often use "ou" where American spellings use "o," such as *savoury/savory, favourite/favorite, mould/mold,* and "re" instead of "er," such as *centre/center, litre/liter.*

**brown/browned** Use either "brown" or "browned," depending on sentence structure and item being cooked. Be consistent within a recipe.

*Cook and stir ground beef until brown; drain.*

*Bake 10 to 12 minutes, or until lightly browned.*

*Cook for 10 minutes, turning to brown evenly.*

**brown sugar** Repeat both words in recipe directions. Indicate firmly packed with cup measures, but not with teaspoon or tablespoon measures. Indicate light or dark if essential to recipe results.

*1 cup firmly packed dark brown sugar*

**broth/stock** Either word is acceptable; decide on one and be consistent. In recipe writing, "broth" usually refers to the canned product, and "stock" to the homemade version. According to culinary dictionaries, stock is usually strained, while broth isn't.

**Bundt** This is a trademark name and must be capitalized. The generic term is "fluted tube pan"; available in 6-cup or 12-cup size.

**butter** Specify only butter when it is important to recipe results.

*6 tablespoons butter (do not substitute margarine)*

In American recipes, butter is presumed to be unsalted butter unless indicated otherwise. (Use the term "unsalted" rather than "sweet.") You can specify unsalted butter each time, if preferred. Specify salted butter when that is the ingredient being used. In other countries, salted butter may be the norm; adjust your ingredient list wording accordingly.

**butter or margarine** Use this wording when either ingredient produces acceptable recipe results. Your style might be to say "margarine or butter"; this is fine, but be consistent. Indicate firm, softened, or melted when necessary.

> *6 tablespoons firm butter or margarine*
>
> *6 tablespoons butter or margarine, softened*
>
> *6 tablespoons butter or margarine, melted*

See MARGARINE/VEGETABLE OIL SPREAD.

**butter or margarine, measurement of** How to indicate the measurement of butter and margarine is a controversial topic. Butter and margarine commonly come in 1-pound boxes containing four 4-ounce sticks or cubes. The sticks and cubes are usually marked off in tablespoons, 8 tablespoons to a stick. A stick or cube equals ½ cup.

Some writers argue that calling for ½ cup butter will cause a novice cook to try to pat the butter into a ½-cup measure—an unnecessary step. However, most writers agree that giving the number of sticks helps to clarify the measure.

The best solution is to give two measurements, when practical. Decide the format that is best for your audience, then be consistent.

> *½ cup (¼ pound) butter*
>
> *½ cup (1 stick) butter*
>
> *½ pound (2 sticks) butter*
>
> *1 pound (2 cups) butter*
>
> *¼ pound (1 stick) butter*

For small measures up to 8 tablespoons, simply call for the number of tablespoons.

Do not substitute reduced-fat butter or margarine for regular products in a cooking or baking recipe without testing the recipe. Reduced-fat butter and margarine, whether in tubs or in stick form, contain more water and/or air than regular products, which will affect the consistency and texture of baked goods, especially cookies. See MARGARINE/VEG-ETABLE OIL SPREAD.

Solid vegetable shortening packaged in 1-cup sticks was introduced in 1994, with widespread consumer acceptance. The reasoning used for butter measurement can be applied to shortening measurement, if referring to the kind packaged in sticks. The 20-ounce package contains three 1-cup sticks. Each stick is marked off in tablespoons for easy measuring.

**butterscotch morsels** Not "butterscotch chips" or "butterscotch pieces."

*1 (6-ounce) package butterscotch morsels (1 cup)*

**cabbage** Specify green, red, or Chinese cabbage. If possible, give the amount in more than one measure: number of heads, number of cups (shredded, chopped, sliced), or weight.

*1 medium head green cabbage (about 1½ pounds)*

*8 cups shredded Chinese cabbage (1 medium head)*

**candy coating** Also called "confectioners' coating." Indicate the flavor rather than the color.

*1 (16-ounce) package vanilla-flavored candy coating*

*1 (16-ounce) package chocolate-flavored candy coating*

Instructions for melting candy coating:

Stovetop method: *Bring water to boiling in bottom of a double boiler or a saucepan. Remove from heat. Place coarsely chopped candy coating in top of double boiler or in a heatproof bowl; place over pan of water. Heat, stirring frequently, until coating melts.*

Microwave method: *Put 1 cup coarsely chopped candy coating in a microwave-safe 2-cup glass measure or bowl. Microwave on High (100 percent power) 1 minute. Stir. Microwave on High 30 seconds, if necessary. Candy coating may not appear to be melted until it is stirred.*

Lumpy candy coating cannot be rescued, so be careful to not add any liquid (liquid food color, alcohol, water-based flavors, margarine, or liquid on utensils) to the melted candy coating. Melted candy coating can be thinned with solid vegetable shortening (1 to 2 teaspoons shortening to 6 ounces coating).

Equivalents: 6 ounces candy coating = about 1 cup coarsely chopped = about ½ cup melted.

**candy doneness tests** Here are examples of standard wording for various candy stages and temperatures:

Soft-ball stage (such as for fondant or fudge): *Cook, stirring occasionally, until mixture reaches 234 degrees on candy thermometer, or until a small amount of mixture dropped into very cold water forms a soft ball that flattens when removed from water. Remove from heat.*

Firm-ball stage (such as for caramels): *Cook over medium heat, stirring frequently, until mixture reaches 245 degrees on candy thermometer, or until a small amount of mixture dropped into very cold water forms a firm ball that does not flatten when removed from water. Remove from heat.*

Hard-ball stage (such as for divinity or marshmallows): *Cook, without stirring, until mixture reaches 260 degrees on candy thermometer, or until a small amount of mixture dropped into very cold water forms a hard ball that is hard enough to hold its shape yet is pliable. Remove from heat.*

Soft-crack stage (such as for butterscotch or taffy): *Cook over medium heat, stirring constantly, until mixture reaches 290 degrees on candy thermometer, or until a small amount of mixture dropped into very cold water separates into threads that are hard but not brittle. Remove from heat.*

Hard-crack stage (such as for peanut brittle): *Cook, stirring constantly, until mixture reaches 300 degrees on candy thermometer, or until a small amount of mixture dropped into very cold water separates into threads that are hard and brittle. Watch carefully to prevent burning. Remove from heat.*

**candy thermometer** See usage examples under CANDY DONENESS TESTS.

**canned foods** List canned ingredients by the number of cans and weight of cans. When possible, give cup measurements, for cooks who are using smaller or larger cans. Indicate drained or undrained, and whether to reserve the liquid.

**caramels** Indicate the flavor rather than the color:

*1 (14-ounce) package vanilla caramels*

*1 (14-ounce) package fudge caramels*

To melt caramels: *Combine 24 caramels with 2 tablespoons liquid (water, milk, or cream). Heat over low heat, stirring constantly, 4 to 5 minutes, or microwave on High (100 percent power) 1 to 3 minutes, stirring every minute.*

**caramelize** Sample wording:

*Heat sugar in a heavy skillet over medium-high heat until sugar begins to melt, shaking skillet occasionally to heat evenly. Do not stir. Reduce heat to low. Cook about 5 minutes, or until sugar melts and is golden, stirring occasionally after sugar begins to melt and as mixture bubbles.*

**carbonated beverage** Used as a generic term for many popular soft drinks.

*1 cup cola-flavored carbonated beverage*

*1 (1-liter) bottle citrus-flavored carbonated beverage*

To retain as much carbonation as possible, add carbonated beverages this way:

*Slowly pour carbonated beverage down side of glass (or bowl, etc.). Gently stir.*

**carbonated water** "Sparkling water" is preferred.

**cardamom** Not "cardamon." Indicate form:
Ground: *1 teaspoon ground cardamom*
Seeds: *20 cardamom seeds (removed from pod), crushed*
Whole: *1 cardamom pod, ground*

**casserole** Use as a noun for food baked and served in a casserole dish. Do not use as a term for a baking dish.

**catsup** Preferred spelling is "ketchup." (The preferred spelling can vary, depending on the project and for whom you're working. Just be consistent throughout each project.)

**cayenne** Same as "ground red pepper." Decide your style and be consistent.

**celery** An individual piece is a "rib"; a bunch of ribs is a "stalk." (Some people prefer to use "stalk" as the individual piece and "bunch" as the composite; decide your use and be consistent.)

*2 ribs celery, sliced*

*1 stalk celery, trimmed and coarsely chopped*

*1 cup finely chopped celery*

**Celsius** A temperature scale, formerly called centigrade, on which freezing is 0 degrees and boiling is 100 degrees. Used in metric recipes. See FAHRENHEIT.

**centigrade** See CELSIUS.

**cheese** There are varying opinions on which cheeses should be capitalized. Here are some commonly used spellings. Use these or consult other sources and determine your own capitalization style; just be consistent.

*Asiago, Bel Paese, blue, Brie, Camembert, Cheddar, chèvre, Colby, cottage, cream, Edam, Emmentaler, feta, fontina, gjetost, Gorgonzola, Gouda, Gruyère, Havarti, Jarlsberg, Liederkranz, Limburger, longhorn, Monterey Jack, mozzarella, Muenster, Neufchâtel, Parmesan, Parmigiano-Reggiano, Port-Salut, provolone, queso fresco, raclette, ricotta, Romano, Roquefort, sapsago, Stilton, Swiss, Tillamook, Tilsit.*

Process cheese items (also called "pasteurized process cheese") include cheese food, slices, spread, sauce, loaf, snack links, product, and imitation. Check labels for generic terms.

As a general rule, soft cheeses are shredded, hard cheeses are grated, blue cheese and feta cheese are crumbled.

Usage examples:

*1 cup shredded sharp Cheddar cheese (4 ounces)*

*1 (8-ounce) package shredded sharp natural Cheddar cheese*

*4 ounces Cheddar cheese, cut into cubes*

*¼ cup grated Parmesan cheese*

**cheesecloth** Specify 100 percent cotton cheesecloth. Some synthetic materials are not food safe.

**cherries** Indicate dark sweet, light sweet, tart, maraschino; indicate fresh, frozen, canned, dried, or candied. Say "dark sweet cherries" instead of "Bing cherries," unless the specific variety is crucial to the recipe.

*1 (16-ounce) can pitted tart cherries, drained*

*1 cup pitted fresh dark sweet cherries*

*1 (16-ounce) package frozen tart cherries, partly thawed*

*8 ounces whole red or green candied cherries, chopped (about 1¼ cups)*

*½ cup dried tart cherries*

**chicken** Be specific about whether the chicken is skinned or boned before or after measuring, whether you mean a chicken breast or a chicken breast half, etc. For example, 1 pound chicken breast, skinned, boned, and cut into cubes is different from 1 pound skinned, boned, cubed chicken breast.

Uncooked:

*4 chicken thighs (about 1 pound)*

*2 pounds chicken wings (about 12)*

*1 (2½- to 3½-pound) broiler-fryer chicken, cut up*

*1 (4- to 5-pound) roasting chicken*

*1 large chicken breast (about 1 pound), skinned, boned, and halved*

*2 small chicken breast halves (about 1 pound), skinned and boned*

Cooked:

*2 cups chopped cooked chicken*

*1 cup shredded cooked chicken*

*5 slices cooked chicken breast*

Canned or packaged:

*1 (5-ounce) can chunk chicken in water, drained*

*1 (2½-ounce) package thinly sliced smoked chicken*

Tests for doneness:

Whole chicken: *Until chicken is no longer pink, juices run clear, and drumsticks move easily.*

Chicken parts: *Until tender and no longer pink.*

For current information about nutrition, food safety, and other chicken issues, contact the National Chicken Council. See Chapter Fourteen, "Resources."

**chicory** A relative of endive (see ENDIVE), it has curly, bitter leaves that are used fresh in salad or cooked as greens. Radicchio is an Italian red-leafed chicory. Roasted chicory is used as a coffee substitute or extender, especially in Louisiana.

**chile(s) or chili(es)** Hot peppers are growing in popularity and availability along with the highly seasoned foods of the American Southwest, Mexico, Thailand, and other countries. Many recipe writers now use the Spanish spelling, *chile(s)*, but others prefer the anglicized version, *chili(es)*. Pick one and be consistent. (The British spelling is *chilli/es*.) "Chili pepper" is redundant, but might be necessary for clarity depending on your audience; likewise for "jalapeño pepper" (or "chile") or "habañero pepper" (or "chile"). The goal is clarity for the end user; decide what best fits your audience and use that term.

> *1 (4-ounce) can diced green chiles, drained*
>
> *1 (4-ounce) can sliced jalapeño chiles, drained*
>
> *1 jalapeño chile, seeded and chopped*

You might want to include a note about the importance of wearing plastic or rubber gloves while handling chiles to protect skin from the oils in the chiles. Avoid direct contact with the eyes. Wash hands thoroughly after handling chiles. See CHILES in Chapter Five, "Cooking Terminology."

**chili** Correct spelling for the spicy stew of that name. Also called "chili con carne" (chili with meat). (British spelling is *chilli*.)

**chili powder/chili sauce** Repeat both words in recipe directions. (British spelling is *chilli powder/sauce*.)

**chill** Use "chill" as a verb when referring to cooling gelatin or custard in a bowl of ice instead of in the refrigerator.

> *Let chill in a bowl of ice water until the gelatin is partly set.*

Otherwise, use the verb *refrigerate*. See REFRIGERATE.

> *Refrigerate until gelatin is partly set.*
>
> *Refrigerate 2 hours, or until well chilled.*

**chilled** Use as an adjective.

*1 (12-ounce) can beer, chilled*

*Refrigerate, covered, about 1 hour, or until chilled.*

It is not necessary to specify chilled for ingredients that are normally kept under refrigeration, such as milk or cream.

**chocolate** See Chapter Five for descriptions of types of chocolate.
Usage examples:

*6 ounces semisweet chocolate*

*2 (1-ounce) squares unsweetened chocolate, coarsely chopped*

*1 (1-ounce) envelope premelted unsweetened chocolate*

**chocolate bars/candy bars** Specify correct size (sizes change frequently) and use the generic term from the label. It might be necessary to include a brand name for clarity. Here are examples of Hershey, Snickers, and Milky Way bars, respectively:

*1 (1.65-ounce) milk chocolate candy bar, separated into pieces*

*1 (2.07-ounce) chocolate-coated caramel-peanut nougat bar*

*1 (2.15-ounce) chocolate-coated caramel and creamy nougat bar*

**chocolate morsels** Use "chocolate morsels" instead of "chocolate chips" or "chocolate pieces." Specify semisweet chocolate, milk chocolate, or mint chocolate.

*1 (12-ounce) package semisweet chocolate morsels (2 cups)*

*1 (5.75-ounce) package milk chocolate morsels (1 cup)*

*¾ cup semisweet chocolate morsels*

**chocolate-flavored syrup** Not "chocolate syrup."

**cider** Specify type:

*1 gallon apple cider*

*1 quart cherry cider*

**cider vinegar** The correct term is "apple cider vinegar," but that terminology can cause confusion in an ingredient listing. Some cooks might read that term as "apple cider" or "vinegar." To avoid confusion, list it as "cider vinegar."

**cilantro** "Cilantro" is the preferred term, rather than "coriander," although cilantro is coriander leaves. Also called "Chinese parsley." See CORIANDER.

*1 tablespoon minced fresh cilantro*

**cinnamon** Indicate form:
Ground: *1 teaspoon ground cinnamon*
Oil: *½ teaspoon cinnamon oil*
Stick: *2 (3-inch) sticks cinnamon, broken into pieces*

**cinnamon candies** Preferred term is "red cinnamon candies," not "red hots."

**citrus peel** See LEMON (LIME) PEEL, ORANGE PEEL.

**clams** Indicate form:
Fresh: *1 pint shucked clams*
*24 hardshell clams (littlenecks, cherrystones, or chowders)*
*2 pounds softshell clams (steamers, razors, or geoducks)*
Canned: *1 (6½-ounce) can minced clams, drained, reserving liquor*

**clam chowder** Manhattan clam chowder is made with tomatoes. New England clam chowder is made with milk or cream.

**cloves** Indicate form:
Ground: *¾ teaspoon ground cloves*
Oil: *½ teaspoon clove oil*
Whole: *1 teaspoon whole cloves*

**club sandwich** Not "clubhouse sandwich."

**cocoa/cocoa powder** Cocoa is the beverage (hot chocolate) and cocoa powder is the dry cocoa. Specify "unsweetened cocoa powder" to be sure that cooks use the correct ingredient. Powdered cocoa drink mixes are usually sweetened and sometimes contain dry milk solids; they are not interchangeable with unsweetened cocoa powder.

In Dutch-process cocoa powder, the natural acidity has been neutralized and the cocoa has a darker color and mellow flavor. Indicate Dutch process in the ingredient list when it is preferred. A satisfactory substitute is achieved by using regular (nonalkalized) unsweetened cocoa powder and adding ½ teaspoon baking soda to the dry ingredients to neutralize the slightly acid taste of the cocoa.

**coconut** In most cases, flaked or shredded coconut can be used interchangeably in recipes. If it makes a difference, be sure to indicate which form. When calling for toasted or tinted coconut, include directions.

*1 cup shredded coconut, toasted*

*1 (3½-ounce) can flaked coconut (1⅓ cups)*

*½ cup flaked or shredded coconut, tinted*

To toast coconut: *Spread coconut in an ungreased pan. Bake in a preheated 350-degree oven 5 to 7 minutes, stirring occasionally, or until golden brown.*

To tint coconut: *Add a few drops food color to coconut in a container with a tight-fitting lid; cover and shake well.*

**coffee** For prepared (brewed) coffee, specify hot or cold and, if important, the strength of the brew.

Indicate freeze-dried, powder, or granules for instant coffee.

*1 cup cold coffee*

*1 teaspoon instant coffee granules*

**cold** Include this modifier only when important for recipe results.

*1 cup cold milk*

**combine** Do not use "combine" if another verb ("stir," "mix," "beat," etc.) is more specific.

**condensed milk** Avoid using this term. Specify "sweetened condensed milk" or "evaporated milk." The two are not interchangeable.

**confectioners' sugar** Preferred; also called "powdered sugar."

**continually/continuously** Use "continually" when you mean over and over again. ("Stir continually.") Use "continuously" when you mean uninterrupted action, without a pause. ("Boil continuously.")

**cook/heat** Use "cook" when the food must go through a cooking process on the top of the stove. Use "heat" when the food is already cooked but must be brought to a warm temperature to be served. Use a more specific term than "cook" ("simmer," "boil," "bake," "broil," "roast," etc.) when appropriate.

**cook and stir** Use this wording instead of "sauté," which means to cook rapidly in a small amount of fat, stirring occasionally.

*Melt margarine in a large skillet. Add onions; cook and stir until tender.*

**cookies** Give the yield in dozens (except for bars and squares, for which yield is given in number of pieces). If the yield is approximate, use about or approximately.

*Yield: About 3 dozen cookies.*

**cooking and baking utensils** A baking dish is a glass utensil, usually round, square, or rectangular. A baking pan is a metal utensil, usually round, square, or rectangular. A pie plate is usually glass; a pie pan is usually metal.

Glass baking utensils generally require a 25-degree reduction in oven temperature (350 degrees for metal pan, 325 degrees for glass dish).

A cookie sheet is flat and open on one, two, or three sides; also called a baking sheet. A jelly-roll pan has a 1-inch rim.

Give exact pan sizes in recipes. If the reader doesn't have the exact size, he or she can use the size information to figure out a suitable substitute. Giving a description of the pan is helpful, such as, "Use a skillet large enough to hold the fillets in one layer."

For detailed information and sizes, see Chapter Thirteen.

**cool** Standard cooling times before removing baked goods from pans: quick breads, 10 minutes; layer cakes, 10 minutes; loaf cakes, 15 minutes.

*Let cool in pan 10 minutes, then turn out onto wire rack and let cool completely before slicing.*

*Let cool on baking sheet 1 minute, then transfer to wire rack with a spatula.*

*Let cool slightly before transferring from cookie sheet to wire rack.*

**coriander** The dried seeds of the cilantro (coriander) plant.
Indicate form:
Ground: *½ teaspoon ground coriander*
Seed: *1 teaspoon coriander seeds*
Coriander leaves are called "cilantro"; see CILANTRO.

**corn syrup** Repeat both words in recipe directions. Indicate light or dark when flavor or color is important to recipe results.

*½ cup light corn syrup*

*½ cup dark corn syrup*

*1 tablespoon corn syrup*

**cornflakes cereal** Not "corn flakes." If cornflakes cereal is crushed, indicate whether it is crushed before or after measuring.

*1 cup cornflakes cereal*

*1½ cups crushed cornflakes cereal*

*2 cups cornflakes cereal, crushed*

Exception: There is no *s* on cornflake in "cornflake crumbs." See Chapter Seven, "Generic Terms."

**cornmeal** Not "corn meal." Specify white or yellow if important to recipe results.

**cornmeal/cornmeal mix, self-rising** In the American South, self-rising cornmeal and self-rising cornmeal mix are popular ingredients. Recipes calling for these items should include a note offering substitutions because cooks in other parts of the country might not have access to these ingredients.

Equivalents: 1 cup self-rising cornmeal equals 1 cup cornmeal plus 1½ teaspoons baking powder and ¼ to ½ teaspoon salt; 1 cup self-rising cornmeal mix equals 1 cup cornmeal plus 1½ teaspoons baking powder, ¼ to ½ teaspoon salt, and 1 tablespoon all-purpose flour (the amount of flour can be reduced depending on the recipe).

**cottage cheese** Indicate small curd, large curd, creamed, or dry, if important to recipe results.

*1 (8-ounce) carton large-curd dry cottage cheese*

**cover** Usage examples:

*Cover; set aside.*

*Cook, covered, over medium heat.*

*Cover and keep warm.*

**cover and simmer** Use this wording instead of "braise," which means to cook, covered in liquid, just below the boiling point.

**crackers** Examples of common generic terminology:

*buttery crackers—oval, round, or rectangular*

*cinnamon graham crackers—squares, crumbs*

*graham crackers—squares, crumbs*

*oyster crackers*

*saltine crackers*

*shredded whole wheat wafers*

*small fish-shaped crackers*

*stone-ground wheat crackers*

*thin wheat crackers*

**cranberries** Package size for fresh cranberries is 12 ounces. Older recipes calling for 16-ounce packages must be revised to reflect current packaging. One solution is to indicate measurement in cups. One 12-ounce package equals about 3 cups (fresh or frozen).

**cranberry juice cocktail** Not "cranberry juice" or "cranberry cocktail."

**cranberry sauce** Specify whole berry or jellied.

**cream** When possible, avoid using this word as a verb—it is misunderstood by many cooks. You can often substitute the verb "beat" ("beat until smooth and creamy," or "beat until light and fluffy"). Some readers think the verb is a noun and will look for cream in the ingredient list.

**cream, types of** See Chapter Five, "Cooking Terminology."

**cream cheese** Repeat both words in recipe directions. Clearly indicate package size and the type of cream cheese; light, soft, and whipped versions produce different results.

*1 (3-ounce) package cream cheese, softened*

*1 (8-ounce) package cream cheese, cut into cubes*

*1 (4-ounce) carton whipped cream cheese*

*1 (8-ounce) carton soft cream cheese*

*1 (8-ounce) carton light cream cheese*

**crème de cacao** Specify dark or white when one is preferred.

**crème de menthe** Specify green or white when one is preferred.

**crème fraîche** A thick, cultured cream with a nutty, slightly tangy flavor and rich texture. Crème fraîche is not readily available in many areas. If it is called for in a recipe, offer basic directions for making a suitable homemade version in a note at end of recipe.

*Crème fraîche: Mix 1 cup heavy cream and 2 tablespoons buttermilk or sour cream in a glass container. Cover and let stand at room temperature (60° to 85°) for 8 to 24 hours, or until very thick. (Mixture can be stored in refrigerator, but fermentation will take longer.) Stir well. Cover and refrigerate for at least 4 hours, or up to 10 days.*

**crisp-tender** Not "tender-crisp." This is a popular and acceptable way to word the current preference to cook vegetables until they are still crisp, yet barely tender.

**crockery cooker** Use this term or "slow cooker" instead of "Crock-Pot," which is a brand name.

**crush/crushed** To change the form of an ingredient by pounding, pressing, grinding, or squeezing.

*¾ cup finely crushed graham crackers (about 10 squares)*

*30 vanilla wafers, crushed (1 cup)*

**crushed red pepper/hot red pepper flakes** Either term is correct; pick one and be consistent.

**cubed/cubes** Indicate size when important to results of recipe.

*1 cup cubed cooked chicken*

*2 pounds chicken breast meat, cut into 1-inch cubes*

*1 potato, cubed*

**cucumber** Indicate peeled or unpeeled if one is preferred. If it makes no difference, it is not necessary to specify either.

**cumin** Indicate form:
Ground: *1 teaspoon ground cumin*
Seed: *1 teaspoon cumin seeds*

**curdle** Some mixtures have a tendency to curdle if cooked at a temperature that is too high or when mixed with certain ingredients.

*Sour cream or yogurt: If a sauce or gravy made with sour cream or yogurt must be boiled, stir in at least 2 tablespoons flour or 1 tablespoon cornstarch per 1 cup sour cream or yogurt before cooking. Otherwise, the mixture will probably curdle if boiled.*

To add sour cream to a hot mixture, stir a little of the hot mixture into the sour cream (or sour cream–flour mixture) and then stir sour cream into the hot mixture.

*Eggs:* Egg yolks thicken at a higher temperature than egg whites or whole eggs, so egg yolks are somewhat less likely to curdle. When adding egg yolks to a hot mixture, stir about half of the hot mixture into the beaten yolks, then stir yolks into the hot mixture and cook as directed.

If the egg-liquid mixture contains flour or sugar, it is less likely to curdle.

The presence of an acid in an egg mixture speeds thickening, but it also increases the risk of curdling. Vinegar is more likely to cause curdling than lemon juice. Do not add an acid food to an egg and milk mixture before cooking, or it will curdle.

*Wine:* To prevent curdling, do not add wine to a milk-based sauce until after the mixture has been thickened.

**curly endive** See ENDIVE.

**custard powder** A popular ingredient in Canadian and British dessert recipes, it is available in the United States in specialty food shops or by mail order. You can substitute an equal amount of instant vanilla pudding and pie filling mix (dry).

**darkening** To prevent darkening of fruits (such as apples, apricots, avocados, bananas, peaches, nectarines, and pears) upon exposure to air, add this step to the recipe method:

*Dip fruit into a mixture of lemon juice and water or ascorbic acid color keeper to prevent darkening.*

**dash** Less than ⅛ teaspoon of an ingredient. Do not use "dash of."

*Dash salt*

*Dash ground cinnamon*

**defrost** Do not use "defrost" when you mean "thaw," as in thawing frozen foods. ("Defrost" is used as a power setting on some microwave ovens.) See THAW.

**degrees** Depending on the publication, you might want to spell out degrees or use the degree symbol (°). You will need to indicate Fahrenheit (F) and Celsius (C) if giving metric equivalents. Be consistent throughout a publication.

*Preheat oven to 450 degrees.*

*Preheat oven to 450 °F.*

**dice** To cut into small cubes (usually smaller than ½ inch). Many readers do not know this term. Use "finely chopped" instead of "diced."

**dictionaries** Pick a specific edition of a dictionary as the primary source for spellings and definitions; be sure everyone working on a project uses the same dictionary (see Chapter Fourteen).

**Dijon-style mustard** Not "Dijon mustard," unless you really mean mustard from Dijon, France.

**dimensions** Indicate dimensions in descending order.

*Grease a 13 × 9 × 2-inch baking pan.*

**divided** Use this term to alert the cook that an ingredient is used at different times. In the recipe method, indicate "of the" in the first use, "remaining" in the last use. See RESERVE/RESERVING, RESERVED.

**doneness test** If possible, include a test for doneness when giving a cooking or baking time.

*Bake in a preheated 325-degree oven 40 to 45 minutes, or until a wooden pick inserted near the center comes out clean.*

Doneness tests for baked goods:

Bread puddings, quiches, and baked custards: *Until a knife inserted near the center comes out clean.*

Bar cookies and cakes: *Until a wooden pick inserted near the center comes out clean.*

General: *Until brown.*

See EGGS, MEATS, CHICKEN, TURKEY, and FISH AND SHELLFISH for additional doneness tests.

**double boiler** Many cooks do not have a double boiler—or don't like to use it if they do. Call for a double boiler only when absolutely necessary, and briefly explain the process.

*Place mixture in top of double boiler. Place over gently boiling water; upper pan should not touch water.*

**drain** Usage examples:

*Drain on paper towels.*

*Drain well.*

*Drain in a colander.*

*Drain; squeeze to remove excess liquid.*

*Drain fat.*

If ingredients are completely drained or undrained, indicate this in the ingredient list.

*1 (16-ounce) can pinto beans, drained*

To modify the amount drained, do not indicate draining in the ingredient list; explain it in the recipe directions.

*Drain peaches, reserving ¼ cup syrup.*

*Drain pineapple, reserving juice. Measure juice. Add water as necessary to make 2 cups liquid.*

See RESERVE/RESERVING, RESERVED.

**dry** When referring to a packaged mix that is not prepared in its usual manner (i.e., according to package directions), indicate dry in the directions.

*Sprinkle dry cake mix over cherries in pan.*

*Mix milk, dry pudding mix, and vanilla.*

**dry bread crumbs** Not "dried bread crumbs."

**dry mustard** Repeat both words in recipe directions. Not "powdered mustard."

**Dutch-process cocoa** See COCOA/COCOA POWDER.

**edible plants** Consult a poisonous plant guide before using plants or flowers in recipes, as a garnish in photos, or for making chocolate leaves. Toxic plants should not touch foods or plates. Check with the local Poison Control Center (usually listed in the front of the telephone directory) for more information. Common edible flowers include borage, calendulas, carnations, pinks, chives, onions, chrysanthemums, dandelions, fennel, geraniums, nasturtiums, rosemary, roses, salad burnet, and violets.

**eggs** Eggs are presumed to be large unless indicated otherwise. Raw eggs have come under fire in recent years because of possible contamination with *Salmonella enteritidis,* a bacterium responsible for a type of food poisoning. Less than 1 percent of eggs have been found to harbor *Salmonella;* however, all raw animal foods, including eggs, pose the possibility of *Salmonella* food poisoning. The risk is greater for people who are pregnant, elderly, or very young and for those with medical problems that have impaired their immune systems. These individuals should avoid raw and undercooked animal foods. You should include warnings to this effect on such recipes.

For other people, the risk is small and can be reduced by proper food safety practices. Use only properly refrigerated, clean, sound-shelled, fresh, Grade A or AA eggs. Avoid mixing yolks and whites with the shell. Refrigerate or freeze the broken-out eggs, prepared egg dishes, and other foods if they won't be consumed within an hour. Eggnog and homemade ice cream should be based on a cooked stirred custard to ensure safety.

*Raw egg whites:* Although it is possible for egg white to carry *Salmonella,* it does not readily support bacterial growth. Cold soufflés, mousses, and chiffons containing raw beaten whites require refrigeration to maintain their character, an added safety factor. Such dishes might be considered low risk for healthy individuals.

For further safety, combine whites with the sugar in a recipe (using a minimum of 2 tablespoons sugar per egg white) and beat over hot water or over low heat in a heavy saucepan until the whites stand in soft peaks. Without sugar, the whites will coagulate too rapidly and produce an unsatisfactory meringue.

This procedure can be used for frostings ordinarily containing raw whites.

If using an unlined aluminum saucepan, do not add cream of tartar. It will react with the aluminum to produce an unattractive gray product.

*Raw egg yolks:* Egg yolks are a ready growth medium for bacteria. It is best to cook yolks for use in such dishes as cold soufflés, chiffons, mousses, mayonnaise, and Hollandaise sauce.

To cook yolks, a recipe must contain at least 2 tablespoons of liquid per yolk. Less liquid will produce scrambled eggs. Direct the reader as follows:

*Combine the yolks with the liquid in the recipe. Cook in a heavy saucepan over very low heat, stirring constantly, until the mixture coats a metal spoon, bubbles at the edges, or reaches 160 degrees. Cool quickly and proceed with the recipe.*

Tests for doneness: Following are suggested wordings for visual doneness tests for egg recipes, based on current food safety practices.

Fried eggs: *Cook slowly until whites are completely set and yolks begin to thicken but are not hard, covering with a lid and spooning butter over eggs to baste or turning eggs to cook both sides.*

Steam-basted: *Cook until whites are completely set and yolks begin to thicken but are not hard.*

Microwave: *Let stand, covered, until whites are completely set and yolks begin to thicken but are not hard.*

Baked eggs: *Bake in a preheated 325-degree oven 12 to 18 minutes, depending on number of servings being baked, or until whites are completely set and yolks begin to thicken but are not hard.*

Scrambled eggs: *Cook until eggs are thickened and no visible liquid egg remains.*

Microwave: *If necessary, cover with plastic wrap and let stand about 1 minute, or until eggs are thickened and no visible liquid egg remains.*

Soft-cooked eggs: *Let eggs stand, covered, in the hot water 4 to 5 minutes, depending on desired doneness.*

Poached eggs: *Cook 3 to 5 minutes, or until whites are completely set and yolks begin to thicken but are not hard.*

Microwave: *If necessary, let stand, covered, 1 to 2 minutes, or until whites are completely set and yolks begin to thicken but are not hard.*

Omelet: *When top is thickened and no visible liquid egg remains, fill, if desired.*

Puffy omelet: *Bake in a preheated 350-degree oven 10 to 12 minutes, or until knife inserted halfway between center and outer edge comes out clean.*

Soufflé: *Bake in a preheated 350-degree oven 30 to 40 minutes, or until puffy and light brown and soufflé shakes slightly when oven rack is moved gently back and forth.*

Soft (stirred) custard sauce: *Cook over low heat, stirring constantly, until mixture is thick enough to coat a metal spoon with a thin film and reaches at least 160 degrees.*

Baked custard: *Bake in a preheated 350-degree oven until knife inserted near center comes out clean, 25 to 30 minutes for cups or 35 to 40 minutes for baking dish.*

Microwave: *Microwave on Medium-low (30 percent power) 9 to 11 minutes, rotating cups 3 or 4 times, or until puffed in center and slightly moist at edges. Let stand 5 minutes.*

Quiche: *Bake in a preheated 375-degree oven 30 to 40 minutes, or until puffed in center and knife inserted near center comes out clean.*

Microwave: *Microwave on High (100 percent power) 5 minutes, rotating dish a half-turn once or twice. Microwave on Medium (50 percent power) 8 to 12 minutes, rotating dish a quarter-turn 2 or 3 times, or until puffed in center and knife inserted near center comes out clean. Let stand about 10 minutes to complete cooking.*

Hard meringues: *Bake in a preheated 225-degree oven 1 to 1½ hours, or until firm and a cake tester inserted near center comes out clean. Turn off oven. Let stand in oven with door closed until cool, dry, and crisp, or at least 1 hour.*

Soft (pie) meringue: *Bake in a preheated 350-degree oven 12 to 15 minutes, or until peaks are light brown.*

Microwave: *Microwave on High (100 percent power) about 3 minutes (1 minute for each egg white), or until knife inserted horizontally into side comes out clean.*

Poached: *Simmer, uncovered, about 5 minutes, or until firm.*

For up-to-date information on eggs, including cooking techniques and food safety, contact the American Egg Board (see Chapter Fourteen).

**endive** Indicate whether you mean curly endive or Belgian endive. Curly endive, also called "frisée," is a loose head of lacy, green-tipped leaves; it is often mistakenly called "chicory." Belgian endive, also called "French endive" or "witloof," is a cigar-shaped head of whitish, tightly packed leaves with pale yellow-green tips. See CHICORY.

**evaporated milk** Do not confuse with sweetened condensed milk; the two are not interchangeable. Evaporated milk comes in 5-ounce and 12-ounce cans.

**extracts/flavorings** Be specific about which is used. Repeat both words (as in following examples) in recipe directions. (Exception: You can just say "vanilla" in directions.)

*almond extract, almond flavoring*

*butter flavoring*

*peppermint extract*

*vanilla extract*

**Fahrenheit** A temperature scale in which freezing is 32 degrees and boiling is 212 degrees. Used as the standard temperature measurement in the United States. Most U.S. consumer-size conventional ovens register the temperature only in degrees Fahrenheit; therefore it is not necessary to indicate Fahrenheit (or F) in recipes written for a U.S.-only audience, although it is fine to do so if desired.

See CELSIUS. For conversion formula of Fahrenheit to Celsius, see Chapter Eight, "Metrics."

**fats** See FAT in Chapter Five, "Cooking Terminology."

**fish and shellfish** List by weight and/or by the piece. Fish and shellfish are generally raw or uncooked. If cooked, be sure to indicate that in the ingredient listing.

*4 tuna steaks (about 6 ounces each)*

*1 whole trout (about 2 pounds), cleaned*

Tests for doneness:

Fish: *Until fish flakes easily when tested with a fork.*

Whole lobster or crab: *Until shells turn red.*

Lobster tail: *Until meat turns opaque.*

Whole clams, oysters, or mussels: *Until shells open and clams (oysters, mussels) are thoroughly cooked. Discard any that do not open.*

Shucked clams, oysters, or mussels: *Until clams (oysters, mussels) become plump and opaque.*

Scallops: *Until scallops are opaque.*

Shrimp: *Until shrimp turn pink.*

**-flavored** Not "-flavor."

*Apricot-flavored brandy*

*Chocolate-flavored syrup*

**flavorings/extracts** See EXTRACTS / FLAVORINGS.

**flour** List flour in tablespoons and cups, rather than by weight (or give both measures). Weighing flour is the most accurate way to measure it, but most American home cooks do not have kitchen scales and are not used to weighing flour. When sifted flour is important to the recipe results, specify sifting in the method.

See FLOUR in Chapter Five, "Cooking Terminology." When more than one type of flour is used in a recipe, repeat the type in the method.

When calling for self-rising flour or cake flour, be sure to include a note offering substitutions (if appropriate). Many cooks do not have these flours on hand.

Equivalents: 1 cup cake flour equals 1 cup minus 2 tablespoons all-purpose flour; 1 cup self-rising flour equals 1 cup all-purpose flour plus $1\frac{1}{2}$ teaspoons baking powder and $\frac{1}{2}$ teaspoon salt (the amount of salt can be reduced depending on the recipe).

**fold** See Chapter Five, "Cooking Terminology." Many cooks are unsure of how to fold ingredients; it might be helpful to describe the process rather than use the term "fold." When using "fold," make it clear which ingredient is being folded into the other.

*Gently fold flour into beaten egg whites.*

**foil** See ALUMINUM FOIL.

**fondue** Sample wordings:

For hot oil fondue: *Fill a metal fondue pot half full with oil. Heat oil on top of stove to 365 degrees. Carefully transfer pot to fondue burner on table. Using fondue forks, spear meat (or other food) and cook in hot oil 1 to 2 minutes, or until done.*

For cheese, chocolate, or other fondue mixtures: *Assemble and heat the ingredients in a heavy saucepan on top of stove. Transfer hot mixture to fondue pot. Place pot on fondue burner on table. Serve at once with appropriate dippers.*

**food color** Not "food coloring."

**food processor** When possible, give the option of using an electric blender; see BLENDER. Specify which blade to use if it is important to recipe results.

**foreign languages** Foreign words are often used in recipe names, but they can be confusing to inexperienced cooks. When using a foreign recipe name, include a descriptive translation in English in parentheses. Or put the recipe name in English, with the authentic foreign name in parentheses.

There are hundreds of French culinary terms that describe specific dishes and cooking preparations and techniques. However, not all cooks are familiar with the meanings of the French terms. An English title should contain a descriptive, not a literal, translation of the term. Recipe directions should describe a technique.

See Chapter Five, "Cooking Terminology," for definitions of many foreign terms. See BRITISH CULINARY TERMS for some differences between American and British English.

**fractions** Use numerals in the ingredient list and in the recipe method when the fraction refers to an amount, such as ½ cup or ¾ pound. Spell out fractions in the method when they refer to portions of ingredients or mixtures.

*Add one-fourth of the egg whites.*

*Stir in half of the batter.*

*Reduce by one-third.*

*Fill halfway up the sides of the pan.*

**frankfurter** Not "hot dog" or "wiener."

**frisée** See ENDIVE.

**frosting** Generally preferred instead of "icing." "Frosting" indicates a consistency that is thick enough to spread. "Icing" can be used to describe a thin, translucent glaze. See GLAZE.

*Beat in enough of the remaining milk to make frosting smooth and of spreading consistency.*

**frozen whipped topping** Originally, this term identified nondairy whipped toppings, but many brands now contain some dairy products. Specify dairy or nondairy only if crucial to recipe results.

*1 (8-ounce) container frozen whipped topping, thawed*

*1 cup thawed frozen whipped topping*

**fruit** List by weight and/or by the piece. Include a description of size (small, medium, or large) or a measure (3-inch diameter). See Chapter Twelve, "Purchasing Information."

**fruit pectin** There are three types of commercial fruit pectin products; they are not interchangeable in recipes. Specify the type of pectin.

Liquid: *Available in boxes containing two 3-ounce packages.*

Powdered: *Available in 1¾-ounce boxes.*

Light powdered: *Available in 1¾-ounce boxes; requires less sugar.*

**frypan/frying pan** Preferred term is "skillet."

**-fuls** *Canfuls, cupfuls, tablespoonfuls, teaspoonfuls.*

**garlic** Usage examples:

*1 clove garlic, finely chopped*

*1 clove garlic, crushed*

You might choose to say "1 garlic clove, finely chopped." This is fine; just be consistent.

**garlic salt/garlic powder** Repeat both words in recipe directions.

**garnish** If the garnish is an important or essential part of a recipe or requires special preparation, mention it in the ingredient list. If not, there is no need to list the garnish; simply refer to it in the directions with the phrase "if desired."

In ingredient list:

*1 red bell pepper, cut into strips, for garnish*

If using subheads in ingredient list:

*For garnish:*

*1 lemon, cut into wedges*

In directions:

*Garnish with parsley sprigs, if desired.*

**gelatin** Not "gelatine." Specify flavored or unflavored. One (¼-ounce) envelope contains 1 tablespoon unflavored gelatin, which will gel 2 cups of liquid and up to 1½ cups of solids.

Note the difference in preparation methods.

For one envelope unflavored gelatin:

*Sprinkle gelatin on cold water in saucepan. Let stand 5 minutes to soften. Heat over low heat, stirring constantly, until gelatin is dissolved.*

*Microwave: Sprinkle 1 envelope unflavored gelatin over ¼ cup water in a microwave-safe glass measure. Let stand 1 minute. Microwave on High (100 percent power) 15 seconds; stir. Microwave on High 25 seconds; stir.*

If sugar is added to unflavored gelatin (at least ¼ cup sugar per envelope of gelatin), softening is not necessary:

*Mix sugar and gelatin in a saucepan. Stir in water (or other liquid). Heat over low heat, stirring constantly, until gelatin is dissolved.*

For 1 (3-ounce) package orange-flavored gelatin:

*Pour boiling water over gelatin in bowl; stir until gelatin is dissolved.*

Some fresh fruit (pineapple, papaya, figs, kiwi fruit, and prickly pears) and fresh ginger should not be added to gelatin salads because they contain an enzyme that affects gelling. Canned or cooked versions of these fruits (except kiwi fruit) can be added to gelatin salads.

**gelatin, unmolding** Carefully loosen gelatin from side of container with the tip of a sharp knife. Dip the container into warm (not hot) water almost to the depth of the gelatin contents for about 5 seconds; tilt or shake container gently to loosen the gelatin. Invert serving dish on top of container. Hold both firmly together and turn over (to right-side up). Shake gently until gelatin slips from container onto serving dish. If gelatin doesn't come loose easily, repeat the process. (It's a good idea to wet the serving dish. If the mold comes out off center, it can be moved carefully into place.)

**gelling, stages of** Chilling time varies, depending on the quantity of the mixture, the container used, and the temperature of the refrigerator.

*Refrigerate until partly set:* Allow 20 to 45 minutes. (At this stage, the gelatin is the consistency of unbeaten egg whites. Solids are added at this stage. If whipped, the mixture will become fluffy and will mound.)

*Refrigerate until almost firm:* Allow 30 to 60 minutes. (The gelatin mixture appears set, but will tend to flow if tipped to one side. It is sticky to the touch. Layering is done at this stage.)

*Refrigerate until firm:* Allow 3 hours or longer. (The gelatin mixture can now hold a distinctive cut. The gelatin doesn't move when the mold is tilted.)

**generic term** A common descriptive name for a brand name product. A generic term is available for common use, is not protected by trademark registration, and is printed in lowercase letters. See Chapter Seven.

**ghee** *Ghee* is the Hindi word for fat. It refers to a form of clarified butter that originated in India but now is used around the world as both an ingredient and a cooking medium.

**ginger** Indicate form:

> Fresh: *1 (1-inch) piece fresh ginger* (not ginger root, gingerroot, or gingeroot)
>
> Ground: *1 teaspoon ground ginger*
>
> Crystallized (same as candied): *1 tablespoon crystallized ginger*

**glaze** A glaze is usually of pouring or drizzling consistency. Thinner glazes can be drizzled; thicker glazes can be spooned or spread.

> Typical directions:
>
> *Beat until smooth and of desired consistency. Spoon glaze on top of cake, letting some drip down the sides.*
>
> *Drizzle glaze over cookies.*

**granulated sugar** If the only sugar used in a recipe is granulated sugar, there is no need to specify granulated (although it is fine to do so). However, if confectioners' sugar or brown sugar is used in addition to granulated sugar, specify each type; repeat both words in recipe directions. Do not use "white sugar" for granulated sugar.

**grapes** Indicate green or red and seedless, if important to recipe results.

**grated** Hard cheeses and fruit peels are grated, not shredded.

**grease** You can make greasing the cooking and baking utensils a separate step in the recipe method in all cases, or only for critical mixtures that should not stand, such as cakes, muffins, soufflés, or popovers. Decide your style and be consistent.

It is also important to indicate ungreased, when no greasing is necessary.

> *Grease and flour a 13 x 9 x 2-inch baking pan. Spread batter in prepared pan.*
>
> *Transfer cookies to ungreased baking sheet.*
>
> *Put dough in greased loaf pan.*

**green onions** Preferred instead of "scallions." (Many readers confuse scallions with shallots; see SHALLOT.) Indicate green part only or white part only if that is the case.

*¼ cup chopped green onions (green part only)*

*2 green onions, sliced*

**green pepper** See BELL PEPPER.

**grill** See BARBECUE. Allow about 5 minutes to preheat a gas grill. Allow 20 to 30 minutes for charcoal to reach the white-ash stage.

*Grill 4 to 5 inches from hot coals 10 to 12 minutes, turning once, or until fish flakes easily when tested with a fork.*

**ground beef** Use this term to refer to raw ground meat. Use "hamburger" to refer to the cooked patty.

**half-and-half** Not "half and half." See CREAM in Chapter Five, "Cooking Terminology."

**hamburger** A cooked patty of ground beef; a cooked hamburger patty served in a split round bun. Use "ground beef" to indicate the raw ingredient.

**hard-cooked egg** Not "hard-boiled egg."

*1 hard-cooked egg, peeled and chopped*

**hazelnut/filbert** These terms are interchangeable and vary according to the region of the country. For recipes destined for a national audience, it is a good idea to indicate both terms.

*½ cup chopped hazelnuts (filberts)*

**healthy/healthful** Use these terms correctly. A person is healthy; a food or diet is healthful.

**heat/preheat** See PREHEAT/HEAT.

**heavy cream** Use instead of "whipping cream." See CREAM in Chapter Five, "Cooking Terminology."

**herbs** Specify fresh, dried, ground, flakes, or other form. Specify leaves only when a ground form also exists, such as marjoram, oregano, sage, thyme; try to use the leaf form because it keeps better than ground. If listing both fresh and dried, put fresh first; you do not have to repeat the herb name after the dried amount.

*1 tablespoon chopped fresh oregano, or 1 teaspoon dried*

As a general rule, call for three times as much fresh as dried. See Chapter Twelve, "Purchasing Information."

**high-acid foods** Some high-acid foods (such as long-cooking tomato sauces or pickling mixtures with a lot of vinegar) should not be cooked in aluminum pans. Specify stainless steel or enamel pans.

**high-altitude** See Chapter Four, "Recipe Testing."

**horseradish** Specify grated fresh horseradish or prepared white horseradish, unless red (beet-tinted) horseradish is used for color.

**hot dog** A heated frankfurter served in a long split roll. Use "frankfurter" as an ingredient listing.

**hot pepper sauce** Use instead of "Tabasco" or "red pepper sauce." Repeat "pepper sauce" in recipe directions. See TABASCO SAUCE.

**ice cream cone/ice cream sandwich/ice cream topping** Not "ice-cream" (no hyphen).

**iced coffee/iced tea** Not "ice coffee," "ice tea."

**ice water** Not "iced water."

**icing** Generally, the preferred term is "frosting." See FROSTING, GLAZE.

**if desired/optional** Used interchangeably in ingredient list. Decide style and be consistent.

In ingredient list:

> ¼ *cup chopped fresh parsley, if desired*
>
> ¼ *cup chopped fresh parsley (optional)*

In directions:

> *Serve pie with ice cream, if desired.*
>
> *Sprinkle grated cheese over each serving and, if desired, garnish with parsley sprigs.*

**indentation** Preferred instead of "impression" or "imprint."

> *Bake about 20 minutes, or until no indentation remains when cake is touched.*

**inexact amounts** Inexact or unspecified amounts of some ingredients are acceptable because they are items presumed to be found in all kitchens: flour for dredging ingredients or shortening for greasing a pan, for example. In most cases, these ingredients do not need to be included in the ingredient list of a recipe; they can just be referred to in the method. For some audiences, such as beginning cooks, listing these ingredients is preferable. Be consistent throughout a project. (See WATER, SALT AND PEPPER.)

> *All-purpose flour, for dredging*
>
> *All-purpose flour, for rolling out dough*
>
> *Butter or shortening, for greasing pan*
>
> *Vegetable oil, for oiling cookie sheet*
>
> *Cornmeal, for coating pan*

**instant** Be sure to include this term when necessary to correctly indentify a specific ingredient.

> *instant rice*
>
> *powdered instant coffee*
>
> *instant pudding and pie filling mix*
>
> *instant mashed potatoes*

**Irish whiskey** Not "whisky."

**Jerusalem artichoke/sunchoke** These terms are interchangeable, but "Jerusalem artichoke" is preferred. Decide on one and be consistent. "Sunchoke" is a marketing term for Jerusalem artichoke.

**kabob** Preferred spelling. "Kebab" and "kebob" are also used. Decide on your style and be consistent.

**keep warm** Don't just say "keep warm." Tell the reader how to keep the food warm.

*Keep warm in a 200-degree oven while preparing the sauce.*

*Cover loosely with foil to keep warm while preparing the gravy.*

*Keep warm over simmering water.*

**knead** Usage example:

*Punch down dough. Turn dough onto lightly floured surface. Knead about 5 minutes, or until smooth and elastic.*

**layer** Usage examples:

*Layer half the beef, all the tomato sauce, and the remaining beef in an ungreased 13 x 9 x 2-inch baking pan.*

*Layer one-fourth each of the noodles, meat sauce, and cheese in an ungreased 9 x 9 x 2-inch baking pan; repeat layers three times using remaining ingredients, ending with cheese layer.*

**leftover** The preferred term is "remaining."

*Cover and refrigerate any remaining sauce.*

**lemon (lime) juice** Repeat both words in the recipe directions. When calling for juice of one lemon (lime), indicate approximate amount.

Equivalents: Juice of 1 lemon = about 3 tablespoons; juice of 1 lime = about 2 tablespoons.

**lemon (lime) peel** Use "peel," not "rind" or "zest." Repeat both words in the recipe directions. Specify freshly grated, dried grated, cut in spirals, strips, or other form.

When the recipe calls for both peel and juice, list the peel first (the cook should grate the peel before juicing the fruit).

*1 teaspoon freshly grated lemon peel*

*Juice of 1 lemon (about 3 tablespoons)*

**lemon pepper seasoning/lemon pepper** Both terms are used as generic descriptions for this seasoning mixture. Select one and be consistent. Repeat complete term in recipe directions.

**let rise** Usage example:

*Let dough rise in warm, draft-free place abount 2 hours, or until double in bulk.*

**let stand** Usage examples:

*Let stand 10 minutes before slicing.*

*Let stand while preparing topping.*

**letters as shapes** Usage examples:

*Use a floured knife to cut an X shape in top of loaf.*

*For each candy, arrange 3 almonds in Y shape on ungreased baking sheet.*

**lime juice, peel** See LEMON JUICE, LEMON PEEL.

**line** Usage examples:

*Line bottom and sides of 9 x 5 x 3-inch loaf pan with aluminum foil or waxed paper; grease foil.*

*Line muffin cups with paper baking cups.*

**liqueurs** Preferred instead of "cordials." See Chapter Seven, "Generic Terms," for suggested terminology.

**loosely packed** Do not hyphenate.

*1 cup loosely packed shredded zucchini (about 1 medium)*

**main dish** The main course at a meal. Hyphenated as a compound adjective, such as "main-dish salad" or "main-dish soup."

**maple-flavored syrup** Use this term unless you are really calling for pure maple syrup. Many cooks don't realize that maple-flavored syrup isn't pure maple syrup—until they taste the real thing.

**margarine/vegetable oil spread** The government's standard fat content for margarine is at least 80 percent. In recent years, most margarine manufacturers have reduced the fat content to below 80 percent, making the product not margarine but a modified margarine or a vegetable oil spread. These spreads range from 70 percent fat to no fat. Modified margarines include reduced-fat (no more than 60 percent fat), light or low-fat (no more than 40 percent fat), and fat-free (less than ½ gram fat per serving); everything else is a vegetable oil spread. Because many of these spreads are sold in 1-pound packages with four sticks, many consumers don't realize that they are not regular margarine. As a general rule for baking recipes, specify a product that contains at least 60 percent fat. Sample wording:

*½ cup (1 stick) vegetable oil spread (at least 60 percent fat)*

See BUTTER OR MARGARINE, MEASUREMENT OF.

**marinade/marinate** Indicate whether a mixture is covered and refrigerated during marinating time. Indicate whether a marinade is reserved or discarded. Follow food safety procedures when marinating raw meats, poultry, fish, or seafood. In general, do not marinate meat, fish, or poultry at room temperature for more than one hour. Marinade that has had raw meat/blood in it should be boiled for 5 to 10 minutes before using for basting or as a sauce.

For additional information, see Chapter Four, "Recipe Testing."

**Marsala** Specify sweet or dry.

**marshmallows**

To melt marshmallows: *To each 10-ounce bag regular marshmallows or 4 cups miniature marshmallows, add 2 tablespoons butter or margarine. Heat over low heat, stirring constantly, 3 to 4 minutes, or until marshmallows are melted. Or, microwave on High (100 percent power) 1½ to 2 minutes, stirring every 45 seconds.*

**meats** List meat by weight and/or by the piece. Provide two measurements when possible. Indicate thickness, bone in or boneless, and other useful information.

*4 boneless center-cut pork chops, cut 1 inch thick*

*1 (4- to 5-pound) beef rump roast*

*4 knockwurst sausages (about 1 pound total)*

Tests for doneness:

Beef top loin or T-bone steaks, 1 inch thick: *8 to 12 minutes for rare, 12 to 15 minutes for medium, 16 to 20 minutes for well done.*

Beef rib roast: *Until meat thermometer registers 140 degrees for rare, 160 degrees for medium, 170 degrees for well done.*

Pork: *Until juices run clear, no pink remains, and meat thermometer registers 160 to 170 degrees.*

Pork chops: *Chops cooked to 160 degrees might be slightly pink, but juices should run clear.*

Pork loin blade, sirloin roasts, and ground pork: *Cook to 170 degrees.*

Veal roasts: *Until meat thermometer registers 160 to 170 degrees for loin and rib roasts, 170 degrees for shoulder and breast roasts.*

Leg of lamb: *Until meat thermometer registers 140 degrees for rare, 160 degrees for medium, 170 degrees for well done.*

Ground meat: *Cook until meat is brown.*

For up-to-date information on standard cuts and correct terminology for beef, veal, lamb, and pork, you can request current meat charts from the American Lamb Council, the National Cattlemen's Beef Association, and the National Pork Producers Council (see Chapter Fourteen).

**meat thermometer** Usage example:

> *Insert meat thermometer in center of thickest part of meat, so tip is not touching bone or fat.*

**microwave cooking** See Microwave Style Sheet, page 94.

**mixer/mixing bowls** *Free-standing electric mixer:* Indicate size of mixer bowl (large or small) in the recipe directions. If ingredients include less than ½ cup fat and less than 2 cups flour, specify a small bowl. For larger amounts, specify a large bowl.

*Portable electric mixer or no mixer:* Indicate size of mixing bowl (small, medium, or large) in the recipe directions.

Small mixing bowl (3 cups)—up to 1 cup flour

Medium mixing bowl (1½ quarts)—up to 2 cups flour

Large mixing bowl (2½ quarts)—more than 2 cups flour

See BOWL.

**mixer, electric** Say "mixer," not "beater."
Common electric mixer speeds:

> *Low:* Used for whipping cream, combining ingredients before increasing speed, and mixtures that might splash.

> *Medium:* Used for creaming butter and sugar or other mixtures, icy mixtures, and salad dressings.

> *High:* Used for candy, egg whites and meringues, egg yolks, and most batters.

Usage example:

> *Beat with an electric mixer on high speed 5 minutes, or until soft peaks form.*

**mojo** A sauce blend of the following four components: any citrus, any member of the lily family (genus *Allium;* onion, garlic, shallot, chive, leek), any herb, and olive oil. A classic mojo combines sour orange, garlic, parsley, and olive oil.

**molasses** Indicate light (mild) or dark (robust) when flavor and color are important to recipe results.

**mushrooms** Restaurant menus and cookbook recipes abound with "wild" mushroom ingredients, although most of the mushrooms called for are harvested on farms rather than foraged in the wild. For authors and menu writers in search of accuracy, "specialty mushrooms" is a useful term that includes both wild and cultivated mushrooms. The term "exotic mushrooms" is also used, but it is losing its meaning as specialty mushrooms become more common. When possible, identify specific varieties, such as wood ears, shiitakes, or oyster mushrooms. See MUSHROOMS in Chapter Five, "Cooking Terminology."

To clean mushrooms, gently wipe with a damp cloth or soft brush to remove particles. Or, rinse quickly with cold water and immediately pat dry with paper towels. Do not soak mushrooms; they are porous and will absorb water.

**mustard** Indicate dry or prepared or other specific type. Repeat "dry mustard" in recipe directions.

**numerals** In text, use figures for numbers 10 and above, and spell out numbers nine and below (follow AP style). In recipe names, follow the same rule. In ingredient lists, use figures for all numbers and fractions. In recipe method, use figures for numbers and fractions that refer to specific measurements (5 inches, 4 dozen, ½ cup).
Exceptions:

Spell out numbers used in a general sense, such as "add eggs, one at a time" or "cut in shortening with two knives."

Spell out fractions used in a general sense, such as "fill the muffin cups two-thirds full."

Avoid using two numbers together, such as "1 8-ounce package," because this can easily be read as "18-ounce package." In the ingredient list, the best way to prevent this is to use parentheses: 1 (8-ounce) package.

In recipe instructions or in a phrase that is already within parentheses, spell out the first number: one 8-ounce package.

Never begin a sentence with a figure; spell out the number or reword the sentence.

**nuts** Be specific about the type of nut: pecan, peanut, almond, walnut, cashew, and so on. Indicate form: cashews, cashew halves, cashew pieces, chopped cashews. Also indicate salted or unsalted, roasted or unroasted, shelled or unshelled, if important to recipe results or necessary for clarity.

*1 pound walnuts, shelled (about 1½ cups chopped)*

*½ cup chopped salted peanuts*

**nuts, toasted** When calling for toasted nuts, include directions.

*2 cups slivered almonds, toasted*

To toast almonds: *Spread almonds in an ungreased pan. Bake in a preheated 350-degree oven 5 to 7 minutes, stirring occasionally, or until brown.*

**oats/rolled oats/oatmeal** "Oats" or "rolled oats" refers to the uncooked ingredient; "oatmeal" refers to the cooked cereal. Be sure to specify quick-cooking or old-fashioned oats in the ingredient list.

**olives** Be specific. See OLIVES in Chapter Five, "Cooking Terminology." "Ripe olive" is the preferred term, instead of "black olive."

**optional** See IF DESIRED / OPTIONAL.

**orange juice** Repeat both words in recipe directions. When calling for juice of one orange, indicate the approximate amount.

Equivalents: Juice of 1 orange = about 4 tablespoons.

**orange peel** Use "peel," not "rind" or "zest." Repeat both words in recipe directions. Indicate freshly grated, dried grated, cut in spirals, strips, or other form. When a recipe calls for both peel and juice, list the peel first (the cook should grate the peel before juicing the fruit).

*1 teaspoon freshly grated orange peel*

*Juice of 1 orange (about 4 tablespoons)*

**organic** The following definition of "organic" was passed by the National Organic Standards Board in 1995: "Organic agriculture is an ecological production management system that promotes and enhances biodiversity, biological cycles, and soil biological activity. It is based on minimal use of off-farm inputs and on management practices that restore, maintain, and enhance ecological harmony."

"Certified organic" means that the grower or processor has met or exceeded defined standards. The confusion lies in the fact that standards vary throughout the world.

The Organic Trade Association (see Chapter Fourteen) is the leading business association representing the organic industry in the United States and Canada.

**oven temperatures** See DEGREES. Some typical oven temperatures:

For baking breads:
    biscuits—450 degrees
    muffins (regular)—400 degrees
    muffins (large)—375 degrees
    quick breads—350 degrees
    scones—425 degrees

For baking cookies:
    bar cookies—350 degrees
    cut-out, drop, shaped, or sliced cookies—375 degrees
    shortbread—325 degrees

For baking casseroles: 350 to 375 degrees

For roasting meats: 325 degrees

**overnight** Instead of just saying "overnight," indicate a specific amount of time if possible, to enable the cook to properly plan the preparation schedule.

*Cover and refrigerate 6 to 8 hours.*

*Cover and refrigerate at least 12 hours but no longer than 36 hours.*

*Cover and refrigerate 8 to 12 hours, or overnight.*

**package directions** When appropriate in recipe method, say, "Prepare according to package directions." This is especially useful when directions vary among different brands of a product.

If the recipe method is slightly different from the package directions, say, "Prepare according to package directions, except add [omit]. . . ."

If the recipe method is totally different from the package directions, give the method without referring to package instructions.

For rice and pasta, say, "Cook according to package directions."

**paper baking cups** Not "paper liners."

**paper towels** Not "paper toweling."

**pared/unpared** See PEELED/UNPEELED.

**parsley** Specify curly parsley or flat-leaf (Italian) parsley, if it is important to recipe results.

**partly** Not "partially." Usage example:

*Partly thawed*

**pasta** Indicate both number of ounces and a cup measure (when appropriate) in ingredient list. For large pasta shapes, such as lasagna noodles, indicate the number of pieces instead of a cup measure. Indicate uncooked or cooked if there is any chance of confusion.

*4 ounces uncooked elbow macaroni (1 cup)*

If calling for a specific amount of cooked pasta, indicate the amount of uncooked pasta that is necessary to obtain the cooked amount. Exception: If a recipe is served over hot cooked pasta, you can simply call for "hot cooked pasta" in the ingredient list, just as you would call for "hot cooked rice."

The National Pasta Association (see Chapter Fourteen) can provide detailed information on types and shapes of pasta, plus preferred spellings.

**pasteurized process cheese** See PROCESS CHEESE.

**pectin** See FRUIT PECTIN.

**peeled/unpeeled** Indicate peeled or unpeeled if one is preferred. If it makes no difference, it is not necessary to specify either way. You might prefer to use "pared" and "unpared"; just be consistent. Some sources recommend "pare" for vegetables and "peel" for fruits.

**pepper** Indicate black, white, or cayenne in ingredient list.

**pies** If a pie shell is to be completely baked before it is filled, prick the bottom and sides with a fork to keep it from puffing during baking. Do not prick the bottom of an unbaked or partly baked pie shell before adding the filling, or the filling will seep under the pastry.

To keep the crust from puffing or shrinking, some cooks line the pastry with aluminum foil; some also fill it with pie weights or dried beans. See BAKING BLIND.

For a baked pie crust (to be filled):

> *Fit pastry into 9- (or 8- or 10-) inch pie pan. Prick bottom and sides of pastry with fork. Line pastry with a double thickness of aluminum foil (or line pastry with aluminum foil and fill with pie weights or dried beans). Bake in a preheated 450-degree oven 8 minutes. Remove foil (and weights). Bake 5 to 6 minutes, or until golden. Let cool. Continue as directed in recipe.*

For a lattice crust:

> *Roll out pastry. Cut into ½-inch-wide strips. Arrange strips over filling to make a lattice crust. Press ends of strips into rim to bottom pastry. Fold bottom pastry over strips. Seal and flute edge.*

**pie weights** Metal or ceramic pellets used to fill a pastry shell in order to bake it without a filling. See BAKING BLIND.

**pineapple** Indicate fresh or canned. For canned, indicate form (crushed, sliced, in chunks), as well as "in juice" or "in syrup."

**place** Use this term when the placement is less specific than would be indicated by the term "arrange."

> *Place rolls on greased baking sheet.*
>
> *Place roast in shallow baking dish.*

**plump** Usage example:

*Cover raisins with hot water; let stand about 15 minutes, or until raisins are plump.*

**popcorn** Be sure to indicate whether the ingredient amount is popped or unpopped.

*3 cups popped popcorn*

*¼ cup unpopped popcorn*

**portabella mushrooms** One of the most popular "new" mushrooms, for both restaurant and home use. In the mid-1980s, some enterprising mushroom growers recognized the potential for selling extra-large crimini mushrooms that were being discarded. Their phenomenal popularity might be attributed to their size (up to 6 inches in diameter), their chewy texture and robust flavor, year-round availability, reasonable cost, and suitability as a meat substitute for vegetarian meals. They were first marketed as "portabella" mushrooms; the "portobello" spelling is also frequently used. Decide on your spelling and be consistent.

Equivalents: 1 pound portabellas = 3 to 4 medium caps (4 inches in diameter) with stems or 4 to 5 medium caps only or 2 large caps (6 inches in diameter) with stems or 3 large caps only.

**potato starch** When using potato starch to thicken sauces or other mixtures, do not let it boil. Potato starch thickens at 160 to 175 degrees and will thin again if boiled.

**powdered sugar** See CONFECTIONERS' SUGAR.

**power levels** See Microwave Style Sheet, page 94.

**preheat/heat** You can say "preheat oven to 300 degrees" or "heat oven to 300 degrees." Decide on your style and be consistent. Put the preheating information in a logical and timely place within the recipe method; it doesn't necessarily have to be the first instruction. Ten to 15 minutes is usually adequate for preheating an oven.

At the same place as you give preheating instructions, include directions for placement of oven rack(s), if necessary.

It is a good idea to repeat the oven temperature when the directions finally call for putting the food in the oven: "Bake in a preheated 300-degree oven."

**process cheese** Preferred term. Available in many types and forms; check package labels for best generic descriptions. Brand names are often helpful to reader because the generic terms are confusing. Among the many process cheese items are cheese food, slices, spread, sauce, loaf, snack links, cheese product, and imitation cheese food. See CHEESE.

**prunes/dried plums** Image is everything, and the California Prune Board is out to change the image of prunes by calling them dried plums. The Food and Drug Administration approved the name change in July 2000.

**pudding and pie mixes** Be sure to indicate instant or regular; specify package size.

**raisins** It's not necessary to specify seedless raisins. Indicate dark or golden if important to recipe results.

**rectangular** Use "rectangular" instead of "oblong" when describing a baking pan or dish.

**red pepper** "Ground red pepper" is the same as "cayenne." "Crushed red pepper" is the same as "hot red pepper flakes." Red bell peppers are sweet (not hot) peppers.

**reduce** Refers to a reduction in temperature; also refers to rapidly boiling a liquid to reduce the quantity and concentrate the flavor.

*Reduce the oven temperature to 350 degrees.*

*Heat to boiling; reduce heat and simmer, covered, 10 minutes.*

*Boil, uncovered, for 10 to 15 minutes, or until mixture has reduced by about half.*

**refrigerate** Preferred instead of "chill" (as a verb). See CHILL.

*Refrigerate about 2 hours, or until thoroughly chilled.*

*Cover and refrigerate any remaining salad.*

**remaining ingredients** It is preferable to repeat each ingredient in the recipe directions as it is used. If space is tight, it is acceptable to say "stir in remaining ingredients" or "mix remaining ingredients" if all of the remaining ingredients are indeed being used. Do not use this wording if one or two ingredients are being retained to be added later, as for a topping. See RESERVE / RESERVING, RESERVED.

**remove** Usage examples:

*Simmer, uncovered, over low heat until smooth and bubbly; remove from heat.*

*Remove roast from pan; place on serving platter.*

**reserve/reserving** Use these terms in recipe directions to indicate that an item or mixture will be not be used until later. Be sure that a reserved item is added to the recipe later; a frequent error in writing recipes is to forget a reserved item.

If the item is going to be used in the next one or two steps, it isn't necessary to indicate "reserve." Keep the reader in mind; don't clutter the recipe with unnecessary or confusing information.

Some writers use "set aside" instead of "reserve." This can cause some confusion because the item will be identified as the "reserved item" when it is used later.

*Mix sugar and cinnamon; reserve.*

*Transfer cooked bacon to paper towels. Let drain. Coarsely crumble the cooled bacon. Reserve.*

*Drain cooked beans, reserving 1 cup liquid.*

Use this term in the ingredient list to indicate that the liquid drained from an ingredient should be saved for use in the recipe.

*1 (8-ounce) can crushed pineapple, drained, reserving juice*

**reserved** When an item or mixture is reserved in the ingredient list or in the recipe directions, identify it as the reserved item when it is used.

*Sprinkle reserved sugar mixture over dough.*

*Garnish casserole with reserved crumbled bacon.*

*Stir drained beans and reserved 1 cup bean liquid into soup; mix well.*

*Add enough water to reserved pineapple juice to measure ¾ cup.*

When a mixture is divided into parts, one to be used right away and the other to be reserved for later use, identify the parts as remaining and reserved.

*Mix brown sugar, flour, butter, and pecans; reserve ½ cup for topping.*

*Spread remaining brown sugar mixture in pan. Pour batter over top.*

*Sprinkle reserved ½ cup brown sugar mixture on top.*

**rice** Indicate whether the ingredient is cooked or uncooked, if there is any chance of confusion. Specify type of rice: brown, white, instant or quick-cooking, parboiled (converted), long-grain, or basmati.

*1 cup cooked white or brown rice*

*1 cup uncooked long-grain white rice*

**room temperature** When it is important that an ingredient be at room temperature, indicate that in the recipe directions:

*Let butter stand at room temperature 30 minutes.*

*Let stand at room temperature 20 minutes, or until slightly thawed.*

Do not let meat, fish, or poultry marinate at room temperature for more than one hour. Do not thaw foods at room temperature.

**rum** Indicate dark or light if flavor or color is important to recipe results.

**saffron** Available in powdered form or filaments. In general, powdered saffron has less aroma than saffron filaments. Powdered is convenient to use and easy to measure, but how do you measure filaments? An average recipe requires about ¹⁄₁₀ gram filaments—impossible to weigh on kitchen scales. The equivalent of ¹⁄₁₀ gram is 40 to 50 filaments. Another way to estimate amounts is to allow six filaments per person plus another six filaments for the pot. If you're using the saffron just for color, you can reduce the amount by about half.

For an infusion, for each 40 to 50 filaments, add 2 tablespoons hot water. Let stand, covered, from 30 minutes to 12 hours. Or, microwave on Medium (50 percent power) for 1 minute.

**salad oil** Use the term "vegetable oil," or indicate a specific oil, such as canola oil or corn oil.

**salmon** Indicate drained or flaked when referring to canned salmon.

*1 (8-ounce) can salmon, drained and flaked*

**salt and pepper** "Salt" and "pepper" are nouns, not verbs. See SEASON.

In ingredient lists, give specific amounts, if possible. For multiple uses or unspecified amounts, list "Salt and pepper" in the ingredient list, then give amounts in the recipe method as ingredients are called for. Coarse salt and kosher salt are interchangeable terms; pick one and be consistent.

**sauce** Sauces with sour cream, yogurt, high butterfat content, or high egg content can break down if cooked too much. If a mixture should not boil, say "do not boil" in the method. If constant stirring is important, say "cook, stirring constantly, . . ." in the method.

When thickening a mixture with flour, gradually stir cold liquid into the flour. (Do not stir flour into a cold liquid.)

**saucepan/saucepot** Specify the size of saucepan in quarts if important to recipe results. Otherwise, simply indicate small saucepan (1 to 1½ quarts), medium (2 quarts), or large (3 to 4 quarts). A saucepot is usually 6 quarts or larger, with a handle on each side.

**sauté/sautéed** Many recipe readers can't give a definition of "sauté." Use "cook and stir" in recipe directions.

*Heat oil in skillet. Add onion; cook and stir until onion is tender.*

**scallions** See GREEN ONIONS.

**scallops** Specify bay scallops (small) or sea scallops (large).

**Scotch whisky** Not "Scotch" or "Scotch whiskey."

**season** Usage examples:

*Season to taste with salt and pepper.*

Not: *Salt and pepper to taste.*

Not: *Adjust seasoning.*

**seasoned salt** Repeat both words in recipe directions.

**self-rising** See FLOUR and CORNMEAL/CORNMEAL MIX.

**sesame seed** Include toasting directions if calling for toasted sesame seed. See BENNE SEED.

> ¼ *cup sesame seeds, toasted*
>
> To toast sesame seeds: *Spread seeds in ungreased pan and bake in preheated 375-degree oven 10 to 12 minutes, stirring occasionally, or until golden brown.*

**set aside/reserve** Generally, the term "reserve" is preferred, but in some instances, "set aside" is more appropriate. Let common sense be your guide. See RESERVE/RESERVING.

**sieve/strainer** Sieves usually have no handles; strainers usually have one handle. Sieves refine texture; strainers separate liquids from solids.

**shallot** A type of onion with an appearance more like garlic. Don't let shallots brown, or they will become bitter. Three to 4 shallots are roughly equivalent to 1 medium onion.

**sherry** Specify sweet or dry.

**shortening** Specify butter, margarine, solid vegetable shortening, lard, oil, or vegetable oil spread. See MARGARINE/VEGETABLE OIL SPREAD. See FAT in Chapter Five, "Cooking Terminology."

**shredded** Soft cheeses and vegetables are shredded, not grated.

**sift/stir** Most modern recipes specify sifting only for cake flour or confectioners' sugar. Stirring before measuring is adequate for most other types of flour. However, if the flour (or sugar) is sifted, be sure to indicate whether the measurement is before or after sifting; 1 cup sifted cake flour is quantitatively different from 1 cup cake flour, sifted.

**silver dragées** A popular candy decoration; small hard silver candy balls. Also called "silver decors."

**skewers** Specify wooden, bamboo, or metal when necessary. For example, wooden or bamboo skewers are used in a microwave oven, whereas metal skewers are often preferred for grilling. When using wooden or bamboo skewers over coals or fire, soak them in water for 30 minutes before use. Indicate this step in recipe directions.

**slow cooker** Use this term or "crockery cooker" instead of "Crock-Pot," which is a brand name.

**softened** Used to indicate the condition of an ingredient.

> *3 tablespoons butter or margarine, softened*
>
> Not: *3 tablespoons softened butter or margarine*
>
> Not: *3 tablespoons soft butter or margarine*

**sour cream** Repeat both words in recipe directions.

**soy sauce** Light or thin are used interchangeably, as are dark and black. Be consistent. Specify reduced-sodium soy sauce when appropriate.

**spices** Indicate form: whole, ground, sticks, or another form. See Chapter Twelve, "Purchasing Information."

> *1 teaspoon whole cloves*
>
> *½ teaspoon ground nutmeg*
>
> *2 (3-inch) sticks cinnamon*

**squares** Use this term (instead of "cookies") in the names and yields of bar cookie recipes that are cut into squares. Indicate the yield in exact numbers instead of in dozens. See BARS, COOKIES.

> *Yield: 15 squares.*

**squash** Specify type: acorn squash, butternut squash, chayote squash, crookneck squash, Hubbard squash, pattypan squash, pumpkin, spaghetti squash, yellow squash, zucchini.

**substitution** When an ingredient substitution cannot be made easily in the ingredient list, it is usually put in a note at the end of the recipe.

**sugar** List by tablespoons or cups, rather than by weight (or give both measurements). See BROWN SUGAR, CONFECTIONERS' SUGAR, GRANULATED SUGAR.

**sunflower seeds** Preferred terminology is "shelled sunflower seeds" not "sunflower kernels" or "sunflower nuts."

**surface** Use "lightly floured surface" rather than "lightly floured board."

**sweetened, unsweetened** Indicate sweetened or unsweetened when calling for frozen fruits and berries, such as strawberries and raspberries.

**sweetened condensed milk** Do not confuse with evaporated milk; the two are not interchangeable. Sweetened condensed milk comes in 14-ounce cans.

**Tabasco sauce** Most stylebooks recommend using "hot pepper sauce" instead of the brand name Tabasco. However, Tabasco is probably one of the most commonly used brand names in recipe writing because there is no specific generic term for it. "Hot pepper sauce" also is used for several Asian, Creole, and Southwestern sauces. Decide your style and be consistent. See HOT PEPPER SAUCE.

**thaw, thawed** Preferred instead of "defrost" when referring to food. (You thaw food; you defrost the freezer.)

*Thaw casserole before reheating.*

*Thaw fish, if frozen.*

*1 (10-ounce) package frozen chopped spinach, thawed and drained*

*1 (8-ounce) container frozen whipped topping, thawed*

**time/timing** In the recipe method, give the timing before the test for doneness.

*Simmer 15 minutes, or until soft and translucent.*

In recipes in which the stage is more important than the timing, as in candy directions, give the stage first and the timing as a guideline.

*Cook until sugar is melted and golden, about 5 minutes.*

Use seconds for times under 1 minute.
Use minutes for times under 1 hour.
Use "1 hour" or "about 1 hour" instead of "60 minutes" or "about 60 minutes."
Use minutes for ranges in time that begin at or under 1 hour and end at or over 1 hour (50 to 60 minutes, 50 to 70 minutes, 60 to 70 minutes).

Use hours and minutes for times that are more than 1 hour but cannot be expressed easily in fractions (1 hour 10 minutes).

Use hours and fractions for times that are more than 1 hour and can be expressed easily in fractions (1½ hours).

**to taste** Include in instructions or in ingredient list, but not in both. Don't say "to taste" if the mixture is something you shouldn't taste, such as raw meat or fish.

**tomato sauce/tomato paste** Repeat both words in recipe directions.

**toothpick/wooden pick** Used interchangeably. Decide your style and be consistent.

**transfer** Use "transfer" (or a similar descriptive word) when moving an object from one place to another.

*Transfer cookies to wire racks to cool.*

**tuna** Indicate whether canned tuna is packed in oil or in water. Indicate drained and flaked.

*1 (6-ounce) can chunk tuna in water, drained and flaked*

**turkey** To estimate the number of servings:

Whole turkey, 12 pounds and under: Allow 1 pound per serving.

Whole turkey, 12 to 24 pounds: Allow ¾ pound per serving.

Boneless turkey breast: Allow ⅓ pound per serving.

Tests for doneness:

Whole turkey: *Until meat thermometer inserted in thigh registers 180 to 185 degrees and drumsticks move easily.*

Turkey parts: *Until tender and no longer pink.*

Turkey breast: *Until meat thermometer reaches 170 degrees* (not 180 to 185 degrees).

For current information about turkey, contact the National Turkey Federation (see Chapter Fourteen).

**uncooked** Indicate that an ingredient is uncooked or raw when it is crucial to measurement and result, as for instant mashed potatoes, rice, oats, or pasta, or if there is any chance for confusion on the part of the recipe user.

**uncover, uncovered** If a utensil is not covered, indicate that in directions.

*Cover and simmer 10 minutes. Uncover and simmer 5 minutes.*

*Bake, uncovered, in preheated 350-degree oven about 30 minutes, or until hot and bubbly.*

**undrained** Used to specify that an ingredient should not be drained.

*1 (29-ounce) can tomatoes, undrained*

For clarity, you also can indicate this in the recipe method.

*Add tomatoes with their liquid, . . .*

**vanilla** Specify vanilla extract, vanilla flavoring, or vanilla bean.

**variation** Variations are usually added in paragraph form at the end of a recipe.

**vegetable oil** Use this term, not "salad oil." Indicate a specific type of vegetable oil (such as olive, corn, or canola) if important to recipe results. See VEGETABLE OIL in Chapter Five, "Cooking Terminology."

**vegetable oil spread** See MARGARINE/VEGETABLE OIL SPREAD.

**vegetable shortening** Use "solid vegetable shortening" in ingredient list;

use "shortening" in recipe directions. See BUTTER OR MARGARINE, MEASUREMENT OF. See FAT in Chapter Five, "Cooking Terminology."

**vinegar** Specify cider, distilled white, white wine, red wine, balsamic, flavored, or other type. See VINEGAR in Chapter Five, "Cooking Terminology."

**warm** A temperature of 105 to 115 degrees for food or liquid.

**water** Water, considered to be readily available, is usually omitted from the ingredient list when an unspecified amount is needed, such as for rinsing an ingredient, cooking pasta, or covering a vegetable before boiling. Water is usually listed when it is a specific ingredient, such as when a specific measure is given, something is dissolved in the water, or when the water is modified in some way, such as cold, hot, warm, or lukewarm. Include the desired temperature of water (or other liquid) in yeast bread recipes.

*¼ cup warm water (105 to 115 degrees)*

**waxed paper** Not "wax paper."

**Welsh rarebit** Melted and seasoned cheese, sometimes mixed with ale or beer, served over toasted bread or crackers. Not "Welsh rabbit."

**whipping cream** Preferred term is "heavy cream."

**whiskey** Spell with an *e* when referring to Irish or American whiskey.

**whisky** Spell without an *e* when referring to Scotch or Canadian whisky.

**white pepper** Repeat both words in recipe directions.

**wiener** "Frankfurter" is preferred.

**wild rice** Repeat both words in recipe directions.

**wine** Indicate dry, medium, or sweet red wine or dry, medium, or sweet white wine. If you call for a specific wine by a varietal or place-name, include a description of the type of wine.

*1 cup cabernet sauvignon or dry red wine*

The rules on capitalization for wines are utterly confusing and vary from source to source. One popular solution is to capitalize wines named for a place that come from that place and to lowercase wines named for a grape, but that rule doesn't always hold.

These are commonly used spellings according to Webster's Collegiate Dictionary, 10th edition:

*Beaujolais, burgundy, cabernet sauvignon, Chablis, champagne, chardonnay, Chianti, claret, gewürztraminer, Lambrusco, liebfraumilch, Madeira, marsala, merlot, pinot noir, port, Rhine, sauvignon blanc, sherry, and zinfandel.*

**Worcestershire sauce** Repeat both words in recipe directions.

**yeast** List active dry yeast by the package and/or by teaspoon or tablespoon; it is available in 2¼-teaspoon packages, 4-ounce jars, and in bulk. List compressed yeast by weight; it comes in 0.6-ounce cakes. See Chapter Twelve and Chapter Five. Liquid should be 120 to 130 degrees for yeast stirred into flour; 105 to 115 degrees for yeast dissolved in liquid.

*2 packages active dry yeast*

*1 (0.6-ounce) cake compressed yeast*

**yield** Give a yield on all recipes. Include both the size and the number of servings when possible, or other descriptive information. For some recipes, a volume measurement is more useful than a number of servings.

*Yield: 4 (½-cup) servings.*

*Yield: Enough to fill and frost a 9-inch 2-layer cake.*

*Yield: 4 servings (two kabobs per serving).*

*Yield: 2 quarts.*

Some approximate yields:

One 13 x 9 x 2-inch cake = 12 servings

One 9 x 5 x 3-inch or 9 x 4 x 3-inch loaf bread = 16 servings

One 9 x 9 x 2-inch or 8 x 8 x 2-inch cake or coffee cake = 9 servings

One 2-layer cake = 16 servings

One 9-inch cheesecake = 12 to 16 servings

One 9-inch pie = 6 to 8 servings

**yogurt** Indicate plain (unflavored) or flavored. Indicate low-fat or nonfat, if important to recipe results.

*1 (8-ounce) carton vanilla low-fat yogurt*

*1 (16-ounce) carton plain yogurt*

# Microwave Style Sheet

Recipes designed for microwave cooking have some special style considerations, which are discussed here. Otherwise, the basic style for conventional recipes applies.

Read the "Microwave Cooking" section in Chapter Four, "Recipe Testing," for useful information.

- Decide which verb you want to use to mean "cook in a microwave oven." The most common term is "microwave." Some use "micro-cook." If the entire project is about microwave cooking, some writers/editors just use "cook," because it is understood that every recipe is a microwave recipe. Be consistent throughout a project.

- Most ovens have at least three power levels, but many have 10 levels. Give a percentage of power, along with the word for the power level, because the percentage will be constant, whereas the word used can vary from brand to brand. Common terminology is:

    **100 percent—High**
    **70 percent—Medium-high**
    **50 percent—Medium**
    **30 percent—Medium-low**
    **10 percent—Low**

- Use High power unless there is a reason for using a lower power. On the first use, give both the percentage and the word; on subsequent uses within the same recipe, just give the word. If a different power level is used in the same recipe, introduce it with both the percentage and the word, and use the word in subsequent references.

  *Microwave, covered, on High (100 percent power) 2 minutes. Give dish a half-turn. Microwave on High 1 minute. Uncover. Microwave on Medium (50 percent power) 1 minute.*

- Indicate whether the food is loosely or tightly covered or uncovered and whether to use a lid, waxed paper, paper towels, or vented plastic wrap as a cover. If specifying plastic wrap, be sure to note that it should be vented at one corner to allow steam to escape. Do not use plastic wrap in microwave ovens with a browning unit; the plastic wrap will melt.

- Indicate stirring, turning, and rearranging as necessary.

- Specify microwave-safe baking dishes (or microwavable baking dishes).

- Include a statement such as this, if possible:

  *Microwave cooking times are based on countertop microwave ovens with 700 to 800 watts of cooking power. Cooking times are approximate because microwave ovens vary. For lower-wattage ovens, allow more time.*

- *Safety tips:* Most paper towels, plates, and other paper containers are safe to use for up to 10 minutes on 100 percent power in moist conditions. Some paper products can be a fire hazard when used for longer times or with high-fat, high-sugar mixtures. If there is a fire in the microwave oven, do not open the oven door. Immediately turn off the oven power. Cover the oven vent with a wet towel to stop the supply of oxygen to the fire.

  Use only white paper products because toxic dyes could be present in colored products and could be transmitted to the food during cooking.

  High-fat and/or high-sugar foods should be cooked in heavy-duty glass cookware that is free from cracks or chips.

Some high-fat mixtures can melt special plastic microwave cookware, so it is best to specify heavy-duty glass for such mixtures.

## Sample Recipes

Throughout this chapter we have included usage examples. The following sample recipes offer additional examples of suggested usage and style. They purposely vary in order to show that there is more than one correct way to write a recipe.

Our purpose in these sample recipes is to illustrate recipe content, not recipe format. Type fonts and styles are design decisions of each publication. Whether to use bold, italics, or small caps for the headnote, subheads, note, yield, and other recipe elements is a design decision that will vary from publication to publication. Whether to put the title before or after the headnote is a design decision, as is whether to put the yield at the beginning or the end of the recipe. There is no right or wrong; what works in one publication might not be appropriate for another.

Study magazines, cookbooks, brochures, and newspapers for examples of good recipe format and use that information to develop a recipe format that is appropriate for your publication.

# Curry Dip

*The original version of this curry dip appeared in one of our first collections of food editors' recipes, submitted by the late Peggy Daum Judge, food editor of the Milwaukee Journal. One of our readers sent us her low-fat adaptation of Peggy's recipe. We tried it and tinkered with it a bit. When we prepared both recipes for a television cooking show, the healthful version was actually preferred by the cast and crew. It just goes to show that better-for-you food can taste good, too.*

1 cup 2 percent low-fat cottage cheese

1 tablespoon lemon juice

2 teaspoons curry powder

$1^1/2$ teaspoons garlic salt

1 teaspoon granulated sugar, or to taste (optional)

2 teaspoons prepared horseradish

2 teaspoons grated onion

1 tablespoon cider vinegar

$^1/2$ cup light mayonnaise-type salad dressing

$^1/2$ cup plain nonfat yogurt

In container of electric blender, blend cottage cheese until smooth and creamy to make "mock sour cream." Add lemon juice; blend well.

Mix curry powder, garlic salt, sugar, horseradish, onion, and vinegar in a medium bowl. Add cottage cheese mixture, salad dressing, and yogurt; mix well. Cover and refrigerate several hours, or overnight.

Serve dip with fresh vegetables for dipping, as a topping for baked potatoes, or with a sprinkling of paprika as a filling for hard-cooked egg whites.

**YIELD: ABOUT 2 CUPS.**

**NOTE:** The original recipe called for 1 cup dairy sour cream and 1 cup mayonnaise instead of the cottage cheese, salad dressing, and yogurt; 2 tablespoons sugar instead of 1 teaspoon; 2 tablespoons cider vinegar instead of 1 tablespoon; and no lemon juice. Use this information as a rule of thumb when modifying other dip recipes.

# Roasted Leg of Lamb

*There is nothing so elegant or so easy to prepare as a roasted leg of lamb. Although I have prepared lamb with many different seasonings, my favorite is a combination of rosemary and garlic pepper. To complete the meal, add steamed red potatoes and a salad of butter lettuce and mandarin oranges with poppy seed dressing.*

1 (5- to 6-pound) leg of lamb, bone in

1 to 2 tablespoons olive oil

1 tablespoon dried rosemary

2 teaspoons garlic pepper (a seasoning blend)

1 teaspoon coarsely ground black pepper (optional)

$^1/_3$ cup chicken broth or water (optional)

Preheat oven to 325 degrees. Put lamb on a rack in a shallow roasting pan. Brush oil over lamb. Sprinkle rosemary, garlic pepper, and black pepper on lamb. Lightly rub seasonings into lamb. Bake in preheated 325-degree oven 25 to 30 minutes per pound, or to an internal temperature of 145 to 150 degrees for medium-rare. Do not cover or baste lamb while it is cooking. Allow roast to stand 10 to 15 minutes, then carve and serve.

If desired, deglaze the roasting pan. To do this, add about ⅓ cup broth or water to drippings in pan. Cook on top of stove, stirring to loosen browned bits on bottom of the pan. Serve glaze over sliced lamb.

YIELD: 6 TO 8 SERVINGS.

# Lean and Luscious Potato Split

*There's no need to turn on the oven and heat up the kitchen with this quick and easy microwave potato dish. Serve it as a meatless main course or as a side dish.*

1 baking potato (about 10 ounces)

$1/4$ cup low-fat cottage cheese

2 to 3 tablespoons low-fat milk

2 tablespoons shelled sunflower seeds

2 tablespoons chopped green bell pepper

2 tablespoons chopped carrot

2 tablespoons sliced green onions

$1/8$ teaspoon black pepper

$1/4$ cup shredded Cheddar cheese, divided

Salt

3 cherry tomatoes, halved

Pierce potato with tines of fork. Place potato in microwave-safe baking dish. Microwave on High (100 percent power) about 4 minutes. Rearrange and turn potato. Microwave on High 3 to 4 minutes, or until potato is fork-tender.

Halve potato; scoop out pulp, leaving $1/4$-inch shells. In medium bowl, mash potato pulp. Stir in cottage cheese and enough milk to make a moist but firm consistency. Stir in sunflower seeds, bell pepper, carrot, green onions, pepper, and half of the Cheddar cheese; stir until thoroughly blended. Season to taste with salt.

Mound mixture in potato shells, dividing equally between the two. Sprinkle remaining Cheddar cheese on top. Place stuffed potatoes in microwave-safe dish. Microwave on High about 2 minutes, or until cheese is melted and potatoes are heated through. Garnish with cherry tomatoes.

YIELD: 2 SERVINGS.

NOTE: Microwave cooking times are based on a 700-watt microwave oven. Adjust cooking times to your own oven.

NUTRITION INFORMATION PER SERVING: 250 calories; 32 grams carbohydrate; 8 grams fat; 10 milligrams cholesterol; 290 milligrams sodium.

# Italian-Style Pepper Bread

*Our testers have kneaded their way through many loaves of bread, but one that especially caught their fancy is this recipe for Italian-style pepper bread. It has a delightful light texture and good flavor. The special ingredient is savory cracklings.*

3/4 pound salt pork

About 6 cups unbleached all-purpose flour, divided

2 packages active dry yeast

2 tablespoons granulated sugar

1 1/2 teaspoons freshly ground black pepper

1 1/2 cups warm water

Cut skin off salt pork; discard skin. Slice pork 1/8 inch thick; dice slices into 1/8-inch pieces. Cook salt pork in a heavy 9-inch skillet over medium heat until brown and crisp. With a slotted spoon, remove the pork bits (cracklings) from the fat; reserve. Drain fat from skillet, reserving 3 tablespoons.

Combine 3 cups of the flour, yeast, sugar, and pepper in a large mixing bowl. Add 2 tablespoons of the reserved fat and the warm water. Beat with an electric mixer on low speed until blended; increase speed to high and beat 3 minutes. With a wooden spoon, stir in the reserved cracklings and enough flour (1 1/2 to 2 cups) to make a smooth dough.

Turn out dough onto lightly floured surface. Knead in enough of the remaining flour to make a stiff dough. Place dough in a greased bowl; turn to grease top. Cover and let rise in a warm (about 80 degrees) place 45 minutes, or until doubled in bulk.

Punch down dough. Cut into three equal pieces. On a lightly floured surface, roll each piece into a 12 x 10-inch rectangle. Roll up tightly; shape into a ring, overlapping ends to fasten.

Place loaves on greased cookie sheets. Brush lightly with remaining 1 tablespoon reserved fat. Cover and let rise 30 minutes, or until doubled. While dough is rising, heat oven to 375 degrees.

Bake loaves in preheated 375-degree oven about 30 minutes, or until bread sounds hollow when tapped with fingers. Let cool on wire racks.

YIELD: 3 LOAVES.

# The Unfruitcake

*This is a fruitcake for people who don't like traditional fruitcake—it contains no cit-*
*ron and no booze. However, you can wrap the fruitcake in a brandy- or rum-soaked*
*cloth and let it age, if you desire. One wise guy suggested adding the brandy by tak-*
*ing a sip between bites of fruitcake—to each his own!*

*This fruitcake has almost no cake at all; there is only one cup of flour in the*
*entire recipe. It is a wonderful concoction of nuts and fruits.*

*The recipe comes from Mabel Ward of St. Clair, Missouri, who got it from her*
*sister in New York, who got it from their sister in Georgia. After tasting Ward's fruit-*
*cake at a church gathering, we asked for the recipe and promptly went home and*
*tried it—and now make it every year. It's expensive, but it's worth every cent.*

2 (3$^1$/$_2$-ounce) cans shredded coconut (or one 7-ounce bag)

2 pounds pitted dates, coarsely chopped

1 pound red and/or green candied cherries, coarsely chopped

1 pound candied pineapple, coarsely chopped

1 pound shelled pecans, halved or coarsely chopped

1 pound shelled English walnuts or Brazil nuts, coarsely chopped

1 cup all-purpose flour

2 (14-ounce) cans sweetened condensed milk (not evaporated milk)

Heat oven to 300 degrees. Grease four 9 x 5 x 3-inch loaf pans. Line pans with waxed paper, leaving a 2-inch overhang; grease paper.

Combine the coconut, dates, cherries, pineapple, pecans, and walnuts in a large bowl; toss to mix. Sift the flour over the mixture; stir to mix well. Stir in sweetened condensed milk. Mixture will be very thick and stiff.

Lightly pack mixture into prepared pans. Bake in a preheated 300-degree oven 1 hour, or until golden brown. Let cool in pans 15 to 30 minutes; while still warm, turn out of pans onto wire rack. Remove waxed paper. (If cake sticks to paper, return to oven for a few minutes.) Let cool completely. Cakes are ready to eat at once; they do not have to age. Store cakes in airtight containers.

YIELD: 4 LOAVES.

NOTE: You can use a food processor fitted with the metal blade to chop the dates, fruits, and nuts. The dates must be processed in small batches to prevent overworking the motor. Add some of the flour or toss in a handful of the nuts with each batch of dates. You need something dry (the flour or nuts) to coat the sticky dates as they are chopped. Use the same procedure for the cherries and pineapple; be careful not to overprocess the fruits. You can purchase chopped, pitted dates, but they are usually sugar coated and can make the end product too sweet.

## German Chocolate Cake Cookies

*These cookies were "invented" by a friend, Susan Manlin Katzman, the day of a Christmas cookie exchange. She combined several recipes to produce these chewy, chocolaty treats, which won first prize at the party.*

**DOUGH**
2 cups confectioners' sugar
2 cups (4 sticks) butter, softened
4 teaspoons vanilla extract
4 cups all-purpose flour
$1/4$ cup unsweetened cocoa powder
1 teaspoon salt

**FILLING**
$2/3$ cup evaporated milk
$2/3$ cup granulated sugar
2 egg yolks, beaten
6 tablespoons butter
1 teaspoon vanilla extract
$3/4$ cup chopped pecans
$1^1/4$ cups shredded coconut

**TOPPING**
$1/2$ cup semisweet chocolate morsels
2 tablespoons water
2 tablespoons butter
$1/2$ cup sifted confectioners' sugar

**For dough:** Combine confectioners' sugar, butter, and vanilla in a large mixing bowl; beat with an electric mixer on medium speed until light and fluffy. Sift flour, cocoa, and salt into another bowl. Gradually add flour mixture to butter mixture, mixing until well blended. Dough will be stiff. Use your hands to knead ingredients together, if necessary. If the dough is not well mixed, parts of it will be too soft and other parts too dry and crumbly.

Preheat oven to 350 degrees. Form dough into balls, using about 2 tablespoons of dough per ball. Put balls on ungreased baking sheets. Make an indentation in center of each ball with your finger. Bake in preheated 350-degree oven 12 to 14 minutes, or until cookies are slightly brown around edges. Remove from baking sheets immediately and let cool on wire racks.

**For filling:** Combine evaporated milk, sugar, egg yolks, butter, and vanilla in a saucepan. Cook, stirring constantly, over medium heat 5 to 8 minutes, or until mixture is slightly thick and gold in color. The mixture will become thicker as it cools. Remove from heat. Stir in pecans and coconut. Let cool 15 to 20 minutes, then spoon a small amount of filling into the indentation in each cookie. Let cool.

**For topping:** Combine chocolate morsels, water, and butter in a saucepan. Heat over low heat, stirring constantly, until smooth. Add confectioners' sugar; beat until smooth. Drizzle topping over cookies. Let cool.

Store cookies in airtight tins with waxed paper between layers, or freeze.

YIELD: 6$^1/_2$ DOZEN.

## Recipes for Children

### Cheery Cherry Shake

*This cool combination will please family and friends. Be sure to ask an adult for help before using the blender and the knife.*

> 1 (10-ounce) jar maraschino cherries
> 3 cups vanilla ice cream
> Whipped topping

**1.** Put a strainer or colander in a bowl. Pour cherries into the strainer. Measure 3 tablespoons of cherry juice from the bowl and put in a small container. You will use these 3 tablespoons of juice to prepare this recipe. You can either discard the remaining juice or save it for another use.

**2.** Put cherries from the strainer onto a cutting board. Count four whole cherries and set them aside to use later as a garnish. With a sharp knife, carefully cut the remaining cherries into small pieces. Have an adult show you how to use the knife.

**3.** Put chopped cherries, 3 tablespoons cherry juice, and ice cream in the container of an electric blender; put lid on blender. Blend until smooth. Do not put a spoon or spatula in the blender while it is running and keep your hands clear of the working parts.

**4.** Pour mixture into 2 tall glasses. Top each shake with a dollop of whipped topping and garnish with the reserved whole cherries.

MAKES 2 (12-OUNCE) SERVINGS.

### Easy Cherry-Mallow Cake

*You'll like this easy-to-make cake—the marshmallows melt and rise to the top for a tasty glaze. Your family will be surprised and pleased when you serve this cake for dessert at a special dinner. Just be sure to ask an adult for permission before you begin to cook.*

> 4 cups miniature marshmallows (about $3/4$ of a $10^1/2$-ounce package)
> 1 ($18^1/4$-ounce) package yellow cake mix
> Ingredients called for on cake-mix package
> 1 (21-ounce) can cherry pie filling

**1.** If you have not cooked before, ask an adult to help you with this recipe. It's an easy recipe, but you might not be familiar with using a mixer, a can opener, or the oven.

**2.** Spray the inside of a 13 x 9 x 2-inch baking pan with vegetable cooking spray. Arange marshmallows evenly in the bottom of the pan. Set the oven temperature at 350 degrees so the oven can heat while you assemble the cake.

**3.** Prepare the cake mix according to package directions, using the ingredients called for on the package. Ask an adult if you need help using the electric mixer to mix the batter. Pour the cake batter over the marshmallows in the pan.

**4.** Spoon the cherry pie filling evenly over the cake batter.

**5.** Bake in the preheated 350-degree oven 45 to 50 minutes. The top of the cake will be bubbly and the marshmallows will be sticky on top of the cake. Wearing oven mitts, carefully remove the pan from the oven. Set the cake pan on hot pads or a rack on the counter. Don't forget to turn off the oven.

**6.** Let the cake cool in the pan, then cut it into pieces with a sharp knife. Have an adult show you how to use the knife.

MAKES ONE CAKE; ABOUT 15 SERVINGS.

## Large-Quantity Recipes

Following are two examples of large-quantity or food service recipes. The format and overall style of professional recipes are different from consumer recipes. The ingredients should be given in weights and measurements, the preparation instructions are generally shorter, and there seldom is a headnote.

As a general rule, the recipes are written for people skilled in professional food preparation who will understand scoop and ladle sizes (for yields) and phrasing (such as 4 x 6), which indicates how the dough should be placed on the baking pan or how the finished dish should be cut.

Large-quantity recipes require as much attention to detail in the testing and writing process as consumer recipes do. As with consumer (home cook) recipes, it is a good idea to study magazines and cookbooks that specialize in large-quantity recipes for examples of appropriate formats.

# Power Bars

YIELD: 96 BARS.

| INGREDIENTS | WEIGHT | MEASURE |
|---|---|---|
| Cherry pie filling | 5 pounds 4 ounces | $9^1/_4$ cups |
| Granulated sugar | 5 ounces | $^1/_2$ cup |
| Cornstarch | 2 ounces | $^1/_3$ cup |
| Almond extract | | 2 teaspoons |
| Margarine | $1^1/_2$ pounds | 3 cups |
| Brown sugar | $1^1/_2$ pounds | 4 cups |
| All-purpose flour | 2 pounds | 8 cups |
| Quick-cooking oats, uncooked | $1^1/_4$ pounds | $7^1/_2$ cups |
| Baking powder | $^1/_2$ ounce | $1^1/_4$ tablespoons |
| Ground cinnamon | | 1 teaspoon |

## DIRECTIONS

Puree cherry pie filling with an electric blender or food processor. Pour pureed filling into a medium saucepan. Combine granulated sugar and cornstarch; stir into cherry filling. Cook, stirring constantly, over low heat until mixture is thick and bubbly. Stir in almond extract.

Combine margarine and brown sugar; beat with an electric mixer until smooth. Combine flour, oats, baking powder, and cinnamon; stir. Add flour mixture to margarine mixture. Beat until crumbly. Spread one half of batter evenly in ungreased 26 x 18 x 1-inch baking pan.

Spread cherry filling evenly over batter layer. Crumble remaining batter over filling. Bake in preheated 350°F. oven 30 to 35 minutes. Cut 8 x 12.

NUTRITION INFORMATION PER SERVING (ONE BAR): 167 calories, 2 g protein, 26 g carbohydrates, 6 g total fat (33% calories from fat), 0 mg cholesterol, 114 mg potassium, 94 mg sodium.

# Cherry Chip Cookies

YIELD: 100 (3-INCH) COOKIES OR 150 (2-INCH) COOKIES.

| INGREDIENTS | WEIGHT | MEASURE |
|---|---|---|
| Butter or margarine, softened | 1 pound | 2 cups |
| Granulated sugar | 10 ounces | 1$^1$/$_2$ cups |
| Brown sugar, firmly packed | 10 ounces | 1$^1$/$_2$ cups |
| Whole eggs, slightly beaten | 7 ounces | 4 |
| Vanilla extract | | 2 teaspoons |
| All-purpose flour | 1 pounds 6 ounces | 4$^1$/$_2$ cups |
| Baking soda | | 2 teaspoons |
| White baking chocolate, chopped | 1 pound 2 ounces | 3 cups |
| Dried tart cherries | 1 pound | 3 cups |
| Cashews, broken pieces | 8 ounces | 2 cups |

## DIRECTIONS

Combine butter, granulated sugar, and brown sugar with an electric mixer on medium speed. Add eggs and vanilla; mix well.

Combine flour and baking soda; add to butter mixture. Mix thoroughly. Stir in white baking chocolate, dried cherries, and cashews.

Portion batter with No. 40 scoop 4 x 6 onto lightly greased or parchment paper–lined 26 x 18 x 1-inch baking pans.

Bake in preheated 350°F. oven 10 to 12 minutes, or until light golden brown. Do not overbake.

NOTE: For 2-inch cookies, portion batter with No. 70 scoop 4 x 6 onto lightly greased or parchment paper–lined 26 x 18 x 1-inch baking pans. Bake in preheated 350°F. oven 8 to 10 minutes, or until light golden brown. Do not overbake.

## Carolyn O'Neil, USA

Former director of Nutrition News, *CNN On the Menu*

A good recipe is one that's been tested. In addition, the recipe should tell me what the dish is supposed to look like at various points along the way. I really appreciate knowing why I'm doing something; for instance, "Press the water out of the cooked eggplant or the extra liquid will make the mixture too soggy."

Chapter Four

# Recipe Testing

LET'S FACE FACTS. IN ORDER to write or edit recipes, you must begin with kitchen-tested recipes. This is the key to accuracy. You might not have tested the recipe yourself, but as the recipe writer or editor, you must have access to recipe development and testing information and, if possible, the person or persons who created and tested the recipe.

## Know Your Audience

To begin recipe testing, you need to know the target audience. Is this a recipe for a typical home cook? Is this a recipe for a special group of consumers, such as beginning cooks or people with special dietary requirements? Is this a recipe or group of recipes using a certain type of equipment, such as a microwave oven or gas grill? Is this a recipe for a food service operation? If so, is it for a catering company, school food service, an upscale café, or a buffet restaurant?

The intended audience or purpose can affect the number and kinds of ingredients, the amount of detail needed in the instructions, whether alcohol can or cannot be used, and serving sizes.

Defining the audience for the recipe also helps to target the type of equipment available to that audience. A college student will have different equipment than an older homemaker. A child preparing recipes will have limited access to kitchen equipment, such as knives, electric blender, food processor, and can opener. Caterers often have different equipment than restaurants. It is also important to make sure that all of the equipment, such as ovens and scales, is calibrated accurately.

Products also vary, depending on the target audience. Products for professional cooks in restaurants or food service operations are often different from consumer products. Products used in school meals are different from those used by chefs in upscale restaurants. No matter what the target audience, you need to know the availability of products, especially fresh produce.

Some produce items are available only during certain seasons. If you are writing or developing recipes using fresh produce, check whether the product is available fresh year-round. If not, the testing schedule might have to revolve around the time when the product is available, and mention of product availability should be made in the recipe. Food promotion organizations, such as those listed in Chapter Fourteen, can provide useful information on product availability.

If you are the recipe developer, ask about the target audience and appropriate products and equipment at the beginning of the project. If you are the writer or editor, give clear instructions to the recipe developer about the target audience before the testing begins. The more precisely you define the target audience, the easier it will be to develop and write appropriate recipes.

T ime is the one ingredient that everyone is lacking. Cutting out paper-work is often seen as a way of saving time. In recipe testing, this leads to disaster. When testing recipes in the kitchen, write down *everything* you do as you do it. Do not assume anything.

The best way to keep an accurate record of what you are doing in the kitchen is to use a recipe-testing worksheet (page 131). Modify the worksheet to fit specific projects, but use the same worksheet for all recipes that are part of the same project. Generally, you will fill out this form by hand. If you have a computer in the kitchen and can use the computer while you are cooking, the paper trail can be electronic. In either case, write down the information as you prepare the recipe. Do not think that you will remember it. Even a delay of 30 minutes can make a difference in how accurate your information is.

The paper trail for the creation of a recipe actually begins with the idea for the recipe. If the inspiration for a recipe comes from a book or magazine, make a copy of the original recipe. If something tasted in a restaurant gives you the idea for the recipe, jot down as much as you can remember of the original dish. Attach this information to the work-sheet.

Each test should have a different worksheet. Include as many details as possible on each worksheet, and be sure to indicate the date of the test. These worksheets will be a great source of information for the recipe writer or editor, and a good reference if later there are concerns about the recipe.

If the finished recipe is actually made of several parts—a cake, a fill-ing, and a frosting, for example—use a worksheet for each part of the recipe. If there is a variation to the recipe, say a chocolate or vanilla ver-sion, test the variation as you do the original, using a separate work-sheet.

If possible, take a photo of the finished recipe and include this as part of the paper trail. A photo can help the recipe writer visualize the recipe. If the recipe is used in a food service operation, a photo can help the person preparing the recipe know exactly what the end result should look like.

After the original development of a recipe, there should be at least one more test by the originator to make sure the recipe works. The recipe should then be prepared by someone else to double-check results. All of these tests should be recorded on dated worksheets, which will accompany the recipe throughout the writing and editing process. The final piece of the paper trail should be a printout of the edited recipe. All of this paperwork should be filed for future reference. If the worksheets and recipes are on the computer, make a backup of the files and archive them.

## General Tips on Recipe Testing

If you are doing the original development of a recipe, follow the guidelines in this chapter. If you are a recipe editor, use the guidelines to give the recipe tester clear instructions about what is needed during the testing process.

If, during the writing or editing process, you have the least doubt about a recipe, have it tested again. You can spend more time trying to fudge the recipe than in having it tested, and the chances for errors are quite high. Although hiring a professional recipe tester might seem expensive, it is worth it to have accurate results.

If you are a recipe writer or editor and decide to test some recipes yourself, do not underestimate the time that this will require. Also, make sure you have appropriate equipment. This is often a problem in testing large-quantity recipes. Sometimes you can use space in a restaurant or a school kitchen. A budget for recipe testing is a necessary part of any recipe project.

## Tips for Professional or Large-Quantity Recipe Testing

For recipes geared for food service operations, there is a great temptation to multiply recipes to get recipes for 100, 200, or even 500 servings. It is always best to test the recipe in the quantities indicated. However, if it is necessary to scale up a recipe without an actual kitchen test, first begin with a kitchen-tested recipe in a smaller quantity. Then, think before you multiply. Is this recipe really suitable for the type of operation in which it will be prepared? Many great one-order-at-a-time recipes are not good in 100-plus servings.

Remember that most large-quantity recipes give quantities of ingredients in both weights and cup measures. When multiplying, avoid bizarre measurements, such as 18 ounces instead of 1 pound (16 ounces) or 15½ cups instead of 1 gallon (16 cups). These kinds of measures occur when you simply multiply ingredients in a recipe. That is why you have to actually test the recipe or be well versed in how to accommodate changes to make realistic measurements.

In bakery operations and some other food service businesses, many chefs and cooks use a formula called Baker's Percent. This is a way to increase or decrease a recipe primarily based on flour. First, start with a tested recipe. The total flour is always equal to 100 percent. The remaining ingredients are a percent of the flour. More information on this formula is available from the American Institute of Baking (see Chapter Fourteen).

For a recipe that was kitchen-tested in a small quantity (12 servings, for example) then multiplied to 100 or 500 servings, use a recipe tracking sheet (page 133) to test the accuracy of the larger quantities. The tracking sheet shows the results when the recipe is prepared in various quantities. It also is a way to record changes made in a recipe as different cooks prepare it. Over time, the recipe will most likely need to be rewritten and a new tracking sheet used to follow the revised recipe.

A tracking sheet also is useful for recipes prepared off-site. For example, a food company might send a large-quantity recipe to a convention center for preparation by the convention catering company for a food show. The tracking sheet provides information on changes made or problems encountered.

## General Recipe-Testing Guidelines

These guidelines give general information to use in recipe testing. Guidelines for specific foods and cooking situations follow. These lists include many details, some of which might not be used in the final, written recipe. However, it is easier to make the notations during the testing stages rather than to retest the recipe during the final editing process, often under the pressure of a deadline.

- Use standard measurements that are appropriate for your target audience. For U. S. consumer recipes, measure in cups, teaspoons, and tablespoons. Pounds or ounces of meat, poultry, seafood, or fish are acceptable. For large-quantity recipes and some specialty recipes for cakes and breads, indicate amounts in pounds and ounces as well as cup (volume) measures. International recipes use metric measures.

- Measure liquid ingredients in standard glass or clear plastic measuring cups designed for liquids. Measure dry or solid ingredients in standard metal or plastic cups that are the exact capacity needed.

- Be specific about the yield of the recipe. Give a cup measure on sauces, soups, stews, salads, frostings, etc. Indicate the size of the piece for cakes, cookies, pies, or other baked products. For large-quantity recipes, give the scoop size and the weight of the portion. Accurate yield information helps the end-user of the recipe; it also enables the recipe editor to make sure that all recipes in a group have a consistent number of servings.

- Give specific package sizes. List how many cans, cartons, boxes, or envelopes are needed and how many ounces are in each. Be aware that package sizes can vary by manufacturer. You might want to give a range of package sizes, such as 1 (14½- to 16-ounce) can whole tomatoes.

- Try to use the entire package in the recipe, unless the remainder can be stored easily.

- Be specific about:

  — The kind and amount of meat, poultry, or seafood used. Indicate whether the ingredient is boned, skinned, or otherwise prepared before or after measuring.

  — The kind of fat (butter, margarine, shortening, lard, vegetable oil). For butter, indicate whether it is salted or unsalted.

- The kind of flour (all-purpose, whole wheat, rye).
- The kind of sweetener (light or dark brown sugar, granulated sugar, light or dark corn syrup).
- The kind of milk (whole, skim, 2%, soy).
- Whether you use sweetened condensed milk or evaporated milk.
- The kind of cream (heavy, light, or half-and-half).
- The kind of yeast (compressed, active dry, or quick-rising).

- Indicate whether you use the regular or low-fat version of a product. You might need to test the recipe with both versions. This is particularly important with margarine or butter that is used in baked products. A reduced-fat margarine or butter will add liquid to the recipe and not as much fat, which can make a difference in the results. Indicate on the worksheet the exact product used and include the package label.

- If using ethnic or regional products or difficult-to-find ingredients, tell where to purchase them (a type of food store or mail-order source) and try to suggest substitutions. Attach a copy of the label to the worksheet.

- If an ingredient is prepared according to package directions, write down the package directions or attach the package label.

- Indicate whether ingredients are cold, warm, or at room temperature.

- Specify whether an ingredient is chopped before or after measuring. A cup of pecan halves is not the same as a cup of chopped pecans.

- Most recipes do not use brand-name ingredients. However, for testing purposes, specify exactly which brand you use. The recipe editor will make the decision on whether the brand name should be used. Recipes developed for a specific food company will use the company's brand-name products.

- Do not suggest that a recipe can be halved or doubled unless you test it that way.

- Be sure the cookware you use is readily available to the consumer, and that the measure or capacity you indicate is correct. Do not assume everyone has a tart pan or food processor, for example. Suggest other possibilities for cookware and preparation methods (see Chapter Thirteen).

- Try to foresee questions or problems that the recipe editor and recipe user might have. For example, if you have developed a cake recipe with a thin batter, say so on the worksheet.

- Make note of preparation time and cooking time. Find out before you begin testing whether you need to indicate the cost of ingredients.

- For testing purposes, do not abbreviate any words. The recipe editor might or might not use abbreviations, but for the testing notes you want to be as clear as possible.

- Include comments that might be useful in writing the headnote for the recipe.

- Pay as much attention to details in secondary recipes or variations as you do in the main recipe. The recipe writer needs the same information for secondary recipes as for the main recipe.

## Guidelines for Specific Ingredients

Some ingredients require extra attention to detail. If you are working on a project that involves numerous specialized ingredients, develop your own checklist to make sure you have appropriate information on all the ingredients.

### Cheeses

- If cheese is available in both natural and pasteurized process forms, specify the form used.

- If using process cheese spreads, be specific about the product used. Attach a label, if possible.

- Give a cup measure for shredded, grated, or cubed cheese and a weight. For example, "1 cup shredded Cheddar cheese (4 ounces)." Soft cheeses are shredded; hard cheeses are grated; blue cheese and feta cheese are crumbled.

## Elizabeth Luard, Wales

Author of *The Old World Kitchen* and other cookbooks and novels

The proof of the pudding will always be in the eating, and it's this—the need to make food taste good—that makes a great recipe writer. And a great recipe writer cannot help but write good recipes; anything else would be a betrayal of trust. That said, I'm as capable as the next person of listing pecans in the ingredients and forgetting to pop them into the method.

I have a notice stuck up over my desk that reads, "You are not writing the Bible." It keeps me from taking myself too seriously.

- Indicate curd size for cottage cheese. If curd size is not critical, say so.

- Be clear about whether you are using regular, light (reduced-fat), or whipped cream cheese.

- If using rounds of Brie or Camembert cheese, indicate how many and the weight of each.

## Eggs

- Because of possible problems with *Salmonella* in raw eggs, recipes calling for raw or undercooked eggs are not acceptable for many publications. Verify the publication's policy before you begin to create or test recipes.

- Eggs should be cooked to an internal temperature of 165 degrees, or heated to at least 145 degrees for $3\frac{1}{2}$ minutes. Make sure you test the internal temperature and give timings to reach that temperature so the home cook will not need to use a thermometer. As a general rule, home cooks will not use a thermometer to test for the internal temperature on egg recipes, while many professional cooks will. For suggested wording for visual doneness tests for egg recipes, see Chapter Three.

- Standard egg size is Large, Grade A. Specify if you use a different size.

- Indicate whether the eggs are beaten or unbeaten before being added to other ingredients.

- Additional information on eggs or egg safety is available from the American Egg Board (see Chapter Fourteen).

## Fruits and Vegetables

- Give the measure or number, size of units, and the weight for fresh fruits and vegetables. For example, 6 medium potatoes (2 pounds).

- Indicate whether the produce is peeled or unpeeled.

- If using frozen fruit, indicate if it is thawed, partly thawed, drained, etc.

- Specify whether frozen fruits or berries, such as frozen strawberries, are sweetened or unsweetened.

- If canned fruits or vegetables can be used instead of frozen ones, test the recipe that way and say so on the worksheet. Be specific about can sizes.

- If using green onions or leeks, specify whether you use the white or green parts only or both white and green parts.

- Check on the year-round availability of fresh produce. Test the recipe with the fresh product and give information on the worksheet about any special availability problems. For example, fresh sweet cherries are not available during certain times of the year. If appropriate, give a canned or frozen alternative for fresh, having first tested the recipe with that product.

## Pasta, Rice, Grains, and Breads

- Specify exactly what kind of pasta (dry or fresh, packaged or homemade) is used to test the recipe. If you want to suggest that the recipe can be prepared with either fresh or dry pasta, test the recipe both ways to verify taste and cooking times.

- The shapes of pastas available to both consumers and professional cooks have greatly increased. Give the appropriate name along with any alternatives. Rotini, for example, is also sold as twists or spiral pasta. Include a sample of the pasta or the package label.

- Make it clear whether you are listing cooked or uncooked pasta. Most recipes start with uncooked pasta and give cooking instructions.

- List the ounce weight of the pasta first and include a cup measurement, when practical. For example, 8 ounces elbow macaroni (2 cups). A cup amount does not need to be listed for long pasta, such as spaghetti.

- Give the individual number of pieces for such pasta products as lasagna noodles or manicotti.

- Identify rice as white, brown, wild, or other type. Specify whether you are using regular or instant (or quick-cooking) rice. Indicate whether the listed amount is for cooked or uncooked rice.

- Indicate whether bread crumbs or cubes are dry, fresh, or seasoned. Specify fine or coarse, if important to recipe results.

- If using stuffing mix, indicate whether it is seasoned and whether it is crumbs or cubes. Attaching a label is a good idea.

- Give the diameter in inches of pocket pita breads and tortillas.

## Meats, Poultry, and Seafood

- Give the weight of meat and specify the cut. For example, 2 pounds beef top round steak. If the number of slices or pieces, or the thickness of the cut is important, include that information on the worksheet.

- When browning ground meats, indicate whether the fat should be drained from the meat. If some of the fat is reserved, specify how much.

- For shrimp, specify raw or cooked and give the number of shrimp in one pound (the count per pound is an indication of size). Specify whether the shrimp are peeled and deveined before or after weighing.

- Indicate whether oysters, clams, and mussels are in the shell or shucked.

- Be specific about whether you are using the smaller bay scallops or the larger sea scallops.

- If using frozen fish, indicate whether it is thawed before preparing or cooking.

- If using canned tuna, indicate whether it is packed in oil or water and whether it is drained or undrained.

- Indicate the specific part of chicken used—thighs, breasts, wings, etc. Indicate whether the pieces are skinned or boned.

- Be specific about whether you use whole chicken breasts or chicken breast halves.

## Other Ingredients

- Indicate whether canned food is drained or undrained and whether you reserve the liquid.

- Specify the type of chocolate or cocoa used. Give a spoon or cup measure and weight.

- Indicate whether condensed soup is undiluted or diluted. Be sure to give the can size.

- Specify whether herbs are fresh or dried, and whether they are chopped or crushed. Try to include equivalent measures for both fresh and dried.

- For spices, indicate whether they are whole or ground.

- Be specific about the kind of black pepper used—ground, crushed, or cracked. Clearly indicate if you use white pepper. If using a mixed pepper seasoning, such as lemon pepper seasoning, give the exact name.

- If using a seasoning blend, include the label with the worksheet, so the recipe editor knows exactly what was used.

## Guidelines for Recipe Preparation

You need to pay as much attention to details in the preparation of the recipe as in the kinds of ingredients used. Today, many consumers have little cooking experience, so you need to be specific about exactly what you do. Recipes for food professionals also need to be specific, at least in the testing stage. In many cases, inexperienced cooks in food service operations will be preparing the recipe.

## Mixing

- Properly measure dry ingredients. Do not shake or pack them down. For example, lightly spoon unsifted flour into a measuring cup, then level it off. Brown sugar is the exception; it is firmly packed into the measuring cup.

- Indicate, if appropriate, whether the recipe will work with self-rising flour.

- When the recipe says "mix," specify whether you do so by hand or with an electric mixer. If by mixer, specify the kind of mixer (standard, portable, or hand beater), the speed, and the length of mixing time. If the recipe is mixed by hand, include the number of hand strokes as well as the length of mixing time.

- Precisely indicate the technique—stir, fold, beat, mix, knead, toss, pour. Don't just say "add." If necessary, identify the equipment, such as a wire whisk or rubber spatula, used for the procedure.

- Be explicit about actions or results. For example, some batters are thin enough to pour, while others need to be spooned or spread into the pan.

- If part of the mixture, such as a batter, is reserved, give a cup measure in addition to a quantity, such as ½ cup or one-fourth of the batter.

## Baking and Roasting

- Note whether pans are greased, ungreased, floured, coated with nonstick cooking spray, etc.

- Indicate whether the pan is glass or metal (dark colored, black, or insulated) because this can affect cooking time and oven temperature. If appropriate, test the recipe in both glass and metal pans.

- Use standard pan sizes; give the size in inches. Give metric measures, if appropriate. For some baking pans, such as a Bundt pan, you will need to give a cup measure, such as 12-cup or 6-cup (see Chapter Thirteen).

- Specify oven temperatures. In recipes for U.S. consumers, the oven temperature is always in Fahrenheit degrees, but it is a good idea to specify this on the worksheet. If the recipe is to be used by an international audience or in some food service kitchens, you will need to also indicate temperature in Celsius degrees.

- Use an accurate timer, preferably one that indicates seconds as well as minutes, to determine baking times. Recipes usually give a range of baking times, such as, bake in a preheated 350-degree oven 8 to 10 minutes.

- Give a visual test for doneness in addition to a baking time. For example, bake in a preheated 350-degree oven 8 to 10 minutes, or until golden brown.

- Indicate whether the oven is preheated and whether the oven rack needs to be adjusted.

- If the recipe can be prepared in more than one size pan, test the recipe in each pan and give specific cooking times for each size.

- For meats, use a meat thermometer to give a specific internal temperature; also indicate a range of cooking time.

- Indicate what procedures are needed after an item is removed from the oven. For example, indicate whether cookies need to cool a minute on the pan or be transferred at once to a wire rack.

## Stove-top Cooking

- Indicate the size of the saucepan or skillet—small, medium, or large. Indicate size in quarts or in inches (or metric measurements), if important to recipe results.

- Indicate whether the cookware is covered or uncovered.

- Specify length of cooking time and the kind of heat—low, medium, or high.

- If using a double boiler, specify whether the water is boiling or simmering.

## Grilling

- Indicate whether you are using a charcoal or gas grill. It might be necessary to test the recipe on both kinds of grills.

- If using a charcoal grill, indicate how far the grill rack is from the coals, generally 4 to 6 inches. Also specify how hot the coals are—low or slow, medium, or hot.

- If using a gas grill, specify the heat level—low, medium, or high—and whether it is direct or indirect heat. Also indicate whether the grill is covered or uncovered.

- Give a range of cooking time and a test for doneness. Meat and poultry cooked on a grill often brown quickly. Use a meat thermometer to be sure food has reached a safe internal temperature. Note that temperature on the worksheet.

- Indicate whether and how often the food is turned.

- The outdoor temperature will affect the cooking time on grill recipes. The ideal temperature for grilling is 65 to 70 degrees Fahrenheit. On the worksheet, indicate the outdoor temperature at the time of your test.

- Marinate foods in the refrigerator; specify that on the worksheet.

- It is not considered safe to use a marinade or sauce that has had raw meat, poultry, or seafood in it without bringing the marinade or sauce to boiling and simmering it 5 to 10 minutes. You can then use the marinade to baste the food as it is grilling, or serve it as a sauce alongside the grilled food. Make sure you test the sauce or marinade under these conditions. Is there enough liquid to bring it to boiling and simmer? If not, the marinade or sauce recipe should be modified.

- If a marinade will not be reheated, clearly state that it should be discarded.

- Sauces applied during grilling that are not reheated should be discarded, not served with the grilled food. If you want to serve some of the sauce with the cooked food, reserve a portion of it before using the rest as a basting sauce.

- If food is to be precooked, do so immediately before putting it on the grill.

## Microwave Cooking

- Consult a standard microwave cookbook for general information on microwave cooking. Several books are listed in Chapter Fourteen.

- Microwave recipes or microwave variations of conventional recipes should be given when there is an advantage to microwave cooking such as speed, convenience, or a better product.

- Test recipes in a microwave oven with 700 to 800 watts of cooking power.

- Because cooking times, even in ovens of the same cooking power, vary greatly, it is a good idea to test the recipe in several microwave ovens to get an appropriate range of cooking time.

- In addition to a range of cooking time, give a test for doneness. Conventional doneness tests usually work for food cooked in a microwave, but food cooked in a microwave does not always change color the way conventionally cooked foods do and some foods have a different texture. Consult a standard microwave cookbook for examples of doneness tests.

- Indicate the power level. Standard power levels are 100 percent (High), 70 percent (Medium-high), 50 percent (Medium), 30 percent (Medium-low) and 10 percent (Low). Use 100 percent power as much as possible.

- Test all recipes in standard microwave-safe cookware. Indicate on the testing worksheet exactly what size and kind of cookware you use. Round dishes will cook food more evenly.

- Specify when food is stirred or rearranged and when dishes are turned. These procedures help to ensure even cooking, but try to keep these steps to a minimum.

- Certain arrangements of food facilitate even microwave cooking. If you arrange the food in a ring, or put the thickest or most dense portions toward the outside of the container, indicate that on the worksheet.

- Specify whether food is loosely or tightly covered or uncovered. Indicate whether you use waxed paper, vented plastic wrap, a lid, or paper towels as a cover.

- Plastic wrap should be vented at one corner to allow steam to escape. Do not wrap foods in plastic wrap. Do not use plastic wrap with a browning unit; the plastic wrap will melt.

- Make sure the container you use fits into a standard microwave oven. A 13 X 9 X 2-inch baking dish is too large to fit in most ovens.

- Usually, pans are not greased or floured because a wet layer will form on the bottom of the product. (Some Bundt and other specialty cake pans are greased and coated with sugar.)

- Indicate if you line the bottom of pans with waxed paper (for cakes or items that will be unmolded) or paper towels (to absorb moisture from sandwiches or bacon). Use double paper baking cups for muffins to help absorb moisture.

- Standing time is an important part of the microwave cooking process. Indicate how long the food needs to stand and whether it is covered or uncovered.

## Guidelines for Special Audiences

In addition to the general recipe-testing guidelines, the target audience of each recipe is important in determining additional information that might be needed for testing and writing the recipe.

### Recipes for Professional or Large-Quantity Cooking

- Test the recipe in appropriate quantities.
- Test the recipe with the equipment commonly used by professional cooks, such as convection ovens, steam-jacketed kettles,

## Pip Duncan, New Zealand

Past president, New Zealand Guild of Food Writers

A good catering recipe develops into a product that consumers eat and enjoy. It has been pretested in a large-scale operation, is easy to read, has a clear method, and the service and garnish plan is included.

or commercial deep-fat fryers. Take into consideration the equipment available to the many different kinds of food service operations. For example, school cafeterias have different equipment and menu requirements than an upscale restaurant. A multi-outlet bakery with a central kitchen will need a different recipe than a single-unit operation. Make arrangements to test the recipe in an appropriate food service operation.

- Make sure you are using the appropriate pans. For example, bakeries seldom use a 13 x 9 x 2-inch baking pan, but rather a sheet pan (26 x 18 x 1-inch) or half-sheet pan (18 x 12 x 1-inch).

- Know the ingredients that are available to your target audience. Flour, sugar, leavening agents, oils, shortenings, and other ingredients can vary from those commonly available to home cooks.

- Give weights in pounds and ounces (or metric measurements) in addition to volume (cup) measurements for most ingredients.

- Give scoop sizes for cookies, muffins, and meat mixtures. Give dipper sizes for liquid mixtures, such as pancake batter, gravy, or syrup (see Chapter Thirteen).

- Give the weight of what goes into each baking pan. For cakes, give the weight of the batter for each pan; for pies, the weight of the filling for each pie; for casseroles or any food mixture baked or served in a steam-table pan, the weight of the mixture in each pan.

- If you divide dough into portions, such as for breads or pizza, give the weight of each portion.

- Indicate how many you put on a pan. For example, cookies are often baked on a 26 x 18 x 1-inch baking pan, 4 x 6 (six rows per pan with four rows across).

- Be specific about yields; give the weight of each portion. Be precise about how you cut each pan, giving the size in inches of each piece in addition to the weight. For example, cut while warm 5 x 6 (six rows per pan with five rows across).

## Recipes for Children or Beginning Cooks

- Make sure you know your target audience. Recipes for 6- or 7-year-old children require different instructions than those for teenagers or novice adult cooks.

- In general, more explicit details are needed for young or beginning cooks. Recipes should include information on how to remove cookie sheets from the oven, the necessity of setting hot pans on racks or hot pads after removing from heat, etc. Recipes might need to specify procedures, such as peeling onions and garlic, seeding bell peppers, or coring apples. The recipe tester can aid the recipe writer or editor by including these details on the worksheet.

- Because of safety concerns, avoid recipes that involve deep-fat frying and recipes for candy making where hot fat or syrup is involved. In addition, stress safety in all recipes. As the tester, indicate any potential safety problems.

- Allow room for errors (tolerance) in the preparation of the recipe. Recipes that cannot take overmixing or overkneading are not appropriate for a novice audience.

- Stress the importance of food safety, possibly including procedures for cleaning the cutting board, knives, and counters.

## High-Altitude Cooking

- Determine if high-altitude testing is necessary for a particular recipe or project. If so, it is best to let an experienced high-altitude cook (who lives or has access to kitchens at or higher than 3,000 feet above sea level) test the recipe.

- Factors that can be affected by high altitude and that need to be double-checked include baking times and whether ingredients, such as water, flour, leavening agents, sugar, and shortening, have to be increased or decreased to obtain proper results.

- In addition to conventional cookery, recipes prepared in a microwave oven and on a charcoal grill can be affected by high altitudes and need to be retested for the specific conditions. Canning recipes also must be adjusted for altitude.

## Guidelines for Food Safety

As a recipe tester or editor, you should be well informed about current food handling techniques. Follow food safety practices in the kitchen and incorporate these into recipes where necessary. The U.S. Department of Agriculture (USDA) usually has the most up-to-date information. Food safety bulletins and handling information and cooking procedures for most foods are available from the USDA Consumer Information Center (see Chapter Fourteen).

Some major points to keep in mind are:

- During the entire recipe development process, remember that cross-contamination by raw meats, poultry, seafood, and eggs from work surfaces, plates, utensils, or sauces is a serious health risk. Try to eliminate potential dangers in your procedures.

- Handle and store raw and cooked products separately. If necessary, specify handling and storage procedures on the worksheet.

- Cook raw meats, poultry, and seafood to the appropriate doneness indicators. For example, ground meats need to be cooked until well done, or no longer pink. Cook fish until it flakes easily with a fork.

- Raw eggs are not acceptable in recipes for many publications. See more details under "Eggs" in this chapter.

- Indicate when refrigeration is important. For example, a recipe made with dairy products will need to be stored in the refrigerator until it is served and leftovers will need to be refrigerated

## Susan Derecskey, USA

Author of *The Hungarian Cookbook* and copyeditor or line editor of more than 100 cookbooks

For me, a good recipe is one that makes me want to try the dish. Out of the thousands of recipes I read every year, perhaps 20 meet that standard, and not all fulfill their promise. A good recipe is written by someone who likes to eat and who knows how to cook—and that love and knowledge shine through. The rest is writing skill, which very few people are born with, and writing techniques, which almost anyone can learn.

soon after serving. Indicate all storage instructions on the worksheet.

- The Low setting on a slow cooker should maintain a food temperature of about 200 degrees (180 degrees minimum). Otherwise, use the High setting.

- If you suggest using flowers or leaves in a recipe, specify which ones; avoid mentioning any that are inedible, such as holly. Consult a poisonous plant guide.

- For marinades and sauces, see "Grilling" in this chapter.

- Keep live shellfish alive until cooking. Discard any that have died during storage.

- Use nonmetal pitchers for acidic beverages, because the acid in the beverage can react to the metal. Use glass or stainless steel pans if the beverage needs to be heated.

- High-acid foods, such as pickling mixtures with a lot of vinegar or long-cooking tomato sauces, should not be cooked in aluminum pans because the mixture will react with the pan. Use stainless steel or enamel pans.

- For picnic and brown-bag lunch items, include a warning that hot foods need to be held at more than 140 degrees and cold foods at less than 40 degrees.

- For buffet-type recipes, hot or cold foods should not remain at room temperature for more than two hours. On the worksheet, give ideas on how to safely serve such foods.

- Thaw frozen foods in the refrigerator. Indicate this on the worksheet.

- Indicate proper storage of leftovers.

- Jams, jellies, and preserves need to be processed in a boiling water bath because of possible harmful effects of surface mold. Paraffin is no longer recommended for sealing jellies.

- For specific canning procedures, refer to *The Complete Guide to Home Canning and Preserving* by the U.S. Department of Agriculture (Dover Publications, 2nd revised edition, 1999). Food safety guidelines for home canning were completely revised in 1988. If you consult a canning recipe or book published before December 1988, use it for ideas, but test the recipe using the revised methods. Be sure to check recently published books to verify that the recipes are based upon the revised USDA guidelines, and are not just reprints of old recipes.

# Sample Recipe-Testing Worksheet

Use this sample worksheet to develop your own worksheets for specific recipe-testing projects. Modify it for various projects to make it fit what you are testing.

Date _____

Working title of recipe _____

This recipe is part of what project? _____  Test number _____

Original source of the recipe _____

_____

**Ingredients** *(Include brand names. Be specific; attach labels as needed.)*  **Quantities used**

_____

_____

_____

_____

_____

_____

_____

_____

_____

_____

_____

_____

**Preparation procedures** *(List step by step. Be specific and accurate. Use a separate sheet of paper, if necessary.)*

1. _____

2. _____

3. _____

4. _____

5. _____

**Pan size and preparation** _____

**How many or how much per pan** _____

**Yield** _____

_(Give a cup measure on the total quantity or a size in inches of each piece. For example, 5 dozen 3-inch cookies or 1 quart stew. Editor will decide servings, based on information.)_

**Preparation time** _____

**Refrigeration time** _____

**Oven temperature** _____ **Preheated** ___ **Yes** ___ **No**

**Baking time** _____

**Test for doneness** _____

_For recipes prepared on top of the stove, give pan size, temperature of the burner (high, medium, or low), and length of time cooked. A test for doneness also is appropriate._

_____

_____

_____


**Comments:** _(Include information that might be helpful in writing the recipe or ideas that could be used in the headnote.)_

_____

_____

_____

_____

_____

_____

_____

_____


**Was this test a success?** _____

_____

**What further testing is needed?** _____

_____

**Name of the tester** _____

**Tester's telephone number and e-mail address** _____

# Sample Recipe Tracking Sheet

This form will be used primarily in food service operations where recipes are prepared in various quantities. Sometimes a recipe is developed and tested in a small quantity —for example, 24 servings. The recipe might then be multiplied to larger quantities (100, or even 500, servings), but not tested. In actual preparation, the recipe might need modifications, which can be recorded on the tracking sheet. At some point, the modifications are noted on the master recipe and a new tracking sheet follows the revised recipe each time it is prepared. This sheet can be modified to fit specific circumstances.

Tracking sheet for _____

| DATE | EVENT | QUANTITY PREPARED | CHANGES MADE IN RECIPE | COMMENTS; COOK'S INITIALS |
|------|-------|-------------------|------------------------|---------------------------|
|      |       |                   |                        |                           |
|      |       |                   |                        |                           |
|      |       |                   |                        |                           |
|      |       |                   |                        |                           |
|      |       |                   |                        |                           |
|      |       |                   |                        |                           |
|      |       |                   |                        |                           |
|      |       |                   |                        |                           |
|      |       |                   |                        |                           |
|      |       |                   |                        |                           |
|      |       |                   |                        |                           |
|      |       |                   |                        |                           |
|      |       |                   |                        |                           |
|      |       |                   |                        |                           |
|      |       |                   |                        |                           |

## Harvey Steiman, USA

Editor-at-large, *The Wine Spectator,* and author of several cookbooks

A good recipe is closer to a musical notation than to a blueprint. As a musician, I learned that the notes on the page represent what the composer intended but cannot possibly convey all of the nuances. Ultimately, the performer decides just how loud *ff* is, just how short a staccato sequence should sound, or just how bouncy those triplets should be. One can recognize every performance as Mendelssohn's Violin Concerto, but each will reveal a different interpretation.

In the same way, ten cooks can make a classic Burgundian *coq au vin* from the same recipe. Each result will taste like *coq au vin*, but likely no two will taste the same. Why? Ultimately, each cook decides how intense the stock should be, how deeply to brown the chicken or sauté the mushrooms.

# Chapter Five

# Cooking Terminology

T HIS CHAPTER CONTAINS DEFINITIONS OF basic cooking terms and descriptions of types of foods. Use it in conjunction with Chapter Three, "The Style Sheet," and the lists of preferred spellings and generic terms.

Before using any of these cooking terms in a recipe, consider the target audience for your project. An audience with limited cooking experience, which includes many of today's recipe users, might not know the meaning of some of these terms. When we suggest avoiding a term, we mean that an explanation of the term might be more useful than the term itself. Be specific yet descriptive. Try to use the simplest term or wording to describe a process or procedure.

## Ferdinand E. Metz, USA

President, The Culinary Institute of America

Beyond the fact that a good recipe is one that works, its writer must clearly understand who its audience is.

If the recipe is directed to an amateur cook, it should be explicit in describing each step from start to finish. It should never assume that the reader understands culinary terms or how to execute them.

If the recipe is directed to the professional chef, it should be short, clean, and clear. It shouldn't insult the intelligence of the chef and should assume that the reader has an understanding of the fundamentals of cooking. It should make references to basic cooking principles rather than explain them.

**active dry yeast** See YEAST.

**add** This term does not imply mixing or stirring; it is preferable to use a more specific term, such as mix or beat.

**al dente** Refers to food, usually pasta or vegetables, that has been cooked until tender but still firm to the bite.

**amandine** Containing or topped with almonds.

**arugula** Bitter, aromatic salad green with a peppery mustard flavor.

**aspartame** A nonnutritive sweetener that is 180 times sweeter than sugar. Not heat stable; not recommended for baking.

**au gratin** Food that is browned on top, often achieved by topping with bread crumbs, cheese, or a sauce and cooking under a broiler.

**au jus** Refers to roasted meat, poultry, or game served in natural, unthickened meat juices.

**au lait** Refers to foods or beverages served or prepared with milk.

**bain-marie** A hot water bath used to cook food or keep cooked food hot; also a container for holding food in a hot water bath. The term "water bath" is preferred.

**bake** To cook, covered or uncovered, by dry heat, usually in an oven. When applied to meats and poultry cooked uncovered, the process is called "roasting."

**baking powder** A mixture of baking soda, an acid (such as cream of tartar), and a moisture absorber (such as cornstarch), used to leaven baked goods. When mixed with a liquid, baking powder releases carbon dioxide gas, which causes the dough to rise. Double-acting baking powder is the most common kind in the United States. It releases gas twice, first when it is mixed with a liquid, then again when exposed to heat. Single-acting baking powder releases its gas when mixed with a liquid; it is less common than the double-acting kind.

**barbecue** To cook food on a rack or spit over coals or a gas grill. The food is often brushed with a sauce during cooking.

**bars (bar cookies)** See COOKIES.

**baste** To spoon or brush food during cooking with a liquid, such as melted fat, fruit juice, or stock, to keep the surface moist and add flavor. It is often clearer to say "brush" or "spoon."

**batter** An uncooked mixture of flour, liquid, and other ingredients that is thin enough to be poured or spooned. It generally refers to cakes, muffins, or quick breads.

**beat** To stir or mix ingredients until smooth by incorporating air with rapid, circular motions, using a wire whisk, spoon, hand beater, or electric mixer, until mixture is smooth, light, and fluffy.

**béchamel** A basic white sauce usually made with milk and sometimes with stock.

**bind** To stir ingredients, such as eggs, flour, cheese, or bread crumbs, into a mixture, causing it to thicken and/or hold together. Avoid using this term.

**blanch** To immerse vegetables, fruit, or other food briefly in boiling water to help loosen or remove skins or to precook briefly to set color and flavor and to deactivate enzymes prior to freezing or drying.

**blend** To thoroughly combine two or more ingredients. This word is best used when ingredients are combined in an electric blender or food processor. If such appliances are not used, "beat," "stir," or "mix" might be more appropriate words.

**boil** To heat until bubbles rise continuously and break on the surface of a liquid. Boiling water is at approximately 212 degrees Fahrenheit (100 degrees Celsius).

**bone** To remove bones from meat, poultry, or fish. Do not use "debone."

**bouquet garni** A bundle of several herbs, often parsley, thyme, and bay leaf, tied in cheesecloth and used to flavor soups and stews.

**braise** To slowly cook meat or poultry in a covered pan or baking dish in a small amount of liquid. Avoid using this term; say "simmer, covered."

**bread** To coat food with bread or cracker crumbs before cooking, usually after first dipping food into egg or other liquid so that crumbs adhere.

**broil** To cook by direct heat in the broiler of an electric or gas oven.

**brown** To cook food in a small amount of fat, generally over medium or high heat, until brown on all sides.

**butter** See FAT.

**butterfat** The fatty particles in whole milk that are separated out to make cream and butter. The higher the butterfat content of a milk-based product, the richer and more caloric it is.

**butterfly** To cut a piece of meat, fish, or poultry in half horizontally, leaving one side attached.

**candy** To cook fruit or vegetables in sugar or syrup.

**canola oil** See RAPESEED OIL under VEGETABLE OIL.

**caramelize** To melt sugar over low heat, without burning, until it turns golden to dark brown and develops a caramel flavor. This term also refers to a type of browning that occurs during cooking, such as with onions or meat.

**chiles** This term covers a wide variety of pungent pods that are members of the genus *Capsicum;* available fresh and canned. They range in size from almost a foot long to less than ¼ inch. The heat of these peppers varies from mildly warm to mouth-blistering hot.

> *Ancho:* The ripened and dried form of the poblano chile; has a wrinkled skin and deep reddish-brown color.
>
> *Chilaca:* Long, slim, black-green pepper; moderately hot.
>
> *Chipotle:* A jalapeño pepper that has been ripened, dried, and smoked. Light-brownish red in color, with a wrinkled skin. Used to season soups and stews.
>
> *Habañero:* A small pepper shaped like a lantern; very hot. Also called "Scotch bonnet."
>
> *Jalapeño:* Smooth, dark-green pepper with a rounded tip ranging from hot to very hot; seeds and veins are hottest parts. Used in a variety of sauces and sometimes stuffed with cheese, fish, or meat.
>
> *Pasilla:* Dried form of the chilaca chile; blackish-brown in color. Very hot. Often used with seafood.
>
> *Poblano:* A dark-green pepper with a relatively mild flavor; best known for its use in *chiles rellenos.*
>
> *Serrano:* Small, smooth-skinned green chile, often with a pointed tip. Flesh has a strong flavor; seeds and veins are very hot. Used fresh, boiled, or roasted.
>
> *Tabasco pepper:* Small, red, very hot pepper. Used to make Tabasco sauce, a trademarked name for a hot pepper sauce.

**chill** To refrigerate food until cold, or to let stand in ice or ice water until cold. Preferred term is "refrigerate."

**chocolate** A product (food) made from ground roasted cacao beans.

*Chocolate-flavored syrup:* A combination of cocoa, corn syrup, and flavoring.

*Bittersweet:* Chocolate to which sugar, lecithin, and vanilla have been added; must contain at least 35 percent chocolate liquor.

*Mexican:* Sweet chocolate flavored with cinnamon, almonds, and vanilla; has a grainy texture. Used in Mexican hot chocolate drinks and other Mexican recipes, such as *mole.*

*Milk:* Sweetened chocolate to which dry milk powder has been added; must contain at least 12 percent milk solids and 10 percent chocolate liquor.

*Semisweet or sweet:* Chocolate to which sugar, lecithin, and vanilla have been added; contains 15 to 35 percent chocolate liquor.

*Unsweetened:* Unadulterated chocolate, containing 50 to 58 percent cocoa butter; also called baking or bitter chocolate.

*Unsweetened cocoa powder:* This is pure chocolate powder with no ingredients added. Powdered cocoa drink mixes contain cocoa powder, sugar, flavoring, and sometimes milk solids; mixes should not be used as substitutes for unsweetened cocoa.

*White:* Not true chocolate because it contains no chocolate liquor and little chocolate flavor; usually a mix of sugar, cocoa butter, milk solids, lecithin, and vanilla.

**chop** To cut into pieces with a knife or other sharp utensil.

**coat** To cover food with, or dip it into, a substance, such as flour or sauce, until it is covered.

**coconut** White, sweet meat of fresh coconut. Flaked coconut is made up of longer and moister pieces, and shredded coconut of shorter and drier pieces. Usually, either kind can be used interchangeably in recipes.

**combine** To stir two or more ingredients together. Avoid using this term; "beat," "mix," or "stir" is more explicit.

**cookies** Small, flat, or slightly raised cakes that range from crispy to soft.

*Bar:* A type of cookie baked in a pan with sides. The finished product is cut into rectangular shapes.

*Drop:* Made by dropping spoonfuls of dough onto a baking sheet.

*Molded:* Made by shaping dough by hand into balls, logs, crescents, and other shapes.

*Pressed:* Formed by pressing dough through a cookie press or pastry bag to form fancy shapes.

*Refrigerated:* Made by shaping the dough into a log, which is refrigerated until firm, then sliced and baked.

*Rolled:* Shaped by rolling the dough out flat, then cutting it into decorative shapes with cookie cutters.

**cordial** See LIQUEUR.

**core** To remove the center of a fruit or vegetable.

**couscous** Fine-grained semolina that is a staple of North African recipes. It can be cooked and served plain as a side dish or combined with other ingredients for main dishes, salads, or desserts.

**cream** To mix one or more foods (usually fat and sugar) with a spoon or electric mixer until soft and smooth. Avoid using this term as a verb; use "beat."

**cream** The yellowish part of milk containing from 18 to 40 percent butterfat.

*Half-and-half:* A mixture of equal parts milk and cream with 10 to 12 percent butterfat. This product will not whip. It is often used in recipes interchangeably with light cream.

*Heavy:* Contains 36 to 40 percent butterfat; the high butterfat content allows it to be whipped, doubling in volume. Often called "whipping cream."

*Light:* Contains about 20 percent butterfat; this product will not whip. Avoid using the term "coffee cream."

*Sour:* A milk mixture that contains 18 to 20 percent butterfat and has been treated with lactic acid culture; low-fat and nonfat versions are available.

**cube** To cut food into small pieces (usually about ½ inch). In regard to meats, this term means to pound with a special tool that breaks down meat fibers to increase tenderness (cube steak is an example).

**curdle** To form clots in a smooth liquid. The original substance separates, resulting in a liquid containing small solid particles. Usually caused by overcooking or too much acid, heat, and/or agitation.

**cut in** To distribute solid fat in dry ingredients by chopping with knives or a pastry blender until finely divided.

**cut up** To cut into pieces with a knife or scissors.

**cut** To divide with a knife or scissors.

**dash** Less than ⅛ teaspoon of an ingredient.

**deep–fat fry** To cook in hot fat in a large, deep pan. Also "deep-fry." In general, specify the depth of the oil or shortening in the pan instead of giving a cup measure.

**defrost** For conventional cookery, use the term "thaw." For microwave cookery, "defrost" refers to various power settings.

**deglaze** To dissolve small particles of cooked food remaining in a skillet by adding a liquid and heating. Remove the cooked meat (or other food) and excess grease from the skillet, then add a small amount of liquid (usually wine or broth) and heat and stir to loosen browned bits on the bottom of the pan. The mixture is often used as a base for a sauce.

**degrease** To skim fat from the surface of a liquid.

**dice** To cut into very small pieces, usually smaller than ½ inch.

**dilute** To make less strong by adding a liquid.

**dissolve** To make a solution, such as sugar in water, or to melt or liquefy.

**dollop** To spoon a small portion of a mixture over a food.

**dot** To scatter bits of an ingredient, such as butter, over the surface of food.

**dough** A mixture of flour and water that is stiff enough to knead or to be shaped with hands.

**drain** To remove liquid from a food; a term used extensively in reference to canned products.

**dredge** To coat or cover food lightly with flour, sugar, or another substance.

**drippings** A combination of fat and meat particles.

**drizzle** To pour melted fat, sugar syrup, or other liquid in a fine stream over food.

**drop** To allow batter or dough to fall from a utensil, such as a spoon, onto a baking pan or other surface. Also, a small quantity of a liquid.

**dust** To sprinkle lightly with confectioners' sugar or flour. Avoid using this term; say "sprinkle."

**emulsion** A liquid mixture in which fatty particles are suspended, causing it to thicken.

**evaporated milk** See MILK.

**farina** A cream-colored meal made from hard wheat other than durum; generally used as a hot cereal, but also used in recipes for dumplings, gnocchi, or puddings.

**fat** The generic term for butter, margarine, lard, solid vegetable shortening, oil, and the rendered drippings of meat or poultry.

*Butter:* Cream that has been churned into a semisolid state; must contain at least 80 percent butterfat. Available in salted and unsalted forms. Do not call unsalted butter "sweet butter."

*Margarine:* A kind of spread made with a variety of vegetable oils, including corn and soybean; must contain 80 percent fat.

*Butter-margarine blends:* Made from 60 percent margarine and 40 percent butter.

*Lard:* Pork fat that has been processed and refined. It is softer and more oily than butter or margarine.

*Reduced-fat butter or margarine:* Products that contain at least 20 percent less fat than regular butter or margarine and have water and air added. See MARGARINE/VEGETABLE OIL SPREAD in Chapter Three, "The Style Sheet."

*Vegetable oil:* Pressed from a variety of seeds or kernels, such as canola, corn, safflower, sunflower, and soybean; generally low in saturated fat, contains no cholesterol. Also see VEGETABLE OIL.

*Vegetable shortening:* Solid fat made from vegetable oils that have been processed with air.

**filé powder** A seasoning made from the ground dried leaves of the sassafras tree; often used to flavor and thicken Creole cooking, such as gumbos.

**filet mignon** An extremely tender, boneless cut of beef from the small end of the tenderloin.

**fillet** As a noun, this refers to any boneless cut of meat or fish. As a verb, it means to cut the bones from a piece of meat or fish, thereby creating a fillet. *Filet* is the French spelling of the word.

**fines herbes** A mixture of equal amounts of fresh or dried herbs, traditionally parsley, tarragon, chervil, and chives; usually not removed before serving.

**flake** To break into small, thin pieces, usually with a fork.

**flambé** Food served flaming; produced by warming brandy, rum, or other liquor, then pouring it over the food and igniting it.

**floret** A small flower from a cluster of composite flowers, such as broccoli or cauliflower. Not floweret or flowerette.

**flour** A finely ground meal made from wheat, cereal grains, or edible seeds.

*All-purpose:* A blend of high-gluten hard wheat and low-gluten soft wheat milled from the inner part of the wheat; contains no germ or bran. It is enriched, by law, with niacin, riboflavin, thiamin, and iron.

*Bleached and unbleached:* Two different forms of all-purpose flour.

*Bread:* A specially formulated, high-gluten blend made from hard-wheat flour, a small amount of malted barley flour, and vitamin C or potassium bromate to increase the gluten's elasticity. Bread flour is ideal for yeast breads.

*Cake or pastry:* A fine-textured, soft-wheat flour with a high starch content that makes particularly tender cakes and pastries.

*Graham:* Coarse whole wheat flour.

*Instant or quick-mixing:* A granular flour that dissolves quickly in hot or cold liquids; used primarily for thickening sauces and gravies.

*Oat:* Cleaned, toasted, rolled oats that have been ground into a powder. Contains no gluten. Used in baked products in combination with other flours.

*Pumpernickel:* Coarsely ground dark rye flour.

*Rye:* Made from hardy cereal grass. Contains less gluten than all-purpose and whole wheat flours; usually combined in recipes with another flour.

*Self-rising:* All-purpose flour to which baking powder and salt have been added.

*Whole wheat:* Contains wheat germ, which means it has a higher fiber, nutrient, and fat content. Store in refrigerator.

**flute** To make a decorative pattern around the edge of pastry. Also used to describe indentations cut into vegetables or fruit.

**fold** To combine ingredients lightly by a combination of two motions: one cuts vertically through the mixture, the other slides the spatula across the bottom of the bowl and up the side, turning the mixture over (chiffon cakes, soufflés). Fold the heavier mixture into the lighter mixture. Also, to place one part over another part.

**fondant** A simple sugar-water mixture cooked to the soft-ball stage. After cooling, the mixture is beaten and kneaded until pliable. Used as both a candy and an icing.

**freeze** To chill at 32 degrees Fahrenheit, or lower, until solid.

**fricassee** To cook cut pieces of food, such as poultry, rabbit, or veal, by braising in a sauce. Avoid using this term; say "simmer, covered."

**frosting** A sweet, sugar-based mixture used to fill and coat cakes, pastries, cookies, and other foods; also called "icing." Frosting can be uncooked, such as buttercream frosting, or cooked, such as boiled icing.

**fry** To cook in hot fat. Cooking in a small amount of fat is called pan-frying or sautéing; deep-fat fried foods are completely submerged in hot fat.

**gel** To congeal a substance until it is firm enough to retain the shape of the container.

**glaze** To coat with a glossy mixture, giving food a sheen.

**gluten** A tough, elastic substance created when flour is moistened and mixed; it gives structure and strength to baked foods and is responsible for their volume, texture, and appearance.

**gorp** A snack consisting of high-energy foods, such as raisins and nuts.

**grate** To rub food, such as carrots or cheese, into tiny particles using the small holes of a grater.

**grease** To rub the surface of a pan or dish with fat to prevent food from sticking.

**green onions** See ONIONS.

**grill** To cook on a rack over direct heat, such as on a gas or charcoal grill.

**grind** To pulverize or reduce food to small particles, using a mechanical grinder or food processor.

**grits** Any coarsely ground grain, such as corn, oats, or rice; commonly refers to "hominy grits."

**groats** Hulled crushed grain, such as barley, buckwheat, or oats; more coarsely ground than grits, but can be used interchangeably with grits. The most widely used form is buckwheat groats (also called "kasha"); it is cooked and used like rice.

**heat** To make food or ingredients warm or hot.

**hull** To remove stems and hulls from fruit, especially strawberries.

**invert** To turn upside down.

**irradiation** A process approved by the Food and Drug Administration whereby some foods receive low doses of gamma rays to eliminate microorganisms and thus extend shelf life.

**julienne** To cut in thin, matchlike sticks, about 2 inches long; used especially with vegetables and fruit. Also, a clear soup containing julienne vegetables.

**knead** To work dough by hand or mechanically in a fold-and-press motion to develop gluten.

**lard** See FAT.

**line** To cover the inside or bottom of a baking dish or pan with aluminum foil, parchment paper, waxed paper, or crumbs.

**liqueur** A sweet alcoholic beverage flavored with fruit, spices, nuts, herbs, or seeds. The term "liqueur" is generally preferred instead of "cordial."

**liquor** A distilled alcoholic beverage made from the fermented mash of various grains and other ingredients.

**lukewarm** A temperature that is approximately 95 degrees Fahrenheit. Lukewarm liquids and foods feel neither hot nor cold when in contact with the inside of the wrist.

**Manhattan clam chowder** Made with tomatoes. See NEW ENGLAND CLAM CHOWDER.

**marble cake** A cake made with dark and light batters for a marbled (veined or mottled) appearance.

**margarine** See FAT.

**marinade** A liquid mixture, usually with a vinegar or wine base, often seasoned with herbs and spices, that helps tenderize meats and enhance flavors. Follow appropriate food safety guidelines when using marinades.

**marinate** To soak in a marinade. Follow food safety procedures when marinating raw meats, poultry, or seafood.

**marzipan** A sweet mixture of crushed almonds or almond paste, sugar, and egg whites; used in various shapes for cakes, candies, and other confections.

**mash** To crush to a pulpy, soft mixture.

**mask** To cover completely with a sauce, aspic, mayonnaise, or cream.

**matzo** Unleavened bread eaten especially at the Jewish Passover holiday.

*Matzo meal:* Ground matzo used to make gefilte fish, matzo balls, and pancakes; also a thickening for soups and a breading for fried foods.

**melt** The process by which frozen liquids and certain foods, especially those high in fat, gradually soften, then liquefy when heated.

**meringue** A mixture of stiffly beaten egg whites and sugar that is cooked. Follow appropriate food safety guidelines when preparing a meringue.

**milk** A fluid secreted by the mammary glands of females for the nourishment of their young; cow's milk is the most popular milk consumed by humans.

> *Buttermilk:* A low-fat or nonfat milk that has had a special bacterial culture added to give a tangy flavor and slightly thickened texture.
>
> *Buttermilk powder:* Primarily used for baking.
>
> *Chocolate:* Whole milk with sugar and chocolate added. If cocoa is used instead of chocolate, it's called chocolate-flavored drink.
>
> *Evaporated:* Whole, unsweetened milk that has been cooked to reduce the water content by 60 percent; evaporated skim milk contains 0.5 percent butterfat. Do not substitute sweetened condensed milk for evaporated milk, or vice versa.
>
> *Low-fat:* Contains 1 or 2 percent butterfat.
>
> *Nonfat dry milk powder:* Has most of the butterfat removed; shelf stable until reconstituted.
>
> *Skim or nonfat:* Contains less than 0.5 percent butterfat.
>
> *Sweet acidophilus:* Whole, low-fat, or nonfat milk that has *Lactobacillus acidophilus* bacteria added to it. It tastes and looks like regular milk, but many people believe that the acidophilus culture restores nature's balance to the digestive tract.
>
> *Sweetened condensed:* Milk that has been cooked to reduce the water content by about 60 percent and has 40 to 45 percent added sugar. Do not substitute evaporated milk for this product, or vice versa.
>
> *Whole:* Contains about 3.5 percent butterfat.
>
> *Whole milk powder:* Must be refrigerated in dry form and after reconstituting.

**mince** To cut or chop into fine particles, usually with a knife.

**mix** To combine two or more ingredients so they are evenly dispersed, creating a uniform mixture.

**molds** Algae-like fungi that form long filaments or strands. For the most part, mold affects only the appearance and taste of food; generally, moldy food is safe to eat, but not especially tasty. However, some foods, such as blue cheese, are specially treated with molds to produce a characteristic flavor. The term "mold" also refers to containers used for shaping foods, such as a gelatin mold.

**mountain oysters** The testicles of an animal, such as a calf, sheep, or hog; also called "Rocky Mountain oysters."

**mulled** Heated, sweetened, and flavored with spices; often refers to cider or wine.

**mushrooms** A fleshy fungus that usually consists of a stem and flattened cap. More than 2,500 varieties grow around the world. Mushrooms are available fresh, canned, dried, or frozen. Fresh mushrooms are increasingly popular in contemporary cooking. Cultivated mushrooms are most common, but exotic or specialty mushrooms are growing in popularity, especially on restaurant menus. Some of the most popular mushrooms are:

> Beech or Hon-Shimeji, *Hypsyzygus tessulatus*. Petite stems with white or light brown caps. Crunchy texture; mild flavor that is sweet and nutty. Refrigerate in paper bags 7 to 10 days.
>
> Cepe or porcini or Steinpilze, *Boletus edulis*. Pale brown in color. Caps can range from 1 to 10 inches in diameter. Smooth, meaty texture; woodsy flavor. Usually available dried in United States.
>
> Chanterelle, *Cantharellus cibarius*. Trumpet-shaped wild mushroom that ranges in color from bright yellow to orange. Somewhat chewy texture; delicate, nutty flavor; clean, earthy aroma. Refrigerate in paper bags 5 to 7 days.
>
> Crimini or Italian brown, *Agaricus bisporus*. Similar in appearance to Whites because they're from the same family. Vary in color from light tan to dark brown. Firm texture; deep, earthy flavor. Refrigerate in paper bags 5 to 7 days.
>
> Enoki, *Flammulina veluptides*. Fragile, flower-like mushrooms that grow in small clusters with long, slender stems and tiny caps. Mild, light flavor; slightly crunchy texture. Refrigerate in paper bags up to 14 days.

Maitake or Hen of the Woods, *Grifola frondosa*. A cluster of dark fronds with firm, supple texture at the base, becoming slightly brittle and crumbly at the edges. Woodsy taste and distinctive aroma. Refrigerate in paper bags 7 to 10 days.

Morel, *Morchella esculenta* or *Morchella vulgaris*. Short, thick hollow stems topped with sponge-like pointed caps that resemble honeycombs. Tan, yellow, or black in color, with a woodsy fragrance and rich, nut-like flavor. Refrigerate in paper bags up to 10 days.

Oyster, *Pleurotus ostreatus*. Fluted or fan-shaped mushrooms that grow in clusters. Vary in color from soft brown to gray. Delicate mild flavor and velvety texture. Refrigerate in paper bags 5 to 7 days.

Portabella or portobello, *Agaricus bisporus*. Larger, hardier relative of the White and Crimini; can grow up to 6 inches in diameter. Deep, meat-like flavor and texture. Refrigerate in paper bags 7 to 10 days.

Shiitake or Oak, Chinese, or Black Forest, *Lentinus edodes*. Vary in color from tan to dark brown, with broad, umbrella-shaped caps, open veils, and tan gills. Soft, spongy texture. Woodsy flavor. Refrigerate in paper bags up to 14 days.

White or button, *Agaricus* or *Agaricus bisporus*. Vary in color from creamy white to light brown and in size from small (button) to jumbo. Freshly picked, they have closed veils; mature ones have open veils, darkened caps, and a stronger taste. Refrigerate in paper bags 5 to 7 days.

NOTE: Always use a trusted, reliable source for wild or exotic mushrooms. Risks exist when identifying and eating any wild mushroom. Never eat even the smallest amount if you're not positive it's an edible mushroom.

**New England clam chowder** Made with milk or cream. See MANHATTAN CLAM CHOWDER.

**nondairy creamer** Made with oils, such as coconut and palm, combined with other ingredients; does not contain dairy products. Sold in powdered and liquid forms.

**oenology** The science of growing grapes and making wine.

**olives** The edible fruit of the olive tree; there are two principle types: green and ripe (or black).

*Green:* Fermented and packed in brine, either whole, pitted, or pitted and stuffed with pimento, almonds, capers, or onions.

*Ripe:* Ripe green olives that get their color and flavor from lye curing. Available pitted, unpitted, whole, sliced, or chopped. Also called "black" or "Mission olives."

*Greek* or *Italian:* Dry-cured or salt-cured ripe olives.

*Kalamata:* A kind of Greek olive; purple-black in color. Usually marinated in a vinegar solution and packed in olive oil or vinegar.

*Niçoise:* Tiny, dark-brown olives that are brine cured, then packed in olive oil.

*Spanish:* Small green olives that are picked young, soaked in lye, then fermented in brine 6 to 12 months.

**olive oil** See VEGETABLE OIL.

**onions** Widely cultivated members of the lily family, prized for their edible bulbs. There are two main types: fresh green onions (the small white bulb and green stems are edible; sometimes called scallions) and dry storage onions (bulb is covered with a dry, papery skin). Common storage onion types include:

*Bermuda:* Mild-flavored, dry onions that are white or yellow; available March through June.

*Maui:* Sweet, mild, crisp, dry onions from Hawaii; available April to July.

*Pearl:* Mild-flavored, small, dry onions; available fresh and canned.

## Marlene Sorosky, USA

Author of *The Dessert Lover's Cookbook* and other books

A good recipe is one that is worth the time, effort, and money to make it. When a dish comes out tasting as good as the reader expects it to, it is a good recipe. In short, a good recipe makes a good dish. If the cook is happy with the results and likes what he or she is eating, the recipe is a good one.

*Red:* Have red, purplish skins; available most of the year. Also called "Italian onions."

*Spanish:* Larger, yellow-skinned, dry onions; available most of the year (August through May).

*Vidalia:* Large, pale yellow, dry onions known for their sweetness and juiciness; primarily grown in the area of Vidalia, Georgia. Generally available only during May and June. They lose their sweetness if stored past the season.

*Walla Walla:* Large, round, golden, dry onions grown in the state of Washington; available June to September.

**pan-dressed** A market form of fish in which the viscera, gills, and scales are removed and the fins and tail are trimmed.

**pan-broil** To cook uncovered over high heat, usually in a skillet, without adding additional fat, and pouring off fat as it accumulates.

**pan-fry** To cook over high heat in a small amount of fat. Avoid using this term; use "fry."

**parboil** To boil until partly cooked. Cooking is usually completed by another method.

**parchment paper** A grease- and heat-resistant paper used to line baking pans, wrap food that is to be baked, and make disposable pastry bags.

**peel** To cut off the outer covering with a knife or other sharp tool. "Peel" is generally preferred instead of "pare," which has a similar definition.

**peel** The rind or skin of a fruit or vegetable. "Peel" is preferred instead of "rind" or "zest."

**peppers** See CHILES, SWEET PEPPERS.

**pesto** An uncooked sauce made from fresh basil (or other herbs), garlic, pine nuts, Parmesan cheese, and olive oil; often served with pasta.

**pilaf** A rice-based dish made by browning uncooked rice in butter or oil, then cooking or steaming in stock or other liquid. Meat, seafood, vegetables, herbs, and spices can be added.

**pinch** The amount of a substance that can be held between the thumb and forefinger. If possible, avoid using this as a measurement.

**pit** The stone of a drupacious fruit, such as apricots, avocados, peaches, and cherries. This word also means to remove the pit from such fruits.

**poach** To cook gently in a hot liquid so that food retains its shape.

**poached egg** An egg broken from its shell into simmering water and cooked for about 5 minutes.

**preheat** To heat an oven, griddle, or broiler to the desired temperature before beginning to cook.

**prick** To pierce with a sharp-pointed utensil, such as a fork.

**punch down** To deflate a risen yeast dough by pushing it down with the fist.

**puree** To press food through a fine sieve or food mill, or to blend in an electric blender or food processor, to a smooth, thick mixture. This term also refers to a thick, smooth mixture that has pureed fruits or vegetables as a base.

**reduce** To decrease the quantity and concentrate the flavor of a liquid by rapidly boiling in an uncovered pan. This term also refers to a reduction of temperature.

**refresh** To plunge a food that is hot from cooking into cold water, halting the cooking process.

**render** To cook meats in order to remove the fat. Also, to melt and clarify fat.

**rice** A cereal grass, widely cultivated for its seed.

> *Arborio:* An Italian rice with a short, thick grain; ideal for risottos.
>
> *Basmati:* A fragrant, long-grained rice with a nut-like flavor and aroma; it should be rinsed and soaked before cooking.
>
> *Brown:* Unpolished rice with only the husk removed; requires a longer cooking time than white rice.
>
> *Converted:* White rice that has been steam-treated; also called parboiled.
>
> *Glutinous:* An Asian short-grained rice; becomes sticky when cooked.
>
> *Instant or quick-cooking:* White rice that has been fully or partly cooked before being dehydrated and packaged.
>
> *White:* A polished long-grain or short-grain rice with the husk, bran, and germ removed; the most common rice.
>
> *Wild:* Not a rice; see WILD RICE.

**radicchio** Red-leafed Italian chicory; often used in salads.

**rapeseed oil** See VEGETABLE OIL.

**rinse** To cleanse by flushing with liquid, usually water. Generally, do not say "wash," which implies using soap and water to clean something.

**risotto** An Italian rice specialty made by stirring hot stock into sautéed rice; resulting mixture is creamy.

**roast** To cook meat, uncovered, without additional liquid, in an oven. Also, a cut of meat cooked by this method.

**rolling boil** Refers to heating until bubbles form rapidly and break on the surface of liquid. Generally, use the word "boil."

**roux** A mixture of melted fat and flour, cooked until bubbly to remove the raw starch taste of flour; used to thicken soups and sauces.

**saccharin** A sugar substitute that is 300 to 500 times sweeter than sugar; contains $\frac{1}{8}$ calorie per teaspoon. Not heat stable; not recommended for baking.

**salad oil** The term "vegetable oil," or the name of a specific oil, such as olive or corn, is more accurate. See VEGETABLE OIL under FAT.

**salt** A crystalline compound that is the chloride of sodium; used to season or preserve food.

> *Coarse:* A coarse-grained salt that does not have as intense a flavor as table salt.
>
> *Kosher:* Additive-free, coarse-grained salt.
>
> *Pickling:* Additive-free, fine-grained salt; used to make pickles and other canned goods.
>
> *Rock:* Unrefined salt in grayish, chunky crystals; used mostly for nonedible purposes, such as combining with ice to make ice cream in crank or electric ice cream makers or as a salt bed for shellfish.
>
> *Salt substitute:* Contains little or no sodium.
>
> *Seasoned:* Regular salt combined with spices and herbs.
>
> *Table:* The most common form used in cooking; fine texture and salty taste. Referred to in recipes as "salt."

**sauté** To cook or brown in a small amount of fat. Avoid using this term; say "cook and stir."

**scald** To heat milk to just below the boiling point. Tiny bubbles will form at the edge of the liquid. Also, to pour boiling water over food or to dip food briefly in boiling water.

**scallop** To bake food with a sauce or other liquid. Also, a thin, boneless slice of meat.

**score** To cut shallow gashes across the surface of a food before cooking.

**sear** To brown the surface of foods, often meat, briefly over high heat to seal in juices.

**semolina** See WHEAT.

**sesame oil** See VEGETABLE OIL.

**shell** To remove the shell or tough outer covering of foods, such as nuts, eggs, green peas, and similar items.

**shred** To cut into thin pieces using the large holes of a grater or shredder.

**shuck** To remove the shells from shellfish, such as oysters and clams; also refers to removing the husks from ears of corn.

**simmer** To cook slowly in a liquid just below the boiling point, generally over low heat.

**skim** To remove fat or foam from the surface of a liquid with a spoon or bulb baster.

**slice** To cut food into relatively broad, thin pieces.

**smoke point** The temperature at which fat begins to smoke and emit irritating vapors.

**sorbet** The French word for "sherbet"; sorbet is sometimes distinguished from sherbet by the fact that it contains no milk.

**spoon** To take up and transfer with a spoon.

**spread** To apply a mixture to a surface.

**springform pan** A circular baking pan with a separate bottom and side wall held together with a clamp, which is released to free the baked product.

**steam** To cook food in steam, on a rack or in a steaming basket, in a covered pan over boiling water.

**steep** To let a food stand in liquid below the boiling point of water to extract flavor or color.

**stew** To cook food slowly in simmering liquid in a covered pan.

**stir** To combine ingredients with a circular or figure-eight motion until uniform. See also BEAT, BLEND, and MIX.

**stir-fry** To fry quickly over high heat in a lightly oiled pan, such as a wok, while stirring continuously. Also the name for the food cooked by this technique.

**sugar** A sweet, crystalline material that consists wholly or essentially of sucrose; obtained commercially from sugar cane or sugar beet and sometimes from sorghum, maple, or palm.

> *Brown:* Granulated sugar mixed with molasses; available in light and dark styles.
>
> *Confectioners':* Finely pulverized granulated sugar mixed with a small amount of cornstarch to prevent clumping. Also called "powdered sugar."
>
> *Granulated:* Highly refined cane or beet sugar.
>
> *Raw:* The residue left after sugar cane has been processed to remove the molasses and refine the sugar crystals.
>
> *Superfine:* Very fine granulated sugar.

**sweetened condensed milk** See MILK.

**sweet peppers** A wide variety of mild, not hot, peppers; they range in color from green to red, yellow, and purple.

> *Bell:* Best-known sweet pepper, with a bell-like shape, juicy flesh, and mild, sweet flavor.
>
> *Pimento:* Large red, heart-shaped sweet pepper; most readily available in canned or bottled forms.
>
> *Sweet banana:* Long, yellow, banana-shaped pepper; available fresh or processed.

**syrup** A thick solution of sugar and water.

> *Corn:* A thick, sweet syrup made from hydrolyzed cornstarch; available in light and dark styles.

*Honey:* A flower nectar converted to a syrupy consistency by bees.

*Maple:* The concentrated sap of the sugar maple tree.

*Molasses:* A distinctly flavored syrup made from sugar cane or sugar beet juice; available in light and dark styles. Blackstrap molasses is a more concentrated form of dark molasses.

*Sorghum molasses:* A syrup made from the sap of sorghum, a cereal grass.

**tent** To cover meat, poultry, or other foods loosely with a piece of aluminum foil, generally to prevent overbrowning.

**terrine** An earthenware dish in which foods are cooked and served. Also a mixture of chopped meat, fish, or vegetables cooked and served in a terrine.

**thaw** To bring food from a frozen state to room temperature. Do not use the term "defrost."

**toast** To brown by direct heat in a hot oven or over hot coals.

**toss** To mix ingredients lightly with a lifting motion.

**truss** To secure poultry or meat with skewers or strings so it will retain its shape during cooking. Avoid using this term.

**vegetable oil** See listing under FAT.

*Olive:* Made by pressing the oil from ripe olives. Extra-virgin and virgin olive oil are obtained from the first pressings; refined olive oil comes from additional pressings of the fruit and is filtered to remove impurities. Olive oil is high in monounsaturated fatty acids. Light olive oil has the same amount of monounsaturated fats and calories

## Jennifer Darling, USA

Senior Food Editor, Meredith Corporation

The basic ingredient of every good recipe is clear, concise directions. Without them, the recipe may not turn out as the writer intended, resulting in a dissatisfied customer.

as regular olive oil, but is lighter in color and flavor. Because of the process used to produce light olive oil, it has a higher smoke point than regular olive oil.

*Tropical:* Usually refers to palm or coconut oil. Tropical oils contain more saturated fatty acids than other vegetable oils. Used in food products because they are quite shelf stable.

*Rapeseed/canola:* Made from rapeseeds; commonly marketed under the name canola oil. High in monounsaturated fatty acids.

*Sesame:* Made from pressing the oil from sesame seeds. Light-colored variety has a nutty flavor that is often used in salad dressings; darker, amber-colored oil has a stronger flavor and is used in small quantities in many Asian recipes. Both kinds are high in polyunsaturated fatty acids and have a high smoke point, making them good for frying.

**vegetable shortening** See FAT.

**vinegar** A sour liquid obtained by bacterial activity that converts a fermented liquid to a weak solution of acetic acid; used as a condiment or preservative.

*Apple cider:* Made from fermented apple cider. Refer to as "cider vinegar."

*Balsamic:* Made from white Trebbiano grape juice; its dark color and pungent sweetness come from aging in wood.

*Distilled white:* Made from a grain-alcohol mixture; stronger tasting than cider vinegar.

*Fruit:* Made by steeping fruits (fresh, frozen, or dried) in vinegar.

*Herb:* Made by steeping fresh herbs in vinegar.

*Malt:* Made from malted barley; mild flavor.

*Rice:* Made from fermented rice; has a mild, slightly sweet taste.

*Wine:* Made from red or white wine.

**W**

**water bath** See BAIN-MARIE.

**wheat** A cereal grain used to make flour and pastas as well as animal feed.

> *Bulgur:* Wheat kernels that have been steamed, dried, and crushed. It is often confused with, but not the same as, cracked wheat. Bulgur is used in pilafs, salads (such as tabbouleh), and other Middle Eastern recipes.
>
> *Cracked:* Whole berries that have been broken into coarse, medium, and fine fragments; can be cooked as a cereal or used in pilafs, breads, and other recipes.
>
> *Durum:* High in gluten, but not suitable for baking; most often ground into semolina and used in pasta.
>
> *Hard:* High in protein, which makes a flour rich in gluten; especially suitable for yeast breads.
>
> *Semolina:* Coarsely ground durum wheat obtained by sifting out the finer flour; most good pasta is made from semolina.
>
> *Soft:* Lower in gluten than hard wheat; better suited for baked goods such as cakes and biscuits.
>
> *Wheat berries:* Whole unprocessed kernels of wheat.
>
> *Wheat bran:* The rough outer cover of the unprocessed wheat kernel; adds flavor and fiber to baked products.
>
> *Wheat germ:* The center of the wheat kernel; a concentrated source of vitamins, minerals, and protein. It has a nutty flavor but, because of its high oil content, turns rancid quickly. Store in refrigerator.

**whip** To beat rapidly with a wire whisk or electric mixer, incorporating air to lighten a mixture and increase its volume.

**whisk** To beat with a wire whisk until blended and smooth.

**wild rice** Not really a rice; a long-grain marsh grass with a nutty flavor and chewy texture.

**yeast** A microscopic, unicellular plant that under suitable conditions of temperature, nutrients, and moisture produces carbon dioxide; used in making alcoholic beverages and as a leavening in baking.

*Brewer's:* A special nonleavening yeast used in making beer; also a food supplement that is a good source of B vitamins.

*Baker's:* Refers to three basic types of yeast (active dry, compressed, and quick rising), which are used as leavening agents in recipes.

*Active dry:* A shelf-stable mixture of dehydrated yeast granules and filler. When mixed with warm liquid, the yeast cells once again become active. Use on or before the expiration date stamped on package or jar label. See QUICK-RISING YEAST.

*Compressed:* A moist, perishable mixture of fresh yeast and starch that must be refrigerated and used within one or two weeks; it largely has been replaced by active dry yeast.

*Quick-rising:* A more active form of active dry yeast. It does not need to be rehydrated before mixing; up to 50 percent less rising time is needed with this product than with active dry yeast. It can be used interchangeably with active dry yeast, with adjustments in rising time.

**yogurt** A milk product that has been fermented and congealed; it has a tangy taste and thick texture. Available in a wide range of flavors; can have sugar, flavorings, or fruit added.

**zest** The thin, colored outer layer of citrus peel. Avoid using this term; use the word "peel."

## Aglaia Kremezi, Greece

Author of *Foods of the Greek Islands* and other books

A good recipe for me is one that uses with ingenuity a few basic and simple ingredients to create an exciting dish. I am tired of long lineups with peculiar spices and expensive and exotic fruits, vegetables, and herbs. I have come to believe that the poorer the cooks, the more interesting the dishes they create. They make the most of the local seasonal produce, and use cleverly things that affluent cooks would throw into the dustbin—dried bread pieces, wild greens and weeds growing in the backyard, or the outer rind of a hard cheese—to create utterly delicious foods.

# Chapter Six

# Preferred Spelling of Commonly Used Food Words

THE LIST IN THIS CHAPTER is a handy reference for the preferred spelling and capitalization of food words that are commonly misspelled. Our primary source *is Webster's Tenth New Collegiate Dictionary.* We also used *The Associated Press Stylebook* and several food dictionaries, especially the *Food Lover's Companion.*

For additional reference book suggestions, consult the book list in Chapter Fourteen. Chapters Two, Three, and Five provide information on how to use many of these words. For generic terms of trademarked words or brand names, see Chapter Seven.

Compiling this list was difficult because there is often more than one way to spell a word, especially in transliterations of foreign terms.

## Andrea Bidwell, USA

Senior food editor, *Classic Cookbooks* and *Fast & Healthy* magazine, Pillsbury Publications

Use ingredients that are in national distribution and readily available in both urban and rural areas, use ingredients in season, and make sure that the serving sizes are consistent for all recipes in a menu.

Capitalization is even more capricious. Feel free to consult additional reference books for alternative spellings of these words or for words not listed here.

If you do choose another spelling for a word, be consistent. Make sure you spell the word the same way throughout a project. Jot your additions in the margins of this list, so you'll have a written record of your decisions.

For foreign words not listed here, you can verify accent marks and other diacritical marks with a foreign-language dictionary or computer software.

| | |
|---|---|
| abalone | andouille sausage |
| acidophilus milk | angel food cake |
| à la | aniseed, anise seed |
| albacore | applejack, apple brandy |
| al dente | applesauce |
| alfresco | arugula |
| all-purpose flour | au gratin |
| amandine (not almondine) | au jus |
| amaretti (refers to cookies) | avgolemono |
| amaretto (refers to liqueur) | avocados |
| anadama bread | |

B

baba, baba au rhum
backbone
bain-marie (water bath is the
    preferred term)
baked Alaska
barbecue (not barbeque, bar-
    b-cue, or bar-b-q)
Bartlett pear (indicate Bartlett
    only when referring to spe-
    cific variety)
basmati rice
bearnaise sauce
Beaujolais, Beaujolais
    Nouveau
béchamel sauce
beef stroganoff
beef Wellington
beignet
Belgian endive
Bel Paese
Bibb lettuce
biscotti (plural of biscotto)
bite-size (not bite-sized)
bittersweet
black bottom pie (not black
    bottomed pie)
black-eyed pea (not black-eye
    pea or blackeye pea)
blini (plural of blin)
blue cheese (not bleu cheese)
bologna (not bologne)
bonbon (not bon bon or bon-
    bon)

borscht (not borsch)
Bosc pear (indicate Bosc only
    when referring to specific
    variety)
Boston baked beans
Boston lettuce
bouillabaisse
bouillon (not boullion or bul-
    lion)
bourguignon, bourguignonne
bow-tie pasta
braunschweiger
Brazil nuts
bread-and-butter pickles
bread crumbs
bread cubes
breadfruit
breadstick
breastbone
Brie
broccoli florets (not flow-
    erettes or flowerets)
brussels sprouts (not brussel
    sprouts)
bulgur (also bulghur, bulgar)
burgundy
burrito (plural is burritos)
buttercream
butterfat
buttermilk
butterscotch

Caesar salad
caffeine
Cajun
cake pan
calzone (both singular and
    plural)
Camembert
Canadian-style bacon (not
    Canadian bacon)
canapé
cannellini (refers to large,
    white Italian beans)
cannelloni (refers to large
    pasta tubes)
cannoli (refers to an Italian
    dessert)
canola (refers to a vegetable oil)
caramel (not carmel)
caramel apples (not
    carameled apples)
cardamom (not cardamon)
Caribbean
cappelletti
cappuccino
cashews (not cashew nuts)
catfish
catsup (ketchup is preferred)
cats' tongues (refers to a kind
    of French cookie)
cauliflower florets (not flow-
    erettes or flowerets)
cayenne (same as ground red
    pepper)

Chablis
chamomile (not camomile)
champagne
chanterelle
chardonnay
Chartreuse
Cheddar
cheesecake
cheesy (not cheesey)
chef's salad (not chef salad)
Chenin Blanc
chèvre (also goat cheese)
Chianti
chickpeas (also garbanzo
    beans)
chile, chiles (spelling for
    green or red hot peppers)
chili (spelling for meat-bean
    stew)
chimichanga (plural is
    chimichangas)
chocolaty (also chocolatey)
chopsticks
chop suey (plural is chop
    sueys)
clafouti (plural is clafoutis)
clambake
clam broth
clamshell
claret
Cobb salad
coconut (not cocoanut)
coffee cake

coffeepot
cognac
coleslaw
confectioners' sugar (also
    powdered sugar)
consommé
cookbook
cookie
cook-off
cookout
cookware
Cordon Bleu
corn bread
corncob
corned beef
cornflakes cereal (with an *s*)
cornflake crumbs (no *s* on
    cornflake)
cornhusk
Cornish game hens
cornmeal

cornstarch
corn stick
countertop
couscous
crab apple
crab cakes
crabmeat
cream sherry (not creme
    sherry)
creme soda (not cream soda)
Creole
crepe(s) suzette
crimini
crisscross
cupcake
currants
cutouts (one word as a noun)
cut-out (hyphenate as an
    adjective)
cut-side down

daikon (also Japanese radish)
damson plum
deep-dish (hyphenate as an
    adjective)
deep-fry, deep-fried, deep-frying
deep fryer
demi-glace
demitasse
dietitian
Dijon mustard
Dijon-style mustard

dill seed (not dillseed)
dill weed (not dillweed)
dishwasher-safe (hyphenate as
    an adjective)
double boiler
doughnut (not donut)
dry mustard (not powdered
    mustard)
Dungeness crab
Dusseldorf mustard
Dutch oven

Edam cheese
eggdrop soup
eggnog
egg roll
eggs Benedict
eggshell
Emmentaler cheese (also
    Emmenthaler or
    Emmenthal cheese)

empanada
enchilada
English muffin
enoki
entrée
escargot

fajita (plural is fajitas)
fat-soluble
feta cheese
fettuccine (not fettucine or
    fettuccini)
fillet (not filet, except for filet
    mignon)
filo (phyllo is preferred term)
fines herbes
five-spice powder
flambé
flapjack
flat bread
flatfish
flat-leaf parsley (also Italian
    parsley)

florets (not flowerettes or
    flowerets)
focaccia (refers to an Italian
    bread)
fontina cheese
food color (not food coloring)
freeze-dried (hyphenate as an
    adjective)
freezerproof
French bread
french fries
french-fried onion rings
french fry
fruitcake
fruit-flavored (hyphenate as
    an adjective)

G

gamy (also gamey)
garbanzo beans (also chick peas)
gel, gelled (not jell)
gewürztraminer
ginger (not gingerroot)
ginger ale
gingerbread
gingersnap
glögg
gnocchi

Gorgonzola
Gouda
grapefruit (both singular and plural)
grog
Great Northern beans
green goddess dressing
Gruyère
guacamole
guava
gumdrop

H

half-and-half
Hanukkah
hard-cooked (not hard-boiled)
hash browns, hash-brown potatoes
Hass avocado (not Haas)
haute cuisine
Havarti
hazelnut (also filbert)
heavy-duty aluminum foil
herring (both singular and plural)
highball
hoecake (also johnnycake)

home-baked (hyphenate as an adjective)
homegrown
homemade
home-style (hyphenate as an adjective)
hors d'oeuvre (not hor d'oeuvre)
horseradish
hot cross buns
hot dog
huevos rancheros
hummus
hush puppy

iceberg lettuce
iced tea (not ice tea)
icemaker
ice water (not iced water)

instant-read thermometer
(also rapid-response thermometer)

jack-o'-lantern
jalapeño(s)
Jarlsberg cheese
jelly bean
jelly roll
jelly-roll fashion (hyphenate
as an adjective)

Jerusalem artichoke
jicama
Johannisberg Riesling
John Dory
johnnycake (also hoecake)

kabob (also kebab or kebob)
kaiser roll
ketchup (also catsup)
Key lime
kir
kirsch

kiwi fruit or kiwifruit (not
kiwi)
kolachy
kosher
kuchen
kumquat

ladyfinger
Lambrusco
lasagna, lasagne
lefse (both singular and
    plural)
leftover
lemonade
lemongrass
liebfraumilch
Liederkranz
Limburger

lingcod
linguine (not linguini)
litchi (not litchee)
littleneck clams
longhorn cheese
low-calorie (hyphenate as an
    adjective)
low-fat (hyphenate as an
    adjective)
lyonnaise

Madeira wine
mahimahi, mahi-mahi
maitake
maître d'
maître(s) d'hôtel
mandarin oranges (not neces-
    sary to say segments)
maple-flavored syrup
maple syrup
maraschino cherry
marbled, marbling
marbleize (not marblize or
    marbelize)
margarita
marsala wine

marshmallow (not marshmel-
    low)
marshmallow creme (not
    cream)
marzipan
matzo, matzoh
matzo ball, matzoh ball
meatball
meat loaf
Melba
merlot
microwave-safe (preferred
    instead of microwavable)
milkshake
mincemeat

mince pie (not mincemeat
    pie)
monkfish
Monterey Jack cheese
Montrachet
morel
moussaka
mouth-watering (hyphenate
    as an adjective)

mozzarella cheese
MSG, monosodium gluta-
    mate
Muenster cheese, Munster
    cheese
muesli
mulligatawny

napa cabbage (Chinese cab-
    bage is preferred term)
napoleon (lowercase when
    referring to the dessert)
navel orange
Neufchâtel
navy beans
neapolitan

niçoise
nonalcoholic
nonfat
nonpareil
nonstick
nougat
nouvelle cuisine

oatmeal (refers to cooked
    cereal)
oats (refers to uncooked
    ingredient used in cereal,
    cookies, breads; also rolled
    oats)
old-fashioned (hyphenate as
    an adjective)
omelet, omelette

open-face sandwiches
orange roughy
oriental
osso buco, ossobuco
ovenproof
overbake
overcook
oysters Rockefeller

## Tina Ujlaki, USA

Executive food editor, *Food & Wine* magazine

Regardless of who the intended audience is and what the sophistication level of the recipe may be, two elements are crucial: The information *must be accurate* and it must be *clearly presented.*

paella
Parker House rolls
Parmesan cheese
parsley potatoes (not parslied
    or parsleyed potatoes)
partly (not partially)
passion fruit
pâte (refers to a pastry dough)
pâté (refers to a type of meat
    mixture)
pattypan squash
pea pods
peel (not rind or zest)
peppercorns
petit four (plural is petits
    fours)
pfeffernusse
phyllo (not filo or fillo)
pie crust
pierogi
pilsner, pilsener
pimento (pimiento is Spanish
    spelling)
piña colada
pine nuts, pignoli, piñon
pinot, pinot noir

pizzazz
pomegranate
popover
porcini
port
portabella, portobello
porterhouse steak
Port-Salut
posole, pozole
potluck
potpie
pot roast
pound cake
precook
preheat
prepared mustard (not yellow
    mustard)
pressure cooker
primavera
prizewinning
process cheese (not pasteur-
    ized processed cheese)
profiterole
provolone cheese
puree

quail (both singular and
plural)
quiche lorraine

quick bread

radicchio
ratatouille
ready-to-spread (hyphenate as
an adjective)
ready-to-use (hyphenate as an
adjective)
redeye gravy
restaurateur (not restauran-
teur)
Rhine wine
rib eye (two words as a noun)

rib-eye (hyphenate as an
adjective)
ricotta cheese
Riesling
right-side up
rind (peel is preferred term)
risotto(s)
rolling pin
Romano cheese
root beer
rosé wine

sangria
satay, saté
saucepan
sauerbraten
sauerkraut
sauté, sautéed, sautéing

sauterne
sauvignon blanc
scalloped
sea bass
seam-side down
seaweed

self-rising flour
semisweet
sesame oil (not sesame seed oil)
seviche (not ceviche or cebiche)
shelled sunflower seeds (not sunflower nuts or kernels)
shellfish
sherry
shiitake
shoofly pie
shortbread
shortcake
shortcuts
Sichuan, sometimes Szechwan
smoky (also smokey)
snow pea
soft-shell crab
soufflé
soybeans
spicy (not spicey)
sponge cake

springform pan
star fruit
step-by-step (hyphenate as an adjective)
Stilton cheese
stir-fry, stir-fried
stockpot
stollen (both singular and plural)
stone-ground (hyphenate as an adjective)
store-bought (hyphenate as an adjective)
stove top
succotash
sundae
sun-dried
sweet-and-sour (hyphenate as an adjective)
sweetbreads
Swiss chard
Swiss cheese
Szechwan (Sichuan is preferred)

tabbouleh (not tabbuli or tabouleh)
tablecloth
taste buds
T-bone steak
tea bag
tea ball
teacup

teakettle
teapot
teaspoonfuls (not teaspoonsful)
Thousand Island dressing
ti leaves
Tillamook cheese
time-saver

timesaving
tiramisù
toffee (not toffy)
tomatillo
toothpick (use wooden pick)
tournedos (both singular and
   plural)

tuna (not tuna fish)
turmeric (not tumeric)
turnover
tutti-frutti
tzimmes

underbake
underbeat

until (not til, 'til, or till)
upside-down cake

Valencia orange (indicate
   Valencia only when referring to specific variety)
veggie
vichyssoise

Vidalia onion
vinaigrette (not vinegarette)
vitamin A (capitalize A or B,
   C, D, etc., only)

Waldorf salad
Walla Walla onion
wasabi, wasabe
wassail
waxed paper (not wax paper)

wedge-shaped
Welsh rarebit
whole wheat
wide-mouth jar (not wide-
   mouthed)

wiener (not weiner)
wineglass
wonton
wonton wrapper (preferred
instead of wonton skin)

wooden pick (not toothpick)
Worcestershire (not
Worchestershire)

XXX, XXXX sugar (use con-
fectioners' sugar)

yellowfin tuna

yogurt (not yoghurt)

zabaglione
zest (peel is preferred term)
zinfandel

zucchini (both singular and
plural)
zwieback

## Bonnie Tandy Leblang, R.D., USA

Internationally syndicated columnist with Universal Press Syndicate, *Express Lane Cooking: A Simple Solution to What's for Dinner* and *Supermarket Sampler*

To answer the age-old question of what's for dinner, I prefer recipes with just a few ingredients found on supermarket shelves. Currently I'm trying to simplify and streamline all my recipes. They contain no more necessary ingredients than allowed in the supermarket express lane. To me, a good recipe gets folks cooking. It lets the user feel virtuous about making choices and changes, one that gives them freedom and reminds them that a recipe (other than a precise baking one) is a guideline—it's not written in stone.

# Chapter Seven

# Generic Terms for Brand Names and Trademarks

IF YOU DON'T TAKE BRAND names and trademarks seriously, just wait until you get a letter of warning from the legal department of the company whose trademark you have used incorrectly (albeit innocently). It's a sobering way to begin a workday. It is also a good reminder that recipe writers and editors have a responsibility to respect trademarks and brand names.

In most publications, generic terms are used whenever possible instead of brand names or trademarks. This gives the reader the option of using whatever brand he or she prefers.

For most products, the generic term, or common descriptive name, is readily understood and should be used. Sometimes, however, a generic name is so convoluted and confusing that the reader wouldn't have the slightest idea what is meant. In such cases, it is a reader service to give both the generic term and the brand name or trademark. When a certain brand-name product produces a measurably better recipe result, it is again a reader service to indicate that product by name.

Generic terms are not protected by trademark registration and are printed in lowercase letters. Trademarks and brand names should be capitalized and written exactly the way the company indicates.

The following list is a good starting point for developing your own generic terms resource file. You can write to the consumer service departments of major food companies and ask for their generic terms lists, which usually are updated annually. These lists include brand names, suggested generic terms, and package weights or sizes for each product.

*Webster's Third New International Dictionary* (unabridged) lists the correct spelling of many well-established trademarks and descriptions of the products. You also can check with the legal department of your company or publication if you have any questions about the use of trademarks or brand names.

A.1. steak sauce—steak sauce
Accent—monosodium glutamate
All Bran—shreds of wheat bran cereal
Almond Roca—buttercrunch confection
Amaretto di Saronno—almond-flavored liqueur
Angostura bitters—aromatic bitters

Bac*Os—imitation bacon bits
Baggies—plastic bags

BAKE-OFF—registered trademark of The Pillsbury Company for a cooking contest; no generic term available

Beau Monde seasoning—a branded product produced by Spice Islands; no generic term available

Bisquick—baking mix

Bits 'O Brickle—almond brickle chips

Bran Buds—morsels of wheat bran cereal

Bran Flakes—wheat bran cereal

Bundt pan—fluted tube pan

Butter Buds—butter-flavored granules

Butterball turkey—turkey

Butterfinger—chocolate-covered crispy peanut-buttery candy

Calvados—dry apple brandy or apple brandy

Certo—liquid fruit pectin

Chambord—raspberry-flavored liqueur

Cheerios—toasted oat cereal

Cheez Whiz—process cheese sauce

Coca-Cola, Coke—cola-flavored carbonated beverage

Coffee-Mate—powdered nondairy coffee creamer

Cointreau—orange-flavored liqueur

Cool Whip—frozen nondairy whipped topping

Corn Chex—crispy corn cereal squares

Corn Flakes—cornflakes cereal; cornflake (no s) crumbs

Corn Pops—puffed corn cereal

Cracker Jack—candied popcorn

Cracklin' Oat Bran—O-shaped, sweetened oat and wheat bran cereal

Cran-Apple or Cranapple—cranberry-apple juice drink

Cream of Wheat—hot wheat cereal

Cremora—powdered nondairy coffee creamer

Crisco—solid vegetable shortening

Crispix—corn-and-rice cereal

Crock-Pot—slow cooker or crockery cooker

## Irena Chalmers, USA

Author of *The Great Food Almanac* and other books

My best definition of a good recipe is a short one—short on ingredients to be used, short on preparation and cooking time, and one that requires only a spirit of enthusiasm and virtually no skill to prepare.

Derby Pie—chocolate chip pecan pie
Dijonnaise—creamy mustard blend
Dr Pepper—no generic term available; no period after Dr

Eagle Brand—sweetened condensed milk
Eagle Brand Low Fat—low-fat sweetened condensed milk
Eggbeaters—cholesterol-free real egg product
Equal—nonnutritive sweetener

Fig Newtons—fig bars
Frangelico—hazelnut-flavored liqueur
Fruit Fresh—ascorbic acid color keeper
Fruit Rollups—chewy fruit rolls

Glad Wrap—plastic wrap
Golden Honey Graham Cereal—honey graham cereal
Grand Marnier—orange-flavored liqueur
Grape Nuts—nutlike cereal nuggets
Gummi Bears—bite-size bear-shaped chewy fruit snacks

Handi-Wrap—plastic wrap
Hawaiian Punch—red fruit punch
Heath Bars—English toffee-flavored candy bars
Hershey's Hugs—foil-wrapped white and milk chocolate pieces
Hershey's Kisses—foil-wrapped milk chocolate pieces

Jell-O—flavored gelatin
Jimmies—sprinkles

Kahlúa—coffee-flavored liqueur
Kikkoman—soy sauce
Kitchen Bouquet—browning sauce
KitchenAid—electric mixer

Kitty Litter—cat box litter
Kleenex—facial tissue
Koolaid—sweetened (or unsweetened) flavored soft drink mix powder

Lifesavers—ring-shaped hard candy

M & M's—candy-coated chocolate pieces
Mazola oil—vegetable oil
Milnot—dairy soya blend
Minute Rice—instant or quick-cooking rice
Mrs. Dash—salt-free herb-and-spice blend

Nescafé—instant coffee powder (granules)
NutraSweet—nonnutritive sweetener

Old English Cheese—sharp process cheese spread

PAM—vegetable cooking spray

Peanut M & M's—candy-coated chocolate-covered peanuts

Pepsi—cola-flavored carbonated beverage

Pernod—anise liqueur

Perrier—sparkling mineral water

Pyrex—heat-resistant (or ovenproof) glass container

Quaker Oat Squares—crisp oat cereal squares

Raisin Bran—wheat bran flakes cereal with raisins

Redi-Whip—aerosol whipped dessert topping

Reese's Peanut Butter Cups—chocolate-covered peanut butter cups

Reynolds Wrap—aluminum foil

Rice Chex—crisp rice cereal squares

Rice Krispies—crisp rice cereal

Roquefort—blue cheese; use the word "Roquefort" only if you are
   using the real thing

Rubbermaid—plastic containers

Saran Wrap—plastic wrap

Seven-Up, 7Up—lemon-lime flavored carbonated beverage; no hyphen in 7Up

Shredded Wheat—large (or mini) shredded whole wheat cereal biscuits

Silk—soy milk

SilverStone—nonstick cookware

Smithfield ham—dry-cured smoked ham

Snickers—chocolate-coated caramel-peanut nougat bar

Special K—high-protein rice-and-wheat cereal

Styrofoam—plastic foam

Sure-Jell—powdered fruit pectin

Sure-Jell Light—powdered fruit pectin for reduced sugar

Sweet*10—noncaloric liquid sugar substitute

Sweet 'n Low—low-calorie granulated sugar substitute

Tabasco—hot pepper sauce

Tang—orange-flavored drink mix

Teflon—nonstick coating

Tender Quick—meat cure mix

thermos—formerly a trademark, now a generic term for any vacuum bottle; do not capitalize

Tia Maria—coffee-flavored liqueur

Toll House cookies—chocolate chip cookies

Triple Sec—orange-flavored liqueur

Tupperware—plastic containers

V-8 juice—tomato-vegetable juice cocktail
Velveeta—process cheese spread

Wheaties—whole wheat flake cereal
Wondra—quick-mixing all-purpose flour

Ziploc bags—resealable plastic bags

## Jeanne Voltz, USA

Former food editor, *Woman's Day, Los Angeles Times,* and *Miami Herald,* and author of several cookbooks

A good recipe suits the reader in regard to the time, the place, and the ingredients available; it suits the reader's skill or will to cook; and its taste meets acceptance by his or her family and guests. A good recipe is a commonsense solution to a reader's need for food and sustenance. No one recipe is universally appealing, and a good recipe may not satisfy an individual in all culinary situations. It is the recipe that I or another reader want now!

# Chapter Eight

# Metrics

THE UNITED STATES USES A system of measures based on cups and quarts, ounces and pounds, and inches and yards. In most of the world, however, measurements are based on the metric system—meters for length, grams for weight, and liters for volume.

Despite the fact that the Metric Conversion Act of 1975 called for a conversion to metric, Americans have resisted the metric system. Today most recipes written for U.S. consumers use American Standard measurements; some cookbooks have metric conversion tables in a glossary and some give dual measurements in recipes.

Recipes with dual measurements can be difficult to write because a

## Carol Haddix, USA

Food Guide editor, *Chicago Tribune*

As for what makes a good recipe, I believe that any recipe that makes someone want to cook is good. The rest is just details. Obviously, that means it must be appealing, probably short, and practical.

cup (or other U.S. measure) does not equate exactly to standard metric measures.

In Canada and the United States, metric measuring cups and spoons, similar to the American Standard cups and spoons with which we are familiar, were developed in the 1970s as a means of easing the conversion to metric. These measures are readily available in housewares departments in the United States and Canada.

In Europe, however, cooks use a different approach to measuring most ingredients, one that is based on weight rather than volume. The exception is that European cooks often use soup spoons or coffee spoons for small measures; our standardized teaspoons and tablespoons are more precise.

The suggestions given here are based on the approach to metric measures developed in the United States and Canada because that is how most cookbooks with dual measurements are being written. If you trained in Europe, you will have a different approach to metrics.

It is important to note that you can't rely solely on mathematical conversions to develop metric equivalents. You must kitchen-test a recipe using metric measures, making sure the measurements are realistic for home cooks and that the results are similar to those produced by the original recipe. This is especially true for precise baking recipes.

Books with dual-measurement recipes should include a note to readers that when measuring ingredients, one system should be followed throughout.

Users of American cookbooks outside the United States can avoid the problem of converting measurements by buying and using an inexpensive set of American cup measures, which are sold in cookware shops around the world or on the Internet.

The metric system is based on the decimal system, with large measures being subdivided into units of 10.

For liquid ingredients, the liter is the basic unit of measure. A liter is a little more than a quart. Recipes usually use milliliters ($\frac{1}{1000}$ of a liter), centiliters ($\frac{1}{100}$ of a liter), or deciliters ($\frac{1}{10}$ of a liter). One teaspoon equals 5 milliliters; 1 tablespoon, 15 milliliters; and 1 cup, 250 milliliters. Metric measures in these sizes are readily available in the United States and Canada.

Solid ingredients are weighed. The gram is the basic unit of measure for these ingredients. One ounce equals 28.35 grams; 2.2 pounds is 1 kilogram. Ingredients such as meat, butter, cheese, and most packaged goods are measured in grams in metric recipes. In addition, many dry ingredients, such as flour and sugar, are measured in grams. In the United States and Canada, sugar and flour are frequently measured in liter-measuring utensils instead of being weighed.

For length, width, and depth measurements, the meter is the basic unit. A meter is a little longer than 36 inches (1 yard). In recipes, the centimeter, which is $\frac{1}{100}$ of a meter, is used more often than the meter. There are 2.5 centimeters in an inch.

Temperatures, including oven temperatures, are given in degrees Celsius (formerly called centigrade) in the metric system. Water boils at 100 degrees Celsius (212 degrees Fahrenheit) and freezes at 0 degrees Celsius (32 degrees Fahrenheit).

## How to Adapt U.S. Recipes to Metric

On paper, do the mathematical calculations to convert the U.S. measurements (cups, etc.) for each ingredient to metric units (milliliters, grams, etc.).

Solid ingredients will have to be weighed on a gram scale. (Gram scales are usually available at moderate cost in housewares departments in the United States and Canada.) You can get an estimated metric amount by doing a mathematical calculation, if you know the weight in ounces or pounds.

$^1/_2$ cup butter = 4 ounces

4 ounces x 28.35 = 113 grams

Compare the mathematical results to standard metric measures. The 250-milliliter measure with 25-milliliter graduations is the standard metric measure; "measuring spoons" are available in 1, 2, 5, 15, and 25 milliliters. The amount of an ingredient is usually rounded off so that it can be measured conveniently.

$^3/_4$ cup broth = 180 milliliters, which would be rounded off to 175 milli-liters, a more standard metric measure.

Mathematically convert any measurement of thickness (especially for doughs and meats) or any dimensions of ingredients. Convert pan sizes; check that pan sizes are available in metric.

After you have calculated the approximate metric equivalents, test the recipe using metric measures. Do not rely only on the mathematical conversions. In preparing a recipe, adjustments are often needed to produce results similar to those of the original recipe. Make sure the metric amounts are realistic for a home cook to measure with basic equipment. Double-check the cooking temperature and time and the yield of the recipe.

## Conversion Formulas—U.S. Measures to Metric

Ounces to grams: multiply ounces by 28.35

4 ounces x 28.35 = 113.4 grams

Pounds to grams: multiply pounds by 453.5

2 pounds x 453.5 = 907 grams

Cups to liters: multiply cups (or fraction thereof) by 0.24

$^1/_4$ cup

Convert $^1/_4$ to a decimal = 0.25

0.25 x 0.24 = 0.060 liters or 60 milliliters

Inches to centimeters: multiply inches by 2.54

9 x 9 x 2-inch baking pan = 23 x 23 x 5-centimeter pan

Fahrenheit to Celsius: subtract 32 from the Fahrenheit temperature, multiply by 5, then divide by 9

350 degrees Fahrenheit − 32 = 318

318 x 5 = 1590

1590 ÷ 9 = 176.66 degrees Celsius, which is rounded to 175 degrees Celsius

## Grammatical Points

The term "measure" replaces "teaspoon," "tablespoon," and "cup" in metric recipes, although this usage varies from country to country. Some countries still use the familiar terms ("teaspoon," "tablespoon," "cup") to refer to the metric-size versions of these measures.

**1 tablespoon = 15 milliliter measure**

Unlike American Standard measurements, which are usually spelled out, metric measurements are commonly abbreviated, especially in recipes with dual measurements. Depending on your audience, it might be preferable to write out the metric measurement and/or provide a list of metric terms and their abbreviations in a glossary. The abbreviation for liter is a lower case l, which is easily confused with the numeral one (1). For this reason, some countries use a capital L or a script lowercase $\ell$ as the abbreviation for liter. The following are standard abbreviations:

| | |
|---|---|
| gram | g |
| kilogram | kg |
| millimeter | mm |
| centimeter | cm |
| milliliter | ml or mL |
| deciliter | dl or dL |
| liter | L, l, or $\ell$ |
| degrees Celsius | °C |

Metric abbreviations do not have a period at the end.

**kg (not kg.)**

When spelling out a metric measurement, add an *s* for the plural. When using an abbreviation, do not add an *s*.

**kilograms          kg**

Generally, metric terms begin with a lowercase letter, except those derived from proper terms.

| C | Celsius |
| g | gram |

For numerical values less than 1, place a zero before the decimal point for clarity. (When possible, avoid the fraction and call for the appropriate metric measurement. For example, 0.5 meter is the same as 5 decimeters.)

## Sample Dual-Measurement Recipe

### Creamy Zucchini Casserole

1 pound (450 g) zucchini, cut into $^1/_2$-inch (1-cm) slices
Water
2 eggs, slightly beaten
1 cup (250 ml) heavy cream
Salt and black pepper
$^1/_4$ cup (30 g) grated Gruyère cheese

Preheat oven to 400°F (200°C). Put zucchini slices in a medium saucepan; cover with water. Bring to a boil. Reduce heat and simmer 5 minutes. Drain well. Spread zucchini in a greased 9 x 9 x 2-inch (23 x 23 x 5-cm) baking pan.

Mix eggs and cream in a small bowl; season to taste with salt and pepper. Pour egg mixture over zucchini. Sprinkle cheese over mixture in pan.

Bake in preheated 400°F (200°C) oven 10 to 15 minutes, or until the egg mixture is set and the top is brown.

YIELD: 4 SERVINGS.

# For More Information on Metrics

American National Standards Institute
11 West 42nd Street
New York, NY 10036
212-642-4900
www.ansi.org

# Metric Conversion Charts

These are not exact equivalents, but have been rounded up or down for easier measuring. Metric conversion systems for recipes are often found on food-related Web sites.

## Volume Measurements

| | |
|---|---|
| $1/8$ teaspoon | 0.5 ml |
| $1/4$ teaspoon | 1 ml |
| $1/2$ teaspoon | 2 ml |
| $3/4$ teaspoon | 4 ml |
| 1 teaspoon | 5 ml |
| 1 dessertspoon (2 teaspoons) | 10 ml |
| 1 tablespoon (3 teaspoons) | 15 ml |
| $1/4$ cup | 60 ml |
| $1/3$ cup | 75 ml |
| $1/2$ cup | 125 ml |
| $2/3$ cup | 150 ml |
| $3/4$ cup | 175 ml |
| 1 cup | 250 ml |
| 2 cups | 500 ml |
| 1 quart (4 cups) | 1000 ml or 1 L |
| 1 gallon (4 quarts) | 4 L |

Note: In Australia, 1 tablespoon equals 20 ml, and there are 4 teaspoons in a tablespoon.

# Weight Measurements

Conversion charts commonly found in cookbooks use amounts that are rounded up or down for easy measuring. Common weight ranges found in such charts are included here.

| | |
|---|---|
| $^1/_2$ ounce | 15 g |
| 1 ounce | 25 g or 30 g |
| 3 ounces | 90 g |
| 4 ounces | 115 g or 125 g |
| 8 ounces | 225 g or 250 g |
| 12 ounces | 350 g or 375 g |
| 16 ounces (1 pound) | 450 g or 500 g |
| $2^1/_4$ pounds | 1 kg |

Note: Some countries use 25 grams = 1 ounce as a base because it is easier arithmetic. It is important that readers understand the smallness of a gram or milliliter so they will realize that rounding off is sensible. Because few kitchens have scales, a handy technique is to use a stick of butter (4 ounces or 115 grams) as a standard. Because working with multiples of 115 is not practical, the cook can round it off to 100 grams or 125 grams. Non-baking type recipes can be converted loosely; low-tolerance (such as pastry) or very small quantity recipes require more precise conversions. All converted recipes should be kitchen-tested.

# Oven Temperatures

| Fahrenheit | Celsius | Gas Mark |
|---|---|---|
| 250° | 120° | 1 |
| 300° | 150° | 2 |
| 325° | 160° | 3 |
| 350° | 180° | 4 |
| 375° | 190° | 5 |
| 400° | 200° | 6 |
| 425° | 220° | 7 |
| 450° | 230° | 8 |
| 475° | 240° | 9 |
| 500° | 250° | 10 |

# Commonly Used Temperatures

| | | |
|---|---|---|
| Water freezes | 32°F | 0°C |
| Water boils | 212°F | 100°C |
| Scalding liquid | 175°F | 80°C |
| Lukewarm liquid | 110°F | 45°C |
| Refrigerator storage | 40°F | 4°C |
| Freezer storage | 0°F | -18°C |
| Yeast dough rising | 85°F | 30°C |

# Baking Pan Sizes

Bakeware is sized by either base dimension or volume capacity.

| | |
|---|---|
| 8 x 8 x 2-inch baking pan | 20 x 20 x 5 cm or 2 L |
| 9 x 9 x 2-inch baking pan | 23 x 23 x 5 cm or 2.5 L |
| 13 x 9 x 2-inch baking pan | 33 x 23 x 5 cm or 3.5 L |
| 15 x 10 x 1-inch baking pan | 38 x 26 x 3 cm |
| 26 x 18 x 1-inch baking pan | 66 x 46 x 3 cm |
| 20 x 12 x 2-inch steam table pan | 50 x 30 x 5 cm |
| 12 x 10 x 2-inch steam table pan | 30 x 25 x 5 cm |
| 9 x 5 x 3-inch loaf pan | 23 x 13 x 6 cm or 2 L |
| 8-inch round baking pan (1$^1/_2$ inches deep) | 20 x 4 cm or 1.2 L |
| 9-inch round baking pan (1$^1/_2$ inches deep) | 23 x 4 cm or 1.5 L |
| 8-inch pie plate | 20 cm |
| 9-inch pie plate | 23 cm |
| 10-inch pie plate | 25 cm |
| 10-inch tube pan (4 inches deep) | 25 x 10 cm or 4 L |
| 1$^1/_2$-quart baking dish | 1.5 L |
| 2-quart baking dish | 2 L |

## Common Can and Package Sizes

By volume:

| | |
|---|---|
| 4 ounces | 114 mL |
| 5$^1$/$_2$ ounces | 156 mL |
| 7$^1$/$_2$ ounces | 213 mL |
| 10 ounces | 284 mL |
| 14 ounces | 398 mL |
| 19 ounces | 540 mL |
| 28 ounces | 796 mL |

By mass:

| | |
|---|---|
| 3$^3$/$_4$ ounces | 106 g |
| 4 ounces | 113 g |
| 5 ounces | 142 g |
| 6 ounces | 170 g |
| 6$^1$/$_2$ ounces | 184 g |
| 7$^3$/$_4$ ounces | 220 g |
| 15 ounces | 425 g |

T I P S    F R O M    T H E    E X P E R T S

## Sue Dawson, USA

Food editor, *Columbus Dispatch*

At the *Dispatch*, we tend to be very concise with directions, to save valuable space. In view of today's cooking illiteracy, I think we're too concise. I dislike talking down to readers, but I think we should be more specific.

We fought for and won the right to use numerals in the text of recipes (despite traditional journalism style), because it is so much easier for a busy cook to quickly spot the amount or time she or he needs to know.

# Imperial Measures

As if metric and American Standard measurements weren't confusing enough, there are also Imperial measurements, the official British series of weights and measures used in countries that are or were part of the Commonwealth and British Empire. Most of these countries have officially switched to the metric system; however, Imperial measurements continue to be used and referred to, especially in cookbooks.

The major difference is that the Imperial, or British, pint measures 20 fluid ounces, while the American pint measures 16 fluid ounces. Therefore, the British standard cup measures 10 fluid ounces, while the American standard cup measures 8 fluid ounces.

The British tablespoon is larger than the American tablespoon. Two British tablespoons equal three American tablespoons.

British recipes usually indicate amounts of ingredients by weight in pounds, ounces, fluid ounces, or pints, rather than giving measurements in cups as in American recipes.

## Madeleine Kamman, USA

Former director, School for American Chefs, Beringer Vineyards, and author of *The Making of a Cook* and other books

The best thing you can do for yourself is to read as much as you can about the techniques of cooking and try to master them. The best recipe writers are those who have, first and foremost, mastered their techniques in depth.

# Chapter Nine

# Nutrition Analysis of Recipes

W ITH THE EVER-INCREASING EMPHASIS on diet and health, more and more people want to know what is in the food they eat. Nutrition information is on most food products in supermarkets, and many consumers use that information to make purchasing decisions. Consumers also want to know the nutrient content of the recipes they prepare, so some form of nutrition information often is added to recipes. Many food service operators, especially in schools and hospitals, have to meet specific nutrition requirements that require the analysis of all recipes.

Many computer software programs are available to analyze the nutrient content of recipes, but they vary widely. We strongly suggest

## Chuck Williams, USA

Founder, Williams-Sonoma cookware stores, and general editor, *Williams-Sonoma Kitchen Library* cookbook series

It is the responsibility of people writing cookbooks today to bring recipes up to date, to make them relevant to the way people now live. For example, recipes including dried beans have always said to soak the beans overnight, but today who is going to cook them in the morning? I think today's recipes should probably direct the cook to soak beans for five or six hours before cooking them and let the cook plan the timing accordingly.

that you check with other people in your field (newspaper, magazine, nutrition consulting, recipe development, etc.) to find out which programs they use and whether they are satisfied with them.

Most of the nutrition software companies have Web sites on the Internet. You can locate these Web sites by doing a general search for nutrition software companies.

The most comprehensive listing of nutrition analysis software for recipes is part of the Food and Nutrition-Related Software and Multimedia database, produced by the Food and Nutrition Information Center (FNIC) of the U.S. Department of Agriculture (USDA). You can search this extensive database (more than 300 pages) or download the contents of the entire database on the FNIC Web site. Print copies of four subject-specific reports are available, but not the entire database. The four subject areas are diet analysis and clinical nutrition, consumer diet analysis, nutrition education, and food service management and food industry.

At this time, a subject-specific listing of nutrition software programs for recipes is not available in print form from FNIC. However, if you can view the database electronically, you will find detailed information on nutrition software programs for recipes. Each listing gives the name, address, and telephone number of the producer or distributor. It also lists hardware compatibility, cost, and a brief description of the software. The FNIC list might not cite the most recent programs from specific companies because these programs are constantly updated. When contacting a specific company, ask about the most recent programs. Many software companies have trial versions on their Web sites or can send you a sample copy of the database.

To access the FNIC database electronically, or to obtain print copies of the subject-specific reports, contact:

**Food and Nutrition Information Center**
**USDA/National Agricultural Library**
**10301 Baltimore Avenue, Room 304**
**Beltsville, MD 20705-2351**
**301-504-5719**
**Fax: 301-504-6409**
**www.nal.usda.gov/fnic/software/software.txt**

Another way to obtain nutrition analysis for recipes, depending on the project, information needed, and time requirements, is to hire an individual or company that specializes in nutrition analysis. Here again, check with colleagues for their recommendations or consult the directory of your professional association for members who offer that service. Then ask the individual or company specific questions about how the nutrition analysis is performed. Some major points to discuss are the deadlines (when you can get the recipes to the person and when you need them returned), the quality of the data used, the expertise of the person doing the analysis, and the procedures for proofing and double-checking the entries. Be explicit about the type of information you need and make sure the person or company can meet your requirements.

# Tips on Selecting Nutrition Analysis Programs

Your target audience for the recipes you develop or write will be a determining factor in the kind of nutrition software program you need. Because your projects most likely will vary over time, think about the way you will most often use the program and the most extensive use you could have for the software. You might select a software program that fits your most frequent needs, and make special arrangements for infrequent projects requiring more extensive data. Having a firm idea of how you will use the software is important in making your selection.

Here are some other points that you should consider:

- The food database is a key element. Ask the company selling the software about the original source of the nutrient analysis data. Did they use USDA Handbook 8, Bowes and Church, or a food manufacturer? The quality of the information is critical to being able to do accurate nutrition analysis.

- Many software programs are designed specifically for diet analysis, not nutrition analysis of recipes. If you are going to use the program primarily for nutrition analysis, make sure you purchase a program that does that easily. The program might include other components, such as diet analysis, meal planning, and labeling information.

- Find out how many food items are listed on the program. Ask how often the company updates its data. Inquire about the fees for obtaining database updates and program enhancements.

- Make sure you have the ability to add food items to the database and that it is relatively easy to do. You might be able to use a smaller database (with fewer food items) that could increase computer efficiency if you can easily add food items.

- Depending on the type of recipe writing you are doing, you might want a program with data for brand-name foods. The ability to locate and display all the foods of a particular brand name (or group of brand names) is a time-saving factor.

- Ask whether the program allows you to subtract or add ingredients, such as salt or mayonnaise, from a recipe that you have already analyzed and save the new version without reentering all of the ingredient information.

- If you work with restaurant menu items, you will need to find out whether they are included in the database.

- Most programs allow you to adjust the serving size, but double-check that the program has this important feature.

- Ask whether the food items listed in the database of the program are easy to access or if you must use a code.

- Another important factor, depending on how much nutrition analysis you do, is whether there is a limit on the number of recipes that can be stored as part of the program.

- Ask what nutrients are analyzed. In most cases, you need only the basic nutrients, vitamins, and minerals. Researchers or people with a special project might need individual amino acids, fatty acids, and other items.

- Consider what information prints out in the report. Does the report list the percentages of fat, protein, and carbohydrates from calories? Can all the information be viewed on the screen prior to printing?

- Regarding hardware, make sure that your computer meets the software company's minimum hardware requirements. You will need to know what operating system your computer uses (DOS, Windows, UNIX) and the minimum memory (RAM) and hard disk space requirements for the software.

- Consumer service and technical software support are important in selecting a nutrition analysis program. Is there a toll-free number for assistance? During what hours does it operate?

## Tips on Using Nutrition Analysis Programs

Here are some considerations to keep in mind as you are doing nutrition analysis:

- It is best if the person developing the recipe can do the nutrition analysis. If the recipe does not meet the nutrition requirements for the project, the recipe can be modified and retested immediately, instead of during the editing process, possibly on a tight deadline.

- Someone knowledgeable about food should make the entries in the nutrition analysis program. There are many decisions, such as raw versus cooked portions of food, that must be made on each entry. If a clerical person who is not knowledgeable about recipes and cooking makes the entries, there is a greater margin for errors.

- Be as accurate and consistent with the nutrition analysis as you are with the recipe development, writing, or editing.

- Carefully proof the entries in the nutrition analysis program. Ask someone else to do a second proof.

- If your recipe testing or editing project requires nutrition analysis, allow enough time for this phase of the project. Do not underestimate how much time and attention to detail nutrition analysis takes.

- The format for nutrition analysis information on recipes varies according to the publication, the purpose, the audience, the page design, and graphic capabilities. It can be as simple as a sentence listing calories and/or cholesterol, or as detailed as a chart listing major nutrients, percentages and types of fats, diabetic dietary exchanges, and other information. Study other publications and clip samples of their formats, then use these examples to develop a format that suits your needs and graphic capabilities.

## Karen Haram, USA

Food editor, *San Antonio Express-News*

A good recipe is one that can be prepared in a minimum of time, using a minimum of ingredients and effort, and have the kind of flavor that makes people ask you for a copy so that they can make it themselves.

I don't care how flavorful a recipe is—if it takes multiple trips to markets to get the ingredients or hours to prepare, it's not a good recipe in my book.

## Antonia Allegra, USA

Founder/director, Symposium for Professional Food Writers, and former editor-in-chief, *Appellation* magazine

With prepared food and take-out food making major strides in the pattern of "dining," particularly within the United States, it occurs to me that cookbooks and the recipes within them are truly more books of dreams now, instead of books to assist the cook. Think of how often you hear, "I love that cookbook! I read it at night in bed; it's better than any novel and the pictures are terrific." Yet, ask the same home cook which recipes from that same book he or she has enjoyed cooking and a common response might be, "Well, I don't actually have time to cook the dishes, but did you see the picture of the lemon tart?"

Chapter Ten

# Copyright, Plagiarism, and the Ethics of Recipe Writing

**Copyright.** The exclusive legal right to reproduce, publish, and sell the matter and form (as of a literary, musical, or artistic work).
**Plagiarize.** To steal and pass off (the ideas or words of another) as one's own.
**Ethic(s).** (a) a set of moral principles or values (b) a theory or system of moral values (c) the principles of conduct governing an individual or a group.

—*Webster's Tenth New Collegiate Dictionary*

IN RECENT YEARS, THE ETHICS of recipe writing have moved from the back burner to the front of the stove. A series of cookbook scandals that involved large numbers of recipes reprinted verbatim without credit has brought a long-hidden subject into the open. Although recipe pilfering has been a problem for years, only recently have food professionals begun speaking up.

Although the origin of a recipe might not be important to a casual reader, it is to food writers and cooks. For many, the issue isn't money, but attribution: giving credit where credit is due. Acknowledging that an idea came from someone else or was inspired by another recipe doesn't make your work any less original—and might even give it credibility.

Sharing—ideas, recipes, the prepared food—is part of the pleasure of cooking, and sharing credit should be a natural part of writing about cooking. Readers like to know about a recipe, where it comes from, what makes it special. This information easily can be included in a headnote and can help draw the reader into the recipe.

The general rule of thumb is that three major changes are required to make a recipe "yours." However, even if you make such changes, it is a professional courtesy to acknowledge the source of or inspiration for the recipe.

If a recipe is loosely based on numerous other recipes, you might choose to cite the sources in a bibliography rather than giving credit in the recipe itself. When you honestly don't know the source of a recipe, this can be explained in an appropriate place.

Standard recipes—such as pie crust, white sauce, mayonnaise, and omelets—are so basic they are generally considered to be in the public domain and do not need attribution.

If you want to use a previously printed recipe more or less intact in your own cookbook, you will need to get written permission from the original publisher. Verbal permission from the author is not adequate. Your publisher can provide an example of a permission request letter.

The International Association of Culinary Professionals (IACP) takes the matter of attribution—of recipes and other proprietary material—seriously. In *IACP Ethical Guidelines,* a booklet produced by the ethics committee of IACP (see Chapter Fourteen), there are specific guidelines for attribution of recipes, whether published, demonstrated, taught, or used on menus. In summary, the guidelines say, "When in doubt, give credit." It is sound advice.

Professional courtesy and ethics aside, what about the legality of "borrowing" recipes? The legal position on the ownership of recipes is somewhat murky.

By definition, a copyright protects only the particular manner and form of the expression of an idea; it does not extend to the idea itself. In the broadest sense, recipes are ideas. That interpretation would mean that recipes—the titles, lists of ingredients, and procedures—are not subject to copyright.

## Barbara Haber, USA

Curator of Books, Schlesinger Library, Radcliffe Institute for Advanced Study, Harvard University

I see recipes as historical documents to be treated as respectfully as historians view letters, diaries, court records, or any other documents deemed useful for understanding and interpreting a given time and place.

However, many attorneys argue that the recipe method, the exact wording of the recipe procedure, constitutes a creative and original literary work and thus can be copyrighted. In that sense, copying a recipe verbatim would be a violation of copyright.

To the extent copyright exists in your work, it arises automatically when the work is written. Certain additional advantages attach to your copyright, however, when you place a copyright notice on your work and register the copyright with the U.S. Copyright Office.

Although the legal question is a bit unclear as to whether or not copyright exists in recipes, it is nevertheless a good idea to give your readers notice of your assertion of copyright in your original work and to register the work. To do this, put a copyright mark, the year of first publication, and your name on the article or recipe. To apply for registration of your copyright, complete and mail the appropriate registration form to the Copyright Office along with the appropriate number of copies of the work and the required filing fee (currently $30 for most applications).

You can request registration forms and information from:

**Information Section, Room 401**
**Copyright Office**
**Library of Congress**
**101 Independence Avenue SE**
**Washington, DC 20559**
**www.loc.gov\copyright**

To order Circular I, *Copyright Basics,* or for other information, call the Copyright Office 24-hour automated hotline, 202-707-9100. To speak with an information specialist during business hours (8:30 A.M. to 5 P.M. ET Monday through Friday), call 202-707-3000.

## Betty Fussell, USA

Author of *The Story of Corn* and other books

The recipe suggests the form, but the cook must do the shaping to create the particular work of art, whether it's a jar of raspberry jam or a pâté en croûte. That's where the cook puts his or her thumbprint and says, "It's mine." The best recipes make the cook want to rush to the kitchen to make them "mine" in order to give the finished works to the eater.

The best recipes are formulas for sharing—this dish, this meal, this moment—with the recipe maker, the cook, and the eater, all three of whom may be you.

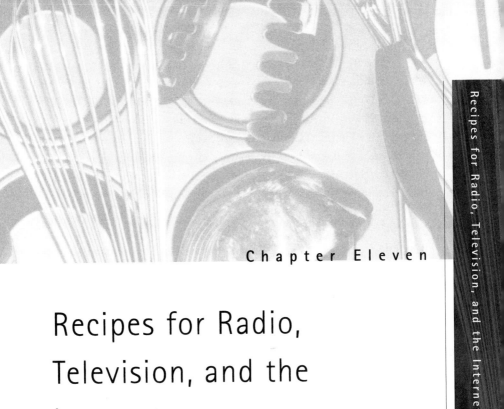

Chapter Eleven

# Recipes for Radio, Television, and the Internet

*What makes a good recipe for the electronic media? When we asked Rick Rodgers, he generously shared tips based on his extensive experience in television, radio, and the Internet. Rodgers has written more than 20 cookbooks, including* **Thanksgiving 101,** *and does many media appearances as a cookbook author and product spokesperson. He works behind the scenes on other cookbooks as a co-author, recipe tester, and general "cookbook doctor."*

In today's cookbook world, exposure to the media is an integral part of the book's success. There are three major areas—television, radio, and the Internet. If you're camera shy, have microphonephobia, or lack computer skills, you might want to think twice about writing a cookbook.

If you are doing a television show, keep this word in mind: *sizzle*. Make food that has theatricality—people love to hear the sizzle of meat hitting a hot skillet or see the flame of a propane torch finishing off a crème brûlée. (But beware of the irritatingly loud whirl of the food processor or blender.) Choose a recipe with a lot of action or something that shows a skill. For desserts, seeing someone decorate a cake (pouring chocolate glaze over a Sachertorte or piping swirls on a birthday cake) is more engaging and interesting than seeing a batter being prepared.

Time constraints are always a problem on television, especially on local shows that run live without editing. If you must resort to an overly simple recipe (I call these "Dump Recipes" because the cook has time only to dump little bowls of ingredients into one big bowl and stir them together), pick one with unusual ingredients so you can keep the viewer's interest by teaching with words, if not by actions.

For example, take salsa. Instead of the common jalapeño, use a chipotle or habañero chile so you can discuss its qualities. The average viewer doesn't know that a chipotle is a smoked jalapeño or about the Scoville system of measuring chile heat or how a habañero is different from a Scotch bonnet pepper. Even if you use a jalapeño, you can discuss wearing plastic gloves to avoid skin irritation, how capsaicin doesn't dissolve in water so milk products reduce the heat in your mouth more readily, and leaving in the chile seeds and ribs to give more heat. This makes you a teacher and not just a cook, and increases the recipe's interest factor as well. And be sure the dish is attractive. Rustic recipes are great for television because they often have a minimum of ingredients, but be sure that you garnish them well to compensate for the lack of frills.

Radio shows are wonderful places to get your book's message across, but recipes are rarely the right way to do it. Many people drive while they listen, and aren't able to jot down the recipe measurements. Also, reciting measurements is boring! While on publicity tours, I was frequently a guest on a popular Midwestern radio show where the host repeated every measurement. I'd say, "One tablespoon of baking powder," and he'd intone, "One Tee-Bee of baking powder. . . ." Imagine two-and-a-half minutes of that gripping conversation. I never left that studio thinking that the listener had any idea what my book was really about, even though I'd try to slip in some hard information.

If the radio show's manager insists on a recipe, be sure that the listeners have an easy way of getting it (other than buying your book). Most radio shows will provide printed recipes on request, but check to be sure. Come with a printout of the recipe you plan to share, including the name of the book, your name, and the publisher, and leave it with the station so they can copy and send it out. Sure, you want to sell a book, but it is unfair to recite a recipe over the air and not give it out.

I prefer to tell listeners they can find the recipe on my Web site, which draws them to the site, as well. Also, I am hooked up to Amazon.com on my site, making it easy for people to buy my books there. In general, it is best to draw the radio listener to your book via anecdotes and facts rather than recipes per se.

Every cookbook author should have a Web site. It's an invaluable marketing tool for your book and is a good way to find new readers and to keep in touch with your fans. I get a lot of e-mail from my readers, and I will answer any culinary question they throw my way, even if it doesn't concern my recipes. Sure, it's a little extra work, but the bonding is worth it.

When choosing recipes for the Internet, almost anything goes, but visuals are especially important. Use a recipe from your book that has been professionally photographed (as a matter of courtesy, check with your publisher and photographer to clear any rights, although if you paid the photographer yourself, you may already own them). If you don't have a photograph to scan, use a free clip-art site to download appropriate graphics—apples for that apple pie recipe, for example. Use a lot of fonts and colors to keep the page lively. You are restricted to how many recipes from a book you can post, so check your contract for the exact number. If you're in doubt, consider your site the same as a usual print outlet, like a newspaper, and keep it to three recipes per book.

No matter what venue, choose a recipe that teaches. A successful recipe illustrates points that make the viewer say, "Gee, I never knew that." They'll want to buy your book because it promises to teach them something along with the recipes.

*Lynne Rosetto Kasper, host of public radio's national food show,* The Splendid Table, *and award-winning author of several cookbooks, shares some thoughts on recipes for the radio.*

Recipes on the radio raise a thorny question—does every listener care? If they do, how do you hold the audience while you go into tortured detail about each measurement and step? My guess is you lose your listener.

Of course, the style of the show guides much of this. Because my show, *The Splendid Table,* is a show about the larger subject of food and not solely cooking, I handle recipes of our guests or ones that tie into a segment by offering an address and a Web site where people can get them.

In answering call-in questions about cooking, I always place the recipe in the setting of a technique that invites variation. This comes down to teaching how food works and encouraging the listeners to trust their common sense and own tastes.

For instance, someone asks how to make a real Italian dressing. My response might be:

"You know, if you stepped over the border from Italy into France, they'd call this a vinaigrette. The idea is to blend together about one part wine vinegar with two to three parts good olive oil—olive oil you'd like to eat with a spoon. Blend them to taste.

"You can add herbs, garlic, minced onion . . . and almost anything else you'd like, but the oil and vinegar are the keys. Mind you, there's never any sugar or sun-dried tomatoes or other odd stuff in a real Italian dressing.

"Some people blend the dressing by whisking the oil into the vinegar, but in most Italian homes, it's done right at the table. You have the bowl of salad. You have a bottle of olive oil and a bottle of vinegar.

"You sprinkle it with salt and pepper. You take a generous tablespoon or two of olive oil and toss until the leaves are barely shining—better too little at first than too much. Then you toss in vinegar to taste. And always taste; it is the most important step. Then add a little more of whatever is needed. And that's how you make Italian dressing. It's easy and really quick."

The emphasis is always on building the confidence of the listener and offering them information that might be helpful by stressing the idea behind the recipe along with the trick or tip that makes it all come together. Of course, what you can't tell from the written word is having fun with it. Tone is everything on radio.

*Harvey Steiman, host of food talk shows on KCBS and KNBR in San Francisco for 11 years, is the author of* **Harvey Steiman's California Kitchen,** *a collection of recipes from his radio shows. He offers the following tips for radio recipes.*

The ideal radio recipe contains three tantalizing ingredients and takes about three minutes to describe. Nothing bores most listeners more than a bland recitation of ingredients, but a step-by-step process creates a word picture that allows the dish to take shape in the mind's eye.

The recipe itself may look no different from a well-written newspaper, magazine, or book recipe, but presenting it works better if the structure is modified.

Remember that most radio listeners are not sitting at a desk, pencil poised over paper to write down what they hear. They are driving through city traffic, jogging, exercising, or working at something else, with the radio playing in the background. Unlike television, radio cannot count on undivided attention. So keep it simple and describe the process with an ear for the important details.

Ten key factors for a successful radio recipe are:

1. Start by describing the finished dish, its appearance, its texture, its flavors. Tell a story about the dish, how you arrived at the recipe, anything to give a reason to keep listening.

2. Repeat the ingredients and their amounts as you say them, and allow a couple of beats for people to write.

3. Fill the time between ingredients, if possible, with any specifications or shopping notes. For example, don't just say, "Two pears." Add something appropriate, such as, "I like to use Bosc pears because the crisp texture lets them cook longer and absorb more flavor." This gives the listener useful information and a little more time to write.

4. Try to keep the ingredients to six or fewer (not counting salt, pepper, or water). If you must use more, try to group the ingredients into smaller clusters to make several interim recipes that finally combine into one.

5. Use normal conversational English to describe the process. Try not to sound as though you're reading a set of instructions.

6. Describe the look, the feel, and, if appropriate, the taste at each step. It helps listeners visualize what's happening as the recipe takes shape.

7. Repeat the amounts as you mention each ingredient in the process.

8. Any notes about ingredients, portions of the process that can be done in advance, alternate ingredients or steps, and so forth, should come at the appropriate point in the linear description of the process. Avoid waiting until the end. Remember, most listeners cannot rewind the tape or look back at what somebody else just read to them.

9. Finish by suggesting an appropriate presentation or accompaniment.

10. In general, try to sound as though you're engaged in the process of cooking, not just reading a recipe.

*Anne Byrn, author of* The Cake Mix Doctor *and other cookbooks, was cohost of the weekly* Food Bites *radio show on WNAH in Nashville, Tennessee. She appears often on television cooking shows. Here are her thoughts on recipes for both radio and television.*

Best recipes for radio: Instead of bringing already prepared food on air, you want the hosts to bake your recipes, if possible. This really allows them to get into the book, to become a part of it. You will have a much better interview. If not possible to bake on air, bring something with a catchy name, or a recipe that is near and dear to the radio station area but with a slight twist. Example: Red Velvet Cake anywhere. It draws lots of calls. Pound cakes are good down South, citrus cakes in the Southwest. Catchy names work well, too. Everyone was curious about

Darn Good Chocolate Cake. On air, you need to make the listener hungry. Don't just talk about the cake, describe how it looks, how it smells, how the crumb is moist, making everyone out there listening very hungry.

Best recipes for TV: You want color and height. My triple-decker strawberry cake has been a solid TV hit because it is tall and bright pink. When cut open to reveal a slice, and when surrounded by big red strawberries, it is gorgeous and generates a lot of calls and interest. You want three-dimensional food, food that appears like that anchorperson—with big hair and a lot of makeup!

## Recipes for Television

*Susan Purdy, author of* The Perfect Pie *and many other cookbooks, cooks frequently on television. She also teaches cooking classes as well as food and recipe writing classes. She shares her experiences here.*

A recipe that is "good for television" (meaning for use in a television cooking demonstration), has different requirements than one destined for print or other media intended for use in real time in a real kitchen. Television itself is visual, fast, and unforgiving. (Even taped shows prefer not to do retakes.) A recipe selected for television must be concise, clear, creative, and complete. This recipe is a success when it works visually, not when it is well written in a literary, stylistic, or even culinary sense. It must work the first time (and so must you, the author/chef). It must appear to be easy, quick, fun to make, and fabulous to look at.

The trick? Keep it simple. Select a dish that is less complex than you would, on first thought, have preferred to do. Ideally, the dish will:

- have few ingredients (five or fewer, if possible),
- have few steps (three is best, or plan to condense several steps),
- be bright and colorful (contrasting colors and textures; avoid white on white or dark pieces of meat on a dark plate that cannot be seen clearly by the camera),
- be highly visual (you must show, not tell; i.e., combine, stir, fry, serve . . . usually in under four minutes).

The "hero" or beauty shot of the completed dish must be dramatic and mouthwatering even if the recipe is never shown.

Avoid any introduction [recipe headnote]. Get right into the procedure and add hints and amusing tidbits as you mix and stir. Tell the recipe's story in one sentence while feeding a bite to the host at the end of your three-minute demonstration:

"This moist chocolate buttermilk cake was the legacy of my grandmother, who ran a bakery for immigrant orphans in Cleveland in the 1930s."

When writing a recipe for television, remember:

1.  Few ingredients, fewer steps, big finish. If your recipe is too long, the producer will probably suggest cutting it to keep down air time. The story editor may condense it still further for use as captions or a sidebar on screen, or for the station newsletter mailed to viewers. If you don't edit it, they will do it for you, and probably make fatal cuts. Bring a printed version of the recipe, approved by you, to leave at the studio. If appropriate, be sure to include book title, publisher, and ordering information.

2.  Count on your air time being short (four minutes, maybe), then prepare for the producer to cut it at the last minute (three minutes, if lucky), just before you go on camera. For this, write a fall-back, condensed version of the recipe that is half the original length, and practice preparing the recipe in half the time, just in case. On camera, this will appear to be a sort of sleight-of-hand cooking-magic show performed while speaking shorthand (as opposed to talking through a full-length, scripted, "real time" recipe). In a worst-case scenario, a television recipe may be no more than show-and-tell: "Here is the finished piece of cake. Here's how I made it"—in twenty words or less.

3.  Count on the host playing with your food. Television sees food as entertainment, usually comedy. Select a recipe that "talks well," has hints, tips, and humor, and invites anecdotes that inform and/or amuse. Don't be too serious yourself, and have fun!

*Melanie Barnard, author of* Short and Sweet *and several other cookbooks, is a monthly columnist for* Bon Appetit *magazine. She appears frequently on both radio and television.*

A good recipe for television is one that has few steps, can be clearly done in only a few minutes, has great visual appeal with bright colors, and also has a lot of "sizzle"—meaning that a skillet dish is especially appealing. On the other hand, plain noise such as blenders or food processors is not nearly as appealing as "sizzle" and can indeed distract from the food and the message.

For radio, it is important to bring the finished food to the host, for the "yum, yum" of tasting is the sizzle needed here.

Recipes that have an element of familiarity, such as new takes on traditional ideas, fare best on television and on radio, because people need to be able to relate to and trust the recipe without really knowing the writer. It is even better to remember that the host of the program is the true friend of the viewer or listener, and if he or she loves the food and relates to it, so will the audience.

While television and radio are great tools for recipe promotion, they are but an adjunct to other media. Finally, remember that you are selling yourself and your credibility as much as the recipe. So be yourself, love the food you cook, and communicate same.

*Nathalie Dupree is a veteran of hundreds of television and radio cooking shows, as well as a prolific cookbook author. She is a past president of the International Association of Culinary Professionals.*

To me, one writes a recipe for the user. My mental picture of my user is quite a different one if I'm on a radio program during drive time, where I might talk about things generally—heating up the grill and cooking a chicken breast, a simple marinade, how to tell if it is done, and some safety hints along with a joke or two—versus my radio show for one hour a day five days a week, where my listeners sat with pencil in hand and wrote down the recipes and called in extravagant ones of their own. Only a few of those listeners (users, readers—call them what you will) were on the road, whereas during drive time many were. So, the mental picture is important, and consistency is important.

For television, my methodology is equally adapted to the viewer. My first three years on the *P.M. Magazine* show, I did two-minute tips—what we call "dump-dump" recipes in the trade. Heat a pan, grease a bowl, turn on a mixer, perform some action to engage the viewer (reader), say what you are doing, then add something (*x* cups of *x*), add another action, "dump" something else (herbs, seasoning, etc.), then move to a conclusion, offering a recipe if allowed.

For my first hundred shows on PBS and subsequently the Learning Channel, my goal was to give as much information as possible, to show every step. I considered myself in the viewer's kitchen as a mother or neighbor. Although entertaining is always part of television, I wanted primarily to motivate the viewer into thinking "I can do that" or "I didn't know that." We provided endless research and displayed the recipe on the screen.

The next hundred or so were for the Food Network, where the desire on the part of the network was to do as little real cooking as possible, just showing the sizzle. Everything was premeasured, and little research was done. All I did was dump, dump, but on a grander scale, for a half-hour show rather than a two-minute spot.

Because I have always had my books written before my television series, I have always followed my books with my series, not the other way around. Most of my editors have insisted that I describe the pot or how long something takes to cook, often at the expense of the poetry of the recipe, but to reach out even more to the cook.

For the last 100 shows, I have had to change my style of recipe presentation yet again, not putting the recipe on the screen and showing all of every recipe but making it quicker.

In summary, the recipe is in the eye of the beholder or the ear of the listener, and must be true to the personality of the deliverer. Sometimes rules are silly.

*Marie Simmons, author of* **The Good Egg** *and many other cookbooks and a traveling cooking teacher, often finds herself cooking on television.*

I'm just back from a book publicity tour for which I did television and it was fun, especially since there was an audience in the studio and the anchor "helped" me. He was cute and funny and created a bit of a mess, which made the audience laugh. It reminded me of other TV spots I have done and how those with a lighter side were more memorable.

One example is the show on which I asked the anchor to take a pan from the oven. We all know that the ovens are not on and the pans are not hot for TV. But, to make it authentic, I told him not to forget to use the mitts because the pan was hot. He played to the camera (there was a live audience for this one, too) and pretended the pan was even too hot for his mitts. Then I had to pretend I cared that he had burned his fingers. It was successful because we laughed, talked, and interacted, and the audience, once again, really seemed to be entertained.

I think there are perhaps two things to remember in terms of recipes for television:

1. Use a recipe that is interactive.
2. Try to show at least one simple but clever technique.

*Carolyn O'Neil, former Director of Nutrition News for* CNN **On the Menu,** *shares these thoughts on recipes for television.*

N othing is more frustrating to the food lover than a recipe for a delicious-looking dish that just whizzes by on television. There's no time to jot down whether it was a half-cup or quarter-cup or whether the onions were supposed to be minced or chopped. Therefore, the first goal of a recipe shown on TV must be to let viewers know that they can either send for the complete recipe or refer to its printed version in an accompanying cookbook or brochure.

On CNN, we have only about two and a half minutes to illustrate what goes into a recipe and how it goes together. We focus on the techniques and equipment needed, rather than the ingredient measures. Television does an even better job, I think, of showing how to do something, like fold or dredge, than an explanation in print or illustrations in a book.

Television is at its best when it inspires and motivates. We can do that effectively when we show a fabulous-looking dish and couple it with comments from the chef or cook describing the taste or how it should be served.

Color is, of course, important in choosing which recipes to use on television. We don't do too well with pâtés that are grayish in color or recipes featuring all white ingredients, such as an angel food cake with whipped cream—visually boring!

## Recipes for the Internet

*Kate Heyhoe, executive editor of the* **Global Gourmet** *Web site, www.globalgour-met.com, offers her unique perspective on making Web recipes readable. Heyhoe is also author of* **Cooking with Kids for Dummies.**

In 1994, my partner and I launched the *Global Gourmet* (then known as the eGG or electronic Gourmet Guide), as the first food and cooking e-zine. One of the best aspects about the Web back then was that there were no rules to follow. This was also one of its worst aspects.

I used to teach magazine and print graphics to journalism students. The point of the material was to skillfully use graphic elements and type to get the reader into the copy. The eye has a tendency to avoid long blocks of text, so breaking up the text with visual elements—even white space—can do a lot to hold the reader's attention.

When it came to putting recipes on the Web, I realized that you can't just plop a printed recipe up online. But we had no models to follow when it came to Web readability. So we questioned everything we did: How does this affect the user experience? What does this page look like on a PC versus a Macintosh? Will the Netscape browser present the page the same way as Microsoft Explorer or other browsers? Often, we've made major design changes simply because a particular element is not universal.

My experience in journalism graphics paid off. By following the tenets of readability rather than the hard-core rules, I gradually came up with little things that we think make recipes appear better on a computer screen. We also pay attention to other aspects that only Web editors have to face, like the nuances of HTML coding and the differences in computer platforms.

Here are a few examples:

- **Keyboard symbols.** Avoid using keyboard commands for degrees, fractions, and special symbols. Not every computer reads these commands the same way. If you've ever seen a recipe online that lists "% cup sugar" instead of, say "$^1/_2$ cup sugar," then the writer had typed in a keyboard command. At the *Global Gourmet*, we always use manual fractions, typing in a number then a slash key and a number, like this: 1/2. Then we save the copy as a TEXT or ASCII file. We do this to preserve the manual fraction; otherwise some word processing programs may automatically convert manual fractions to symbols.

- **Hyphens between fractions.** Because we manually type in fractions, we then have to deal with the readability problem caused by two numbers appearing close to each other, as in 1 1/2 cups. To make the amount more readable, we add a hyphen, so it looks like this: 1-1/2 cups. A print editor would strike this, but on the Web, it keeps the number from looking like 11 cups.

- **White space between paragraphs.** Some books do and some books don't add extra white space between paragraphs, but we always do. It makes the copy less dense, and I prefer it even in printed cookbooks. We also like to use bulleted lists rather than long paragraphs of text for the same reason.

- **Hyperlinks for sub-recipes.** Traditional food writing includes references to sub-recipes, such as "See the recipe for Chipotle Salsa on page xxx." Instead, we put a link directly to the referenced recipe from the recipe name, which shows up underlined and in blue (or other color). Click on the blue underlined word and you go directly there, or you can open it up on a new Web page and view both the main recipe and the subrecipe at the same time.

- **Hyperlinks for nonlinear material.** Likewise, we put links into anything that may be unfamiliar to the reader. An ingredient list calling for "tamarind" may include a link to a page that describes tamarind and its uses. That page can be one previously published or never published at all until now. Or we can link to just a section of a Web page. On the Web, recipe writers should think nonlinearly. Adding a link does not increase the length of the recipe, but it may make the recipe more clear to the reader. This is especially handy when calling for a special method, such as how to use a double boiler, as it keeps the recipe short but still provides complete information.

- **Dashes.** A print editor would also strike our use of dashes. Instead of inserting a dash immediately between the words, we add a space before and one after each dash—to keep the text from looking all jammed up. Our style makes sense to us — it looks like this.

- **Yields up front.** We place serving yields at the beginning of recipes to avoid excess mouse action. This way readers don't have to scroll all the way to the end of a recipe to see the yield, then scroll all the way back up to the ingredients. Personally, I prefer print recipes that show the yields at the beginning as well.

- **Temperatures.** Keep in mind that the Web audience is global—some folks use Fahrenheit and some use Celsius, or centigrade. We try to make sure all temperatures are followed by F or C.

- **Avoid two columns.** A print publication may split the ingredient list into two columns to save space, but I find this makes the eye jump around too much, and on the Web, there is no need to save paper. We like one-column recipes, but if the ingredient list is long, we break it up with white space or subheads, such as "Lasagna Ingredients" followed by "Sauce Ingredients."

- **Italics and bold.** Italics can be hard to read on the Web, so we avoid long bodies of text in italics and stick mainly to recipe titles, book titles, or a single word. Boldface is also avoided for long bodies of text, as it looks like you're shouting, but bold type is handy for setting out subheads.

Finally, short recipes are good for short attention spans (like those of Web surfers), but don't sacrifice the integrity of the recipe. In fact, some long recipes can even be more readable online than in print. Online, you can make headnotes briefer and instructions more concise simply by using hyperlinks. But keep in mind that before any recipe gets to the Web, it should follow all the accepted rules of recipe writing in general. A readable Web recipe is ultimately a collaboration of the writer, the editor, and the programmer.

*Sally Bernstein, editor-in-chief of Sally's Place, an Internet Web site at www.sallys-place.com, was one of the pioneers in food Web sites.*

Writing a basic recipe for the Web is not all that different from the accepted rules of "what is a good recipe?" Although you might think "short," that is not always accurate. People come to the Web for all kinds of information, from short, easy recipes to much more detailed and elaborate ones. For instance, when people are entertaining they are willing to spend more time in the kitchen. Everyone's needs are different as are their skill sets. I would err on the side of overexplaining. And because of the Net's international scope, your reader might just as easily be in China or Indonesia as in the United States.

The big difference is that a recipe online can and should be interactive. Color graphics should be included, as we all know "a picture is worth a thousand words." Another addition is hypertext links to ingredient definitions either within the current Web site or to other sites that have helpful information. Links also should be placed to recipes on the same theme or recipes using similar ingredients.

Last, but not least, audio and visual is now available on the Web so it is possible to both see and hear a demonstration of the recipe. And this is what is happening today—just think what tomorrow will bring!

## Antonia Allegra, USA

Founder/director, Symposium for Professional Food Writers, and former editor-in-chief, *Appellation* magazine

To me, the soul of a recipe is in its headnote. This brief introduction to a recipe is the one place that a food writer can interject his or her personality in the recipe text. The headnote might fully attribute the recipe source, fleshing it out with a brief anecdote, or it might discuss a particular ingredient key to the dish. Perhaps the writer uses that brief but important space preceding the ingredients and recipe method to offer suggestions of food or wine that will pair with the dish.

Chapter Twelve

# Purchasing Information

THE PURCHASING INFORMATION IN THIS chapter provides a guide to package sizes, number of pieces in a pound or can, weights, and similar information for ingredients commonly used in recipes.

This information is useful for developing recipes in appropriate quantities or for double-checking amounts used. However, be aware that the weights of packages (cans, bottles, boxes) change frequently. The definitive source of information on can and package sizes, as well as weight and other information, should be actual test results.

## Breads, Crackers, Crumbs, and Doughs

| Ingredient | Market Unit | Measurement |
| --- | --- | --- |
| Biscuit baking mix | 40-ounce package | 9 cups dry mix; 36 (2$^1/_2$-inch) biscuits |
| | 5-pound package | 18 cups dry mix; 65 (2$^1/_2$-inch) biscuits |
| Biscuits, refrigerated | 12-ounce package | 10 biscuits |
| | 16-ounce package | 8 jumbo biscuits |
| Bread | | |
| *regular* | 16-ounce loaf | 16 to 18 slices |
| | 2 slices | 1 cup soft crumbs |
| | 3 slices | 1 cup dry crumbs |
| *sandwich-type* | 24-ounce loaf | 24 to 30 thin slices |
| *crumbs* | 8-ounce package | 2 cups |
| | 15-ounce package | 3$^3/_4$ cups |
| | 24-ounce package | 6 cups |
| Chocolate cookie crumbs (Oreo) | 15-ounce package | 3 cups; enough for 3 (8- or 9-inch) pie crusts |
| Chocolate wafers | 20 wafers | 1 cup fine crumbs |
| Cornflake crumbs | 21-ounce package | 6$^3/_4$ cups |
| Crackers | | |
| *buttery, round* | 24 crackers | 1 cup crumbs |
| *graham* | 16-ounce package | 66 crackers |
| | 15 crackers | 1 cup fine crumbs |
| | 13$^1/_2$-ounce box crumbs | 3$^3/_4$ cups; enough for 3 (8- or 9-inch) pie crusts |
| *meal (crumbs)* | 14-ounce package | 3$^3/_4$ cups |
| *saltines* | 16-ounce package | 130 to 140 crackers |
| | 30 crackers | 1 cup fine crumbs |
| Crescent rolls, refrigerated | 8-ounce package | 8 rolls |

| Ingredient | Market Unit | Measurement |
|---|---|---|
| Croutons | 5$^1/_2$-ounce package | 3$^1/_2$ cups |
| | 40-ounce package | 24$^1/_2$ cups |
| Gingersnaps | 15 cookies | 1 cup crumbs |
| Pie crust | | |
| *frozen* | 10-ounce package | 2 (9-inch) crusts |
| | 12-ounce package | 2 (9-inch) deep dish crusts |
| | 25-ounce package | 5 (9-inch) crusts |
| *refrigerated* | 15-ounce package | 2 (9-inch) crusts |
| *graham* | 6-ounce package | 1 (9-inch) crust |
| | 9-ounce package | 1 (10-inch) crust |
| | 4-ounce package | 6 mini (3$^1/_2$-inch) crusts |
| Pita bread | 10-ounce package | 5 (6- to 7-inch) pitas |
| Puff pastry sheets, frozen | 17.3-ounce package | 2 ready-to-bake sheets |
| Puff pastry shells, frozen | 10-ounce package | 6 ready-to-bake shells |
| Phyllo dough, frozen | 16-ounce package | 22 (14 x 18-inch) sheets |
| Stuffing mix | 6-ounce package | 3 cups |
| Sugar cookie dough, refrigerated, most varieties | 18-ounce package | 32 cookies |
| Taco shells, hard | 4.6-ounce package | 12 regular-size shells |
| | 8.45-ounce package | 12 super-size shells |
| Tortillas | | |
| *flour* | 14-ounce package | 10 (9-inch) tortillas (large, burrito size) |
| | 11$^1/_2$-ounce package | 10 (7$^1/_2$-inch) tortillas (regular size) |
| *corn* | 6-ounce package | 10 (5$^1/_2$-inch) tortillas |
| Vanilla wafers | 30 wafers | 1 cup fine crumbs |

## Cereal, Grains, and Pasta

| Ingredient | Market Unit | Measurement |
| --- | --- | --- |
| Barley, quick-cooking, pearl | 11-ounce package | 2 cups uncooked; 6 cups cooked |
| Bulgur | 1 pound | $2^3/_4$ cups uncooked; 8 cups cooked |
| Cornmeal, yellow or white | 24-ounce package | $4^1/_2$ cups; 24 cups cooked |
| Cornstarch | 16-ounce package | $3^1/_2$ cups |
| | 1 ounce | 3 tablespoons |
| Couscous, quick-cooking | 10-ounce package | $1^1/_2$ cups |
| | $2^1/_4$ ounces | $^1/_3$ cup uncooked; 1 cup cooked |
| Farina (or Cream of Wheat), quick-cooking | 28-ounce package | $4^1/_2$ cups uncooked; 24 cups cooked |
| Flour | | |
| *all-purpose or bread* | 1 pound unsifted | 4 cups |
| | 5-pound bag | 20 cups |
| *cake or pastry flour* | 1 pound unsifted | $3^3/_4$ cups |
| | 2-pound package | 8 cups |
| *rye* | 1 pound | 4 cups |
| *whole wheat* | 1 pound | $3^3/_4$ cups |
| | 5-pound bag | 18 cups |
| Grits, quick-cooking | 24-ounce package | $4^1/_2$ cups uncooked; 18 cups cooked |
| Oats, quick-cooking | 18-ounce package | 6 cups |
| | 1 cup uncooked | $1^3/_4$ cups cooked |
| Pasta | | |
| *egg noodles* | 1 pound | 10 cups uncooked; 12 cups cooked |
| *macaroni* | 1 pound | 4 cups uncooked; 8 cups cooked |

| Ingredient | Market Unit | Measurement |
|---|---|---|
| *spaghetti* | 1 pound | 4 cups uncooked;<br>7 to 8 cups cooked |
| Rice | | |
| *long-grain, converted* | 32-ounce package | $4^3/_4$ cups uncooked;<br>about 14 cups cooked |
| | 1 cup uncooked | 3 to 4 cups cooked |
| *precooked (instant)* | 1 cup uncooked | 2 cups cooked |
| *brown* | 1 cup uncooked | 3 to 4 cups cooked |
| Wheat germ | 12-ounce jar | 3 cups |
| Wild rice | 1 cup uncooked | 3 cups cooked |

## Cheese

| | | |
|---|---|---|
| Blue | 4 ounces | 1 cup crumbled |
| Cheddar | 1 pound | 4 cups shredded;<br>16 slices |
| Cottage | 8-ounce container | 1 cup |
| | 12-ounce container | $1^1/_2$ cups |
| Cream | 3-ounce package | $^1/_3$ cup |
| | 8-ounce package | 1 cup |
| Feta | 4-ounce | 1 cup crumbled |
| Mozzarella | 1 pound | 4 cups shredded |
| Parmesan or Romano | 3-ounce package | 1 cup grated |
| Swiss | 1 pound | 4 cups shredded;<br>16 slices |

## Chocolate and Candy

| | | |
|---|---|---|
| Caramels | 14-ounce package | 50 pieces |
| Chocolate-flavored syrup | 16-ounce can | $1^1/_2$ cups |
| | 8-pound can | 12 cups |
| Cocoa powder, unsweetened | 8-ounce can | $2^2/_3$ cups |

| Ingredient | Market Unit | Measurement |
|---|---|---|
| Hot fudge sauce | 18-ounce jar | 1$\frac{3}{4}$ cups |
| | 7-pound, 14-ounce can | 11$\frac{1}{2}$ cups |
| Red cinnamon candies | 1 pound | 2$\frac{1}{4}$ cups |
| Semisweet chocolate morsels | 6-ounce package | 1 cup |
| | 12-ounce package | 2 cups |
| Unsweetened or semisweet chocolate | 8-ounce box | 8 squares (1 ounce each) |
| | 1 square (1 ounce) | 4 tablespoons grated |

## Dairy Products

| | | |
|---|---|---|
| Buttermilk powder | 16-ounce package | 5 cups |
| Cream | | |
| *half-and-half* | 1 pint | 2 cups |
| *heavy* | 1 cup ($\frac{1}{2}$ pint) | 2 cups whipped |
| Ice cream | $\frac{1}{2}$ gallon | About 8 cups |
| | 1 quart brick | 8 slices |
| Milk | | |
| *buttermilk* | 1 quart | 4 cups |
| *evaporated* | 5-ounce can | $\frac{2}{3}$ cup |
| | 12-ounce can | 1$\frac{1}{2}$ cups |
| *goat* | 12-ounce can | 1$\frac{1}{2}$ cups |
| *instant nonfat dry* | 9.6-ounce package | 4 cups powder; 3 quarts reconstituted |
| | $\frac{1}{3}$ cup powder | 1 cup reconstituted |
| *soy* | 32-ounce package | 4 cups |
| | 64-ounce package | 8 cups |
| *sweetened condensed, regular and low-fat* | 14-ounce can | 1$\frac{1}{4}$ cups |
| *whole* | 1 quart | 4 cups |
| | 1 pound | 2 cups |

| Ingredient | Market Unit | Measurement |
| --- | --- | --- |
| Sour cream | 8-ounce carton | 1 cup |
| Yogurt | 8-ounce carton | 1 cup |

## Eggs

| Ingredient | Market Unit | Measurement |
| --- | --- | --- |
| Whole, large | 5 to 7 | About 1 cup |
| Whites, large | 8 to 10 | About 1 cup |
| | 1 | About 2 tablespoons |
| Yolks, large | 12 to 14 | About 1 cup |
| | 1 | About 1 tablespoon |
| Hard-cooked, peeled and chopped | 1 dozen | $3^1/_2$ cups |
| Cholesterol-free product, frozen | 2 (8-ounce) packages | 2 cups; 4 servings per package |

## Fats and Oils

| Ingredient | Market Unit | Measurement |
| --- | --- | --- |
| Butter or margarine | 1 pound | 2 cups |
| | 1 stick (4 ounces) | 8 tablespoons; $^1/_2$ cup |
| *soft* | 8-ounce package | 1 cup |
| *whipped* | 16-ounce package | 3 cups |
| Lard | 1 pound | $2^1/_2$ cups |
| Oil, vegetable | 16-ounce bottle | 2 cups |
| | 48-ounce bottle | 6 cups |
| Shortening, solid vegetable | 16-ounce can | $2^1/_2$ cups |
| *sticks* | 20-ounce package | 3 sticks; 1 cup each |

## Fish and Shellfish

| Ingredient | Market Unit | Measurement |
| --- | --- | --- |
| Anchovies | | |
| *fillets* | 2-ounce can | 6 to 8 anchovies per can |
| *paste* | 2-ounce tube | 4 tablespoons |

| Ingredient | Market Unit | Measurement |
|---|---|---|
| Clams | | |
| *canned* | $6^1/_2$-ounce can | About $^3/_4$ cup |
| | 51-ounce can | 7 cups |
| *fresh* | 1 dozen in shell | $1^1/_3$ cups shucked |
| *juice* | 8-ounce bottle | 1 cup |
| | 12-ounce can | $1^1/_2$ cups |
| | 46-ounce can | 6 cups |
| Crab, Dungeness | 1 average | 2 to 3 pounds in shell |
| Crab, imitation | 1 pound | 2 to 4 servings |
| Crabmeat | $^1/_2$ pound in shell | About $1^1/_3$ cups flaked crab |
| | 1 pound flaked | $3^1/_2$ cups |
| | 6-ounce can | $^1/_2$ cup |
| Fish | | |
| *fillets, most types* | 1 | 4 to 5 ounces |
| *steaks, most types* | 1 | 6 to 8 ounces |
| Lobster | $1^1/_2$-pound live lobster | $1^1/_4$ cups cooked meat |
| Mussels | 1 pound in shell | 16 to 20 shucked |
| Oysters, shucked | 1 pound | 2 cups |
| Salmon | | |
| *canned* | 6-ounce can | about 2/3 cup |
| | $7^1/_2$-ounce can | about 1 cup |
| | $14^3/_4$-ounce can | $1^3/_4$ cups |
| *fresh* | 1 pound steaks or fillets | 3 to 4 servings |
| | 2-pound whole fish | 3 to 4 servings |
| Sardines | $3^3/_4$-ounce can | 20 pieces |
| Scallops | | |
| *bay* | 1 pound | About 75 |
| *sea* | 1 pound | About 30 |

| Ingredient | Market Unit | Measurement |
|---|---|---|
| Shrimp, in shell | 1 pound jumbo | 6 to 8 |
| | 1 pound large | 12 to 18 |
| | 1 pound medium | 16 to 20 |
| | 1 pound small | 26 to 30 |
| | $1^1/2$ pounds raw | $3/4$ pound cooked in shell and peeled (about 2 cups) |
| | 4-ounce can | About $1/2$ cup |
| | 6-ounce can | $1/2$ cup |
| Squid | 10- to 12-inch piece | $1/4$ to $1/2$ pound cleaned |
| Tuna | | |
| *canned* | 6- /$6^1/4$-ounce can | $2/3$ cup |
| | 9- /$9^1/4$-ounce can | 1 cup |
| | 12-ounce can | $1^1/4$ cups |
| | 4-pound, 5-ounce can | 6 cups |
| *fresh, steaks* | 1 pound | 2 to 3 servings |

## Fruits

| | | |
|---|---|---|
| Apples | | |
| *whole, fresh* | 1 pound | 3 medium |
| | 1 medium, cored | 1 cup chopped |
| *frozen* | 5-pound package | 18 cups slices |
| *applesauce* | 15- /16-ounce jar | $1^3/4$ to 2 cups |
| | 23- /24- /25-ounce jar | $2^1/2$ to 3 cups |
| | 6-pound, 12-ounce can | 12 cups |
| *pie filling* | 20- /21-ounce can | $2^1/3$ cups; enough for 1 (9-inch) pie |
| | 7-pound can | 12 cups; enough for 6 (9-inch) pies |
| *slices, drained* | 20-ounce can | 2 cups |
| | 6-pound, 8-ounce can | About 10 cups |

| Ingredient | Market Unit | Measurement |
|---|---|---|
| Apricots | | |
| *fresh* | 1 pound | 8 to 12 whole; $2^1/_2$ cups sliced or halved |
| *dried* | 11-ounce package | $1^3/_4$ cups |
| *canned* | 16- /17-ounce can | 6 to 8 whole |
| Avocados | 1 pound | 2 medium; $2^1/_2$ cups sliced or chopped |
| Bananas | 1 pound | 3 small or 2 large; 2 cups sliced |
| | 1 medium | $1/_2$ cup mashed |
| | 1 pound dried slices | $4^1/_2$ cups |
| Blackberries | | |
| *fresh* | 1 pound | $3^1/_2$ cups |
| *frozen* | 12-ounce package | $1^3/_4$ cups |
| *canned* | 15-ounce can | $1^3/_4$ cups |
| Blueberries | | |
| *fresh* | 1 pound | 3 cups |
| *frozen* | 10-ounce package | $1^1/_2$ cups |
| *canned* | 15-ounce can | $1^1/_2$ cups |
| *pie filling* | 20- /21-ounce can | $2^1/_3$ cups; enough for 1 (9-inch) pie |
| Candied fruit | 8-ounce package | $1^1/_2$ cups chopped |
| Cantaloupe | 1 melon, 6-inch diameter | About 3 pounds |
| | 12-ounce package frozen balls | $1^1/_2$ cups |
| Cherries | | |
| *fresh sweet* | 1 pound | About 2 cups unpitted; 3 cups halves |
| *frozen sweet* | 12-ounce package | $1^3/_4$ cups |
| *frozen tart, pitted* | 24-ounce package | 5 cups |
| | 5-pound package | 17 cups |

| Ingredient | Market Unit | Measurement |
|---|---|---|
| *canned tart, pitted* | 16-ounce can | 1$^1$/$_2$ cups |
| *dried tart, pitted* | 3 ounces | $^1$/$_2$ cup |
| *pie filling* | 20- /21-ounce can | 2$^1$/$_3$ cups; enough for 1 (9-inch) pie |
|  | 7-pound, 4-ounce can | 12 cups; enough for 6 (9-inch) pies |
| maraschino cherries | 10-ounce jar | About 30 cherries |
|  | 16-ounce jar | 40 to 50 cherries |
|  | 4-pound, 10-ounce jar | 170 with stems; 225 without stems |
| Cranberries |  |  |
| *fresh* | 1 pound | 4 cups |
|  | 12-ounce package | 3 cups |
| *sauce, jellied* | 16-ounce can | 2 cups |
|  | 7-pound, 5-ounce can | 12 cups |
| *sauce, whole berry* | 16-ounce can | 1$^1$/$_2$ cups |
| *juice cocktail* | 48-ounce bottle | 6 cups |
| Currants, dried | 10-ounce package | 2 cups |
| Dates, dried whole | 1 pound | 60 dates; 2 cups unpitted; 2$^3$/$_4$ cups pitted and chopped |
| Figs |  |  |
| *fresh* | 1 pound | 12 medium |
| *dried* | 1 pound | 44 medium; 3 cups chopped |
| Fruit cocktail | 16- /17-ounce can | 2 cups |
|  | 6-pound, 10-ounce can | 12 cups |
| Grapefruit |  |  |
| *fresh* | 1 pound | 1 medium grapefruit; 10 to 12 sections |
|  | 1 medium | $^2$/$_3$ cup juice; 3 to 4 tablespoons grated peel |
| *canned* | 16-ounce can | 2 cups sections |

| Ingredient | Market Unit | Measurement |
|---|---|---|
| Grapes, whole | 1 pound seedless | $2^1/_2$ to 3 cups |
| Lemons | 1 pound | 4 to 6 medium |
| | 1 medium | 2 to 3 tablespoons juice; 1 tablespoon grated peel |
| Limes | 1 pound | 6 to 8 medium |
| | 1 medium | 2 tablespoons juice; 2 teaspoons grated peel |
| Mangoes | 1 medium | About 12 ounces |
| Nectarines | 1 pound | 3 to 4 medium; $2^1/_2$ cups sliced |
| Olives | | |
| *ripe* | $4^1/_4$-ounce can chopped | $^2/_3$ cup |
| | $2^1/_4$-ounce can sliced | $^1/_2$ cup |
| | $5^3/_4$-ounce can whole pitted colossal | About 25 |
| | $5^3/_4$-ounce can whole pitted super colossal | About 18 |
| | 6-ounce can medium pitted | About 55 |
| *Spanish, stuffed* | 2-ounce jar | About 20 |
| | 3-ounce jar | About 30 |
| | 7-ounce jar | About 65 |
| *Spanish, unpitted* | 5-ounce jar | About 20 |
| Oranges | 1 pound | 3 medium |
| | 1 medium | $^1/_3$ to $^1/_2$ cup juice; 1 to 2 tablespoons finely grated peel |
| *juice concentrate* | 6-ounce can | 3 cups reconstituted |
| | 12-ounce can | 6 cups reconstituted |
| | $^1/_4$ cup concentrate | 1 cup reconstituted |

| Ingredient | Market Unit | Measurement |
|---|---|---|
| *mandarin oranges* | 11-ounce can | $1^1/_4$ cups |
| | 15-ounce can | $1^3/_4$ cups |
| | 6-pound, 13-ounce can | 12 cups |
| Papayas | 1 medium | About 16 ounces |
| Peaches | | |
| *fresh* | 1 pound | 3 to 4 medium; $2^1/_2$ cups sliced or chopped |
| | 1 medium | $^1/_2$ cup sliced |
| *frozen* | 16-ounce package | $2^1/_4$ cups slices |
| | 5-pound package | 16 cups slices |
| *canned* | 16-ounce can | 6 to 10 halves; 2 cups slices |
| | 6-pound, 10-ounce can | 12 cups slices or halves |
| *pie filling* | 20- /21-ounce can | $2^1/_3$ cups; enough for 1 (9-inch) pie |
| | 7-pound can | 12 cups; enough for 6 (9-inch) pies |
| Pears | | |
| *fresh* | 1 pound | 3 to 4 medium; 2 cups sliced |
| *canned* | 16-ounce can | 6 to 10 halves |
| Pineapples | | |
| *fresh* | 1 medium | 2 pounds; 3 cups cubed |
| *canned* | 8-ounce can | 4 slices; 1 cup crushed |
| | 20-ounce can | 10 slices; $2^1/_2$ cups crushed or chunks |
| | 8-ounce can crushed, drained | $^3/_4$ cup |
| | 6-pound, 11-ounce can | 11 cups slices; 12 cups crushed or chunks |

| Ingredient | Market Unit | Measurement |
|---|---|---|
| Plums | | |
| fresh | 1 pound | 6 to 20, depending on variety; $2^1/_2$ cups pitted and sliced |
| canned | $15^1/_4$- /16-ounce can | 9 medium plums |
| Pomegranates | 1 medium | $1/_2$ cup juice |
| | 1 medium | $3/_4$ cup seeds |
| Prunes (dried plums) | 12-ounce package, pitted | 54 prunes; $2^1/_2$ cups |
| | 12-ounce package, bite-size, pitted | 64 prunes; about 3 cups |
| Raisins | | |
| baking | 6-ounce package | 1 cup |
| regular | 9-ounce package | $1^1/_2$ cups |
| | 15-ounce package | $2^1/_2$ cups |
| Raspberries | | |
| fresh | 1 pound | 3 cups |
| frozen with syrup | 10-ounce package | 1 cup |
| frozen unsweetened | 12-ounce package | About $1^1/_2$ cups |
| | 5-pound package | $10^1/_2$ cups |
| Rhubarb | | |
| fresh | 1 pound | 4 to 8 stalks; 2 cups cooked |
| frozen | 12-ounce package | $1^1/_2$ cups |
| Strawberries | | |
| fresh | 1 basket | 1 pint |
| | 1 pint | 12 very large to 36 small berries; $3^1/_2$ cups whole; $2^1/_4$ cups sliced |
| frozen | 20-ounce package | About $2^1/_2$ cups whole |
| | 10-ounce package | 1 cup berries in syrup |
| | 5-pound package | 12 cups whole |

| Ingredient | Market Unit | Measurement |
|---|---|---|
| *pie filling* | 20- /21-ounce can | $2^1/_3$ cups; enough for 1 (9-inch) pie |

## Leavening Agents

| | | |
|---|---|---|
| Baking powder | 7-ounce can | $1^1/_4$ cups |
| Baking soda | 16-ounce box | $2^1/_3$ cups |
| Cream of tartar | $1^3/_4$-ounce can | $5^1/_4$ tablespoons |
| Yeast | | |
| *active dry or quick rising* | $^1/_4$ ounce (1 package) | $2^1/_4$ teaspoons |
| | 1 package | 1 (0.6-ounce) cake compressed yeast |
| | 4-ounce jar | 14 tablespoons |
| *compressed* | 0.6-ounce cake | 1 package active dry yeast |

## Meats

For specific information, consult the National Cattlemen's Beef Association, National Pork Producers Council, or American Lamb Council (see Chapter Fourteen).

| | | |
|---|---|---|
| Bacon | 16-ounce package | 16 to 20 slices |
| | 8 slices crisply cooked | $^1/_2$ cup crumbled |
| Beef flank steak | 1 | $1^1/_4$ to $1^1/_2$ pounds |
| Frankfurters | 16-ounce package | 8 to 10 |
| Ham, cooked | 1 pound | 3 cups diced; 2 cups ground |
| | 1 slice, 1 inch thick | About $1^1/_2$ pounds |
| Lamb | | |
| *leg* | 1 | 4 to 5 pounds, bone in; 3 pounds, boned |
| *chops and steaks* | 1, $^3/_4$ inch thick | About 8 ounces |
| Meat, ground | 1 pound | 2 cups uncooked |
| Meat, stew (cut in cubes) | 1 pound | 2 cups uncooked |

## Miscellaneous Foods

| Ingredient | Market Unit | Measurement |
|---|---|---|
| Broth, chicken or beef | $10^1/_2$-ounce can | $1^1/_4$ cups |
| | $14^1/_2$-ounce can | $1^3/_4$ cups |
| | 48- /$49^1/_2$-ounce can | 6 cups |
| Carbonated beverages, most varieties and brands | 1-liter bottle | 33.8 ounces; 1 quart, 1.8 ounces |
| | 2-liter bottle | 67.6 ounces; 2 quarts, 3.6 ounces |
| | 3-liter bottle | 101.4 ounces; 3 quarts, 5.4 ounces |
| | 12-ounce can | $1^1/_2$ cups |
| Chestnuts | 10-ounce can | About 25 whole chestnuts |
| Chili sauce | 12-ounce bottle | $1^1/_2$ cups |
| | 7-pound, 2-ounce can | $13^1/_2$ cups |
| Coconut, shredded or flaked | $3^1/_2$-ounce can | $1^1/_4$ cups |
| | 7-ounce package | $2^1/_2$ cups |
| | 14-ounce package | $5^1/_3$ cups |
| Coffee | | |
| ground coarse | 16-ounce can | 5 cups; 40 to 50 (6-ounce) cups brewed |
| instant | 4-ounce jar | $2^1/_2$ cups; 120 (6-ounce) cups brewed |
| Consommé | $10^1/_2$-ounce can | $1^1/_3$ cups |
| Fruit pectin | | |
| liquid | 3-ounce pouch | Thickens 3 to 4 cups fruit; 2 to 4 cups juice |
| powdered | $1^3/_4$-ounce box | Thickens 4 to 8 cups fruit; 3 to 6 cups juice |

| Ingredient | Market Unit | Measurement |
|---|---|---|
| Gelatin | | |
| *flavored* | 3-ounce package | $1/2$ cup powder; 2 cups prepared |
| | 6-ounce package | 1 cup powder; 4 cups prepared |
| *unflavored* | $1/4$-ounce envelope | 1 tablespoon |
| Hot pepper sauce | 2-ounce bottle | $1/8$ cup |
| | $4 1/2$-ounce bottle | $1/2$ cup |
| | 12-ounce bottle | $1 1/2$ cups |
| Jam or jelly | 18-ounce jar | $1 2/3$ cups |
| Ketchup | 14-ounce bottle | $1 1/2$ cups |
| | 7-pound, 2-ounce can | 12 cups |
| Marshmallows | | |
| *regular ($1 1/4$-inch)* | 16-ounce package | 60 to 70 |
| | 10-ounce package | About 40 |
| *miniature* | 10 | 1 regular |
| | 16-ounce package | 8 cups |
| | $10 1/2$-ounce package | $5 1/2$ cups |
| *creme* | 7-ounce jar | 2 cups |
| | 15-ounce jar | 4 cups |
| Mayonnaise | 8-ounce jar | 1 cup |
| | 1-gallon jar | 16 cups |
| Mincemeat | 1 pound | 2 cups |
| Monosodium glutamate | 1 ounce | 2 tablespoons |
| Onion soup mix | 1 (2-ounce) package | 2 envelopes |
| | 1 envelope | $1/3$ cup dry soup mix; 4 cups reconstituted |
| Peanut butter | 18-ounce jar | 2 cups |

| Ingredient | Market Unit | Measurement |
|---|---|---|
| Pizza sauce | 8-ounce can | $3/4$ cup |
| | 15-ounce can | $1^3/4$ cups |
| | 6-pound, 10-ounce can | $7^1/4$ cups |
| Popcorn | 30-ounce jar | 4 cups unpopped kernels |
| | $1/4$ cup kernels | 5 cups popped corn |
| Potato chips | 1 pound | 4 to 5 quarts |
| | 4 ounces | 2 cups coarsely crushed |
| Pound cake, frozen | $10^3/4$-ounce package | 8 (1-inch) slices |
| Pudding | | |
| *dry mix* | 4-serving size | $1/2$ cup powder; 2 cups prepared pudding |
| | 6-serving size | $3/4$ cup powder; 3 cups prepared pudding |
| *canned* | $15^3/4$-ounce can | $1^3/4$ cups |
| | 7-pound can | 12 cups |
| Salsa, tomato-based | 12-ounce jar | $1^1/2$ cups |
| | 16-ounce jar | About 2 cups |
| | 24-ounce jar | $2^3/4$ cups |
| | 8-pound, 6-ounce jar | 16 cups |
| Seafood cocktail sauce | 12-ounce bottle | $1^1/2$ cups |
| Soup, condensed, most varieties | $10^3/4$-ounce can | $1^1/4$ cups; $2^1/2$ cups reconstituted |
| | 50-ounce can | $5^1/2$ cups; 11 cups reconstituted |
| Taco sauce | 8-ounce jar | 1 cup |
| | 16-ounce jar | 2 cups |
| | 8-pound, 6-ounce jar | 16 cups |
| Tapioca, quick-cooking | 8-ounce package | $1^1/2$ cups; $3^3/4$ cups cooked |

| Ingredient | Market Unit | Measurement |
|---|---|---|
| **Tea** | | |
| *bags* | 3 regular | 1 family-size tea bag |
| *leaves, bulk* | 1 pound | 6 cups; 300 cups brewed |
| *instant* | 3-ounce jar | $2^1/2$ cups; 30 quarts brewed |
| **Vanilla and other extracts** | 1 ounce | $2^1/2$ tablespoons |
| **Vinegar** | | |
| *balsamic* | $12^1/2$-ounce bottle | $1^1/2$ cups |
| | 16-ounce bottle | 2 cups |
| *cider or distilled white* | 16-ounce bottle | 2 cups |
| *red or white wine* | 12-ounce bottle | $1^1/2$ cups |
| | 16-ounce bottle | 2 cups |
| **Whipped topping mix** | 1 (2.8-ounce) package | 2 envelopes |
| | 1 (5.2-ounce) package | 4 envelopes |
| | 1 envelope | 2 cups whipped topping |
| **Whipped topping, frozen** | 8-ounce package | 3 cups |
| | 16-ounce package | 7 cups |

## Nuts

| | | |
|---|---|---|
| Nuts, shelled | | |
| *almonds, whole* | 1 pound | 3 cups |
| *slivered* | 1 pound | 4 cups |
| *peanuts, whole* | 1 pound | 3 cups |
| *pecans, halves* | 1 pound | 4 cups; $3^3/4$ cups chopped |
| *pine nuts, whole* | $2^1/2$-ounce package | $2/3$ cup |
| *walnuts, halves* | 1 pound | 4 cups; $3^1/2$ cups chopped |

| Ingredient | Market Unit | Measurement |
|---|---|---|
| Nuts, in shell | | |
| *almonds* | 1 pound | 1 to $1^3/_4$ cups nut meats |
| *peanuts* | 1 pound | 2 to $2^1/_4$ cups nut meats |
| *pecans* | 1 pound | 2 to $2^1/_4$ cups nut meats |
| *walnuts* | 1 pound | $1^1/_2$ to $1^2/_3$ cups nut meats |

## Poultry

For additional information, contact the National Chicken Council, the National Turkey Federation, or the Duckling Council (see Chapter Fourteen).

| | | |
|---|---|---|
| Chicken | 4- to 5-pound stewing chicken | 5 cups cooked, cubed or chopped |
| | 1 large whole breast | 2 cups cooked, cubed or chopped |
| | 5-ounce can | $^1/_2$ cup |
| | 10-ounce can | $^7/_8$ cup |
| Cornish game hens | About $1^1/_4$ pounds each | 1 serving each |
| Turkey | 1 pound cooked | 3 cups chopped |
| Turkey bacon | 12-ounce package | 24 slices |

## Spices and Herbs

| | | |
|---|---|---|
| Allspice, ground | 1 ounce | $4^1/_2$ tablespoons |
| Basil, dried leaves | 1 ounce | $^3/_4$ cup |
| Bay leaves, dried | 1 ounce | About 200 leaves |
| Cayenne (see Pepper) | | |
| Celery | | |
| *dried flakes* | 1 ounce | $^3/_4$ cup |
| *salt* | 1 ounce | 2 tablespoons |
| *seeds* | 1 ounce | 4 tablespoons |

| Ingredient | Market Unit | Measurement |
|---|---|---|
| Chili powder | 1 ounce | 4 tablespoons |
| Chives, chopped, freeze-dried | 1 ounce | About 3 cups |
| Cilantro, dried leaves | 1 ounce | 1 cup |
| Cinnamon | | |
| *ground* | 1 ounce | 4 tablespoons |
| *sticks* | 1 ounce | 8 to 10 pieces |
| Cloves, ground | 1 ounce | 4 tablespoons |
| Cumin seeds, ground | 1 ounce | $4^1/_2$ tablespoons |
| Dill | | |
| *seeds* | 1 ounce | $4^1/_2$ tablespoons |
| *weed, dried* | 1 ounce | $^3/_4$ cup |
| Fennel seeds | 1 ounce | 4 tablespoons |
| Garlic | | |
| *fresh* | 1 ounce | 6 large cloves; 3 tablespoons minced |
| | 2 medium cloves | 1 teaspoon minced; $^1/_4$ teaspoon garlic powder |
| *powder* | 1 ounce | 3 tablespoons |
| *salt* | 1 ounce | 2 tablespoons |
| Ginger | | |
| *candied, chopped* | 1 ounce | 2 tablespoons |
| *fresh* | 2-inch piece | 2 tablespoons grated or chopped |
| | 4 ounces | $^1/_2$ cup peeled and finely chopped |
| *ground* | 1 ounce | 4 tablespoons |
| | $^1/_2$ teaspoon | 1 teaspoon fresh chopped |
| Herbs, fresh | 1 tablespoon chopped | 1 teaspoon crushed dried |

| Ingredient | Market Unit | Measurement |
|---|---|---|
| Horseradish, prepared | 1 ounce | 2 tablespoons |
| | 1 tablespoon | $1^1/_2$ teaspoon freshly grated |
| Mace, ground | 1 ounce | $4^1/_2$ tablespoons |
| Marjoram, dried leaves | 1 ounce | $^3/_4$ cup |
| Mustard | | |
| *dry* | 1 ounce | 5 tablespoons |
| *prepared* | 1 ounce | 2 tablespoons |
| *seeds* | 1 ounce | $2^1/_2$ tablespoons |
| Nutmeg, ground | 1 ounce | $3^1/_2$ tablespoons |
| Onion | | |
| *powder* | 1 ounce | 3 tablespoons |
| *salt* | 1 ounce | $2^1/_2$ tablespoons |
| Oregano | | |
| *ground* | 1 ounce | 5 tablespoons |
| *dried leaves* | 1 ounce | $^3/_4$ cup |
| Paprika, ground | 1 ounce | 4 tablespoons |
| Parsley | | |
| *fresh, coarsely chopped* | 1 ounce | $^3/_4$ cup |
| *dried flakes* | 1 ounce | $1^1/_3$ cups |
| Pepper, ground, black, white, or red | 1 ounce | 4 tablespoons |
| Peppercorns | 1 ounce | 3 tablespoons |
| Poppy seeds | 1 ounce | 3 tablespoons |
| Poultry seasoning, ground | 1 ounce | 6 tablespoons |
| Rosemary, dried leaves | 1 ounce | 9 tablespoons |
| Saffron | $^1/_{20}$-ounce vial | 1 tablespoon |

| Ingredient | Market Unit | Measurement |
|---|---|---|
| Sage | | |
| *dried leaves* | 1 ounce | $3/4$ cup |
| *rubbed* | 1 ounce | $2/3$ cup |
| Salt | 1 pound | $1^3/4$ cups |
| | 1 ounce | $1^1/2$ tablespoons |
| Sesame seeds | 1 ounce | 3 tablespoons |
| Tarragon, dried leaves | 1 ounce | 1 cup |
| Thyme | | |
| *ground* | 1 ounce | 6 tablespoons |
| *dried leaves* | 1 ounce | $1/2$ cup |
| Turmeric, ground | 1 ounce | 4 tablespoons |

## Sugar and Sweetening Agents

| Ingredient | Market Unit | Measurement |
|---|---|---|
| Corn syrup, light or dark | 16-ounce bottle | 2 cups |
| Honey | 16-ounce jar | $1^1/3$ cups |
| Maple syrup | 12-ounce bottle | $1^1/2$ cups |
| | 16-ounce bottle | 2 cups |
| Molasses, light or dark | 12-ounce bottle | $1^1/2$ cups |
| | 16-ounce bottle | 2 cups |
| Sugar | | |
| *brown, light or dark* | 16-ounce package | $2^1/4$ cups firmly packed |
| *cubes* | 16-ounce package | 96 cubes |
| *granulated* | 1 pound | $2^1/4$ cups |
| | 4-pound bag | 9 cups |
| | 5-pound bag | $11^1/4$ cups |
| *confectioners'* | 16-ounce package | 3 to 4 cups unsifted; $4^1/2$ cups sifted |
| *superfine* | 16-ounce package | 2 cups |

| Ingredient | Market Unit | Measurement |
|---|---|---|

## Vegetables

| Ingredient | Market Unit | Measurement |
|---|---|---|
| Alfalfa sprouts | 1 pound | 6 cups |
| Artichokes | | |
| *fresh* | 2 medium | About 1 pound |
| *canned* | 14-ounce jar | 8 to 10 medium; 5 to 7 large |
| *marinated* | $6^1/2$-ounce jar | $^3/4$ cup |
| Asparagus | | |
| *fresh* | 1 pound | 16 to 20 spears; $2^1/2$ cups cooked pieces |
| *frozen* | 10-ounce package | 2 cups cut pieces |
| *canned* | 12-ounce can | 8 spears |
| | $14^1/2$- /15-ounce can | 14 to 17 spears |
| Beans | | |
| *baked pork and beans, vegetarian* | 15-ounce can | $1^3/4$ cups |
| | 28-ounce can | 3 cups |
| | 7-pound, 5-ounce can | 13 cups |
| *dried (most varieties)* | 1 pound | $2^1/2$ cups uncooked; $5^1/2$ to 6 cups cooked |
| *garbanzo (chickpeas)* | 15-ounce can | 2 cups |
| | 6-pound, 12-ounce can | 12 cups |
| *Great Northern* | 15- /$15^1/2$-ounce can | $1^1/2$ cups |
| *green or wax* | | |
| *fresh* | 1 pound | 4 cups 1-inch pieces |
| *frozen* | 10-package cut | 3 cups |
| | 10-ounce package French-style | 3 cups |
| *canned* | $14^1/2$- /$15^1/2$-ounce can | $1^3/4$ cups |
| | 6-pound, 5-ounce | 12 cups, cut and French-style |

| Ingredient | Market Unit | Measurement |
| --- | --- | --- |
| *kidney* | 15- /15$\frac{1}{2}$-ounce can | 1$\frac{3}{4}$ cups |
| | 6-pound, 12-ounce can | 12 cups |
| *lima (fresh, canned, or frozen)* | 1 pound | 3 cups |
| *pinto* | 15- /15$\frac{1}{2}$-ounce can | 1$\frac{3}{4}$ cups |
| | 6-pound, 12-ounce can | 12 cups |
| *refried* | 16-ounce can | 1$\frac{3}{4}$ cups |
| | 6-pound, 14-ounce can | 13 cups |
| Bean sprouts | | |
| *fresh* | $\frac{1}{4}$ pound | 1 cup |
| *canned* | 16-ounce can | 4 cups |
| Beets | | |
| *fresh, without tops* | 1 pound | 2 cups sliced |
| *canned* | 14$\frac{1}{2}$- /16- /17-ounce can | 1$\frac{3}{4}$ to 2 cups; 14 to 16 whole beets |
| | 6-pound, 8-ounce can | 12 cups sliced |
| Broccoli | | |
| *fresh* | 1 pound | 1 medium bunch; 2 cups florets |
| *frozen* | 10-ounce package | 2$\frac{1}{2}$ cups chopped |
| | 24-ounce package | 16 spears |
| Brussels sprouts | | |
| *fresh* | 1 pound | 4 cups |
| *frozen* | 10-ounce package | 18 to 24; 1$\frac{1}{2}$ to 2 cups |
| Cabbage | | |
| *fresh* | 1 small head | About 1 pound; 3 to 4$\frac{1}{2}$ cups shredded; 2 cups cooked |
| *Chinese* | 1$\frac{1}{2}$ pounds | 6 to 8 cups sliced |
| *red* | 1 medium head | 2 pounds; 4 cups cooked |
| *coleslaw* | 16-ounce package | 7$\frac{1}{2}$ cups |

| Ingredient | Market Unit | Measurement |
|---|---|---|
| Carrots | | |
| *fresh* | 1 pound | 5 to 6 medium; $3^1/2$ cups shredded or chopped; 3 cups cooked |
| *baby* | 1 pound | $3^1/2$ cups; about 20 carrots per cup |
| *frozen* | 10-ounce package | $1^1/2$ to 2 cups |
| *canned* | $13^1/2$- /15-ounce can | $1^1/2$ cups sliced |
| Cauliflower | | |
| *fresh* | 1 large head | About 2 pounds; 3 cups florets |
| *frozen* | 10-ounce package | $1^1/2$ cups florets |
| Celery, fresh | 1 stalk | 1 to $1^1/2$ pounds |
| | 2 medium ribs | 1 cup $1/4$-inch slices |
| Chiles | | |
| *green, whole* | 4-ounce can | 3 |
| *green, chopped* | $4^1/2$-ounce can | $1/2$ cup |
| | 7-ounce can | About 1 cup |
| Corn | | |
| *canned, whole kernel* | $15^1/4$-ounce can | $1^3/4$ cups |
| | 17-ounce can | 2 cups |
| | 6-pound, 10-ounce can | 12 cups |
| *fresh* | 2 medium ears | 1 cup kernels |
| *frozen, whole kernel* | 10-ounce package | $1^1/2$ cups kernels |
| | 4-pound package | 13 cups |
| Cucumber | 1 medium | $1/2$ pound; 2 cups sliced or diced |
| Eggplant | 1 medium | $1^1/4$ pounds; 8 (4-inch) slices |
| | 1 medium | 4 cups diced; $2^1/2$ cups cooked |

| Ingredient | Market Unit | Measurement |
|---|---|---|
| Lentils | 1 pound | $2^1/_4$ cups dry; 5 cups cooked |
| Lettuce | | |
| *endive* | 1 pound | About 4 cups |
| *iceberg* | 1 head | $1^1/_4$ pounds; 6 cups bite-size pieces; 10 cups shredded |
| | 1 pound | 25 to 30 leaves; about 6 cups |
| *Romaine* | 1 pound | 6 cups leaves |
| *salad mix* | 8-ounce package | $3^3/_4$ to 4 cups |
| Mixed vegetables | | |
| *frozen* | 10-ounce package | 2 cups |
| *canned* | $14^1/_2$- /15-ounce can | $1^3/_4$ cups |
| | 6-pound, 10-ounce can | 12 cups |
| Mushrooms | | |
| *fresh button* | 1 pound | 2 to 3 cups sliced |
| *fresh portabella* | 7-ounce package | 12 to 14 ($^1/_4$-inch) slices |
| | 16-ounce package | 3 large caps |
| *fresh shiitake* | $3^1/_2$-ounce package | About 1 cup chopped |
| *canned* | 4-ounce jar | $^2/_3$ cup |
| | 7-ounce can or jar | 1 cup |
| | 4-pound, 4-ounce can | $8^1/_2$ cups |
| Okra | | |
| *fresh* | 1 pound | 2 cups chopped |
| *frozen* | 10-ounce package | $1^1/_2$ cups chopped |
| *canned* | $14^1/_2$- /$15^1/_2$-ounce can | $1^3/_4$ cups |

| Ingredient | Market Unit | Measurement |
|---|---|---|
| Onions | | |
| *white or yellow* | 1 pound | 2 large or 3 medium |
| | 3 large | $2^1/2$ cups chopped |
| | 1 medium | $^1/2$ to $^2/3$ cup chopped |
| | 12-ounce package frozen | 3 cups chopped |
| | 4-pound, 4-ounce package | 18 cups diced |
| | 15-ounce jar | $1^3/4$ cups whole |
| *green* | 1 bunch (6 to 8) | 4 ounces; $^1/3$ cup chopped (white part only); 1 cup sliced (white and green parts) |
| Shallots | 1 large | 1 tablespoon minced |
| Parsnips | 1 pound | 4 medium; 2 cups chopped |
| Peas | | |
| *green, in pod* | 1 pound | 1 cup shelled |
| *green, frozen* | 10-ounce package | 2 cups |
| *green, canned* | 15- /17-ounce can | $1^3/4$ to 2 cups |
| | 6-pound, 12-ounce | 12 cups |
| *split* | 1 pound | $2^1/3$ cups uncooked; about 5 cups cooked |
| Peppers, bell (red, green, or yellow) | 1 large | 6 to 8 ounces; 1 cup chopped |
| *frozen* | 10-ounce package | $2^1/2$ cups chopped |
| Pimentos, diced or sliced | 2-ounce jar | $^1/4$ cup |
| | 4-ounce jar | $^1/2$ cup |
| Potatoes | | |
| *baking, raw* | 1 pound | 1 large |
| *red, raw* | 1 pound | 4 medium |
| *white, raw* | 1 pound | 3 medium |

| Ingredient | Market Unit | Measurement |
|---|---|---|
| *white, cooked* | 1 pound | $2^1/_4$ cups diced or sliced; $1^3/_4$ cups mashed |
| *dried flakes* | $13^3/_4$-ounce package | $5^2/_3$ cups flakes; $8^1/_2$ cups prepared |
| | $^1/_3$ cup flakes | $^1/_2$ cup prepared |
| *hash browns, refrigerated* | 20-ounce package | $3^1/_2$ cups |
| *sweet* | | |
| *raw* | 1 pound | 3 medium; 2 cups sliced |
| *canned* | 15-ounce can | $1^1/_2$ cups |
| | 29-ounce can | $2^1/_2$ cups |
| Pumpkins | | |
| *fresh* | 1 medium | About 5 pounds |
| | 1 pound | 4 cups, pared, cubed; 1 cup cooked, mashed |
| *canned* | 15- /16-ounce can | $1^3/_4$ to 2 cups; enough for 1 (9-inch) pie |
| | 29-ounce can | $3^1/_2$ cups; enough for 2 (9-inch) pies |
| | 6-pound, 4-ounce can | 12 cups; enough for 6 (9-inch) pies |
| Radishes | 12 whole (about 1 bunch) | 1 cup sliced |
| Rutabagas | 1 pound | $2^1/_2$ cups cubed |
| Sauerkraut | 14-ounce can | $1^3/_4$ cups |
| | 32-ounce jar | 4 cups |
| | 6-pound, 3-ounce can | 12 cups |
| Spinach | | |
| *fresh* | 1 pound | About 4 cups leaves; 3 cups torn; 1 cup cooked |
| *frozen* | 10-ounce package | $1^1/_4$ cups chopped or leaf |

| Ingredient | Market Unit | Measurement |
|---|---|---|
| *canned* | 14- /15-ounce can | $1^1/_2$ cups |
| Squash, winter | | |
| *fresh* | 1 pound | 1 cup cooked, mashed |
| *frozen, sliced* | 12-ounce package | $1^1/_2$ cups |
| *canned* | 15- /16-ounce can | About 2 cups |
| Squash, summer | | |
| *fresh* | 1 pound | 3 medium; $2^1/_2$ cups sliced |
| *frozen* | 10-ounce package | $1^1/_2$ cups sliced |
| Tomatillos | 1 pound | 16 medium |
| Tomatoes | | |
| *fresh* | 1 pound | 4 small; 3 medium; 2 large |
| | 1 medium | 1 cup chopped |
| | 1 pound, peeled and seeded | $1^1/_2$ cups pulp |
| *canned, whole* | $14^1/_2$- /16-ounce can | $1^3/_4$ to 2 cups |
| | 6-pound, 6-ounce can | 12 cups |
| *canned, whole* | 10-ounce can | 1 cup |
| *with green chiles* | 10-ounce can | 1 cup |
| | $14^1/_2$-ounce can | $1^3/_4$ cups |
| *canned, diced* | 16-ounce can | 2 cups |
| | $14^1/_2$-ounce can | $1^1/_2$ cups |
| | 6-pound, 6-ounce can | 11 cups |
| *canned, stewed* | $14^1/_2$-ounce can | $1^1/_2$ cups |
| *cherry* | 1 pint | 2 cups (about 25) |
| *sauce* | 8-ounce can | 1 cup |
| | 15-ounce can | $1^3/_4$ cups |
| | 6-pound, 10-ounce can | 12 cups |

| Ingredient | Market Unit | Measurement |
|---|---|---|
| *paste* | 6-ounce can | $3/4$ cup |
|  | $4^1/2$-ounce tube | 5 tablespoons |
|  | 6-pound, 15-ounce can | 12 cups |
| Turnips | 1 pound | 3 medium; 2 cups cooked |
| Zucchini |  |  |
| *fresh* | 1 pound | 3 medium |
|  | 1 large | 2 cups sliced |
| *canned* | $14^1/2$-ounce can | $1^3/4$ cups |

## Karen Weisberg, USA

Feature editor, *FoodService Director* magazine

What's a good recipe? It's one that:

- Has customer appeal (it tastes good);
- Has perceived food value for the price;
- Is not too labor intensive; and
- Has a fairly low food cost.

## Robyn Martin, New Zealand

Food editor, *New Zealand Woman's Weekly*, and author of more than 27 cookbooks

A good recipe is clearly written, not open to interpretation, never assumes a reader has a knowledge of cooking nor underestimates the reader's intelligence. A good recipe is one that works. That means anyone, anywhere, who can read and understand the language in which it is written, can produce an end product as perfect as the recipe's creator intended.

It could probably be argued that the most important thing for a good recipe is for it to inspire, but a recipe is of little use to the cook if it is difficult to understand and does not produce a superb end result.

# Chapter Thirteen

# Standard Pan Sizes

INDICATING THE PROPER SIZE OR type of pan or other piece of equipment is important when writing or editing recipes. Pan size can affect cooking or baking times and recipe yields. Providing the recommended pan size enables the recipe user to determine a suitable substitute if the exact pan is not available.

Give the size of the pan in inches or metric measurements (see Chapter Eight) or, if appropriate, give a volume measurement. For microwave cookware, sizes are usually the same as for conventional cookware. Some pans, such as a 13 x 9 x 2-inch baking pan, are too large to fit in a standard microwave oven.

It is important to indicate whether a pan is glass or metal, whether it has a special nonstick coating, or whether it is insulated. Each of these can make a difference in the cooking time and the final results.

Be sure to note the size and type of pan during recipe testing and write it on the recipe worksheet.

# Commonly Used Pans

Included here are the most commonly used pans for consumer and large-quantity recipes.

## Baking Dishes

Give the quart size and indicate how deep or shallow, if appropriate.

- 1-quart
- 1$^1$/$_2$-quart
- 2-quart
- 4-quart

## Custard Cups

- 6-ounce
- 10-ounce

## Loaf Pans

- 7$^1$/$_2$ x 3$^3$/$_4$ x 2$^1$/$_4$-inch
- 8$^1$/$_2$ x 4$^1$/$_2$ x 2$^1$/$_2$-inch
- 9 x 5 x 3-inch (standard size)
- 16 x 5 x 4-inch; also 8 x 5 x 4-inch (for some large-quantity recipes)
- 4$^1$/$_2$ x 2$^3$/$_4$ x 1$^1$/$_4$-inch (for mini loaves)

## Molds

These sometimes have a center tube or a decorative or removable bottom.

- 4-cup
- 5-cup
- 6-cup
- 9-cup
- 12-cup

## Muffin Pans

The measurements refer to the size of individual muffin cups; pans have 6 to 12 cups per pan.

$1^3/4$ x 1-inch (miniature muffins)

$2^1/2$ x $1^1/4$-inch (standard-size muffins)

3 x $1^1/2$-inch (oversize or jumbo muffins)

Muffin ring (for use in microwave oven)

## Pie and Quiche Pans

8-inch ($1^1/4$ inches deep)

9-inch ($1^1/4$ inches deep)

9-inch (2 inches deep), a deep-dish pan

10-inch ($1^1/2$ inches deep)

## Rectangular Pans

13 x 9 x 2-inch

11 x 7 x 2-inch

12 x $7^1/2$ x 2-inch

15 x 10-inch (often referred to as a cookie sheet or baking sheet)

15 x 10 x 1-inch (often referred to as a jelly-roll pan)

26 x 18 x 2-inch (cake pan for large-quantity recipes)

26 x 18 x 1-inch (sheet pan for large-quantity recipes)

12 x 18 x 1-inch (half sheet pan for large-quantity recipes)

## Roasting Pans

14 x 10 x 2-inch

$15^1/2$ x $10^1/2$ x $2^1/4$-inch

$17^1/4$ x $11^1/2$ x $2^1/4$-inch

## Round Baking Pans

8-inch ($1^1/2$ inches deep)

9-inch ($1^1/2$ inches deep)

## Saucepans

1-quart
1$^1$/$_2$-quart
2-quart
2$^1$/$_2$-quart
3-quart

## Skillets

7- to 8-inch (small)
8- to 10-inch (medium)
11- to 12-inch (large)

## Springform Pans

9-inch (usually 3 inches deep)
10-inch (usually 3 inches deep)

## Square Baking Pans

8 x 8 x 2-inch
9 x 9 x 2-inch

## Stockpots

Used for large-quantity recipes.

9-quart
12-quart
15-quart
20-quart
25-quart

## Tart Pans

4$^1$/$_4$ x 1$^1$/$_4$-inch
9 x 1-inch
10 x 1-inch

## Tube Pans

9-inch ($3^1/_2$ inches deep)
10-inch (4 inches deep)

## Miscellaneous Pans

Bundt—6-cup and 12-cup (Bundt is a registered trademark)
Bean pot—3-quart
Omelet pan—8-inch
Pizza pan—10-, 12-, and 14-inch
Soufflé dishes—$1^1/_2$- to 8-cup
Steam table pans (also called counter or insert pans)
    20 x 12 x 2-inch
    20 x 12 x 4-inch
    20 x 12 x 6-inch
    10 x 12 x 2-inch (half counter pan)
    10 x 12 x 4-inch (half counter pan)

# Miscellaneous Equipment

## Ladles or Dippers

These are used in food service to measure and to control portions. Include the ladle size in the yield of the recipe.

1-ounce ($^1/_8$ cup)—sauces and relishes
2-ounce ($^1/_4$ cup)—gravy and sauces
4-ounce ($^1/_2$ cup)—creamed vegetables
6-ounce ($^3/_4$ cup)—soup, chili, or stew
8-ounce (1 cup)—soup, chili, or stew
12-ounce ($1^1/_2$ cups)—large serving of soup or goulash
24-ounce (3 cup)—kitchen dipper
32-ounce (4 cups)—quart dipper

## Scoops

Generally for large-quantity recipes; the scoop number tells the number of portions per quart of food. Include the scoop number or size in the yield of the recipe.

No. 4 (1 cup)—main course

No. 6 ($^2/_3$ cup)—main course

No. 8 ($^1/_2$ cup)—meat patty or casserole

No. 12 ($^1/_3$ cup)—salads, croquettes, or vegetables

No. 16 ($^1/_4$ cup)—muffins or desserts

No. 24 (8 teaspoons)—sandwich and cream puff fillings

No. 30 (2 tablespoons)—large drop cookies

No. 40 (5 teaspoons)—medium drop cookies

No. 60 (1 tablespoon)—small drop cookies

# Tui Flower, New Zealand

Former cookery editor, *New Zealand Woman's Weekly,* and author of several cookbooks

What is a good recipe? To answer this question is to examine the evolution of the cookbook and of the form in which the recipe is written.

The first recognized cookery book in the English language is that written by an anonymous chef of King Richard II about 1390, called *Forme of Cury.* Not until the eighteenth century does the cookbook, in a form recognizable to us today, make its appearance. At that time women were learning to read and write, industrial development changed living conditions and improved cooking facilities, and agricultural advances meant better-quality produce. Three women, Hannah Glasse (1708–1770), Elizabeth Raffald (1733–1781), and Maria Rundell (1745–1829), saw the need to write for the housewife, and each wrote a best-seller in its time.

All provided knowledge for the reader, helping her to utilize new foods introduced from foreign lands and to use better cooking equipment that resulted from modern technology. They also provided guidance in health and hygiene. Mrs. Glasse is credited with writing recipes with more detailed measures and methods than her predecessors, thus making recipes more available to less experienced cooks.

During the eighteenth century, the English-language cookbooks used in the United States originated in England until, in 1796, an all-American book—the collected recipes of Amelia Simmons—came into print. It was the first cookbook that featured American ingredients (such as cornmeal, corn cobs, and cranberries) and recipes for hoecakes, Indian pudding, cookies, and pumpkin pie. This book gave American cooking its own identity.

Industrial and commercial advances allowed for further changes in food habits in the latter half of the nineteenth century. Again the cookery book changed, this time to encompass the culinary needs of all women, as by now literacy was widespread. Two writers of this period became household names: Eliza Acton (1799–1859) and Isabella Beeton (1836–1865).

At the end of the century, the cookbook writer responsible for the scientific presentation of recipe material was writing her best-seller. Fannie Farmer (1857–1915) and her *Boston Cooking-School Cook Book* impressed on cooks the need for accuracy of measurement to obtain uniform results. From this approach has evolved the highly precise recipe style of today.

## Susan Manlin Katzman, USA

Author of *Kids Cooking: Scrumptious Recipes for Cooks Ages 9 to 13* and other books

What makes a good recipe? "Not much," comes my stream-of-consciousness answer. Not much. The kind of not much that is so labor-intensive for the recipe writer and so taken for granted by the reader. The same not much as in not embellished, not artificial, not complicated, not adorned, not pretentious, not affected, not gilded, and not contrived. The type of not much that serves as a synonym for simplicity. The not-much principle applies to every aspect of a recipe, except, of course, the results, which reverse the theory. I believe that all really good recipes create food touched with magic. Results of good recipes give the cook much—much pride, much gratification, and much, much pleasure.

# Chapter Fourteen

# Resources

OUR GOAL IS TO MAKE this book a one-stop source of information about recipe writing. However, it would not be practical or efficient to reproduce information that is readily available elsewhere, such as in dictionaries and encyclopedias. We encourage you to make use of other resources, including reference books, cookbooks, Internet sites, food promotion organizations, government agencies, and professional groups.

For your basic recipe-writing reference library, we recommend, in addition to this book, four other books:

## Elizabeth Alston, USA

Former food editor, *Woman's Day,* and author of several cookbooks

Above all, a good recipe must please the person who makes it and those who eat it.

- A dictionary, for preferred spellings
- *The Associated Press Stylebook,* for style information including capitalization, spelling, punctuation, and grammar
- A food dictionary, for additional spellings and definitions
- A comprehensive, basic cookbook, to compare proportions, tests for doneness, serving sizes, and other information

Our preferences for these books are listed under "The Basics." With this suggested basic reference library, you would be well equipped to write and edit recipes. Depending on your specialty and your finances, you might want to add other reference books and cookbooks to your library. Our suggestions for such books are listed by categories.

We do not necessarily recommend the recipe-writing formats used in the cookbooks listed here. We do, however, refer to these books often for information about a particular subject, ingredient, or cuisine. We have listed the most current edition of a book, when possible. We have used various editions over the years and often have consulted other books by the same authors. Some of the books are out of print. You might find them at used-book stores or the out-of-print services at bookstores.

Despite the multitude of cookbooks on the market today and the abundance of recipes in newspapers and magazines, there are few books on recipe writing. We have included such books for your information.

If you are working on a project for a food manufacturer or book publisher, ask for the company's style guidelines and raise your concerns and questions about style early in the project.

When writing recipes featuring a particular food, you can obtain useful information from food promotion groups, including the latest nutrition data, proper product terminology, cooking times and temperatures, and tests for doneness. These organizations generally provide information free of charge. The following listings include state, national, and international food organizations, as well as government agencies.

Depending on your specialty, you might want to consider membership in one or more professional organizations. These provide a good way to network with others in your field, and some offer annual conferences with valuable seminars. We have listed some that particularly apply to food professionals.

The World Wide Web, or Internet, is the fastest-growing source of information today. We have included Web addresses when available, as well as a short list of some of the most popular food and recipe Web sites.

# Book List

## The Basics

*Associated Press Stylebook and Libel Manual,* edited by Norm Goldstein. Reading, Mass.: Perseus, 2000.

*Better Homes and Gardens New Cook Book.* 11th ed. Des Moines, Iowa: Meredith Corp., 1996. (Or one of the other books listed under General Cookbooks.)

*New Food Lover's Companion,* by Sharon Tyler Herbst. New York: Barron's, 1995.

*Webster's Collegiate Dictionary.* 10th ed. Springfield, Mass.: Merriam-Webster, 1998.

## Books on Writing and Style

*Chicago Manual of Style.* 14th ed. Chicago: University of Chicago Press, 1993.

*Elements of Style,* by William Strunk, Jr. and E. B. White. 4th ed. Boston: Allyn & Bacon, 1999.

*How to Register a Copyright and Protect Your Creative Work,* by Robert B. Chickering and Susan Hartman. New York: Scribner's, 1987.

*Internet Writer's Handbook,* by Martha C. Sammons. Boston: Allyn & Bacon, 1999.

*New York Times Manual of Style and Usage,* by William G. Connolly and Allan M. Siegal. New York: Times Books, 1999.

*Synonym Finder,* by J. I. Rodale, Nancy LaRoche, and Faye C. Allen. New York: Warner Books, 1986.

*Webster's New World Thesaurus,* prepared by Charlton Laird. 3rd ed. New York: IDG Books Worldwide, 1996.

*Words into Type,* by Marjorie E. Skillin and Robert M. Gay. 3rd ed. Englewood Cliffs, N. J.: Prentice Hall, 1974.

*Writing for the Web,* by Crawford Kilian. Bellingham, Washington: Self-Counsel Press, 2000.

## Food and Beverage Reference Books

*All You Need to Know About the British Kitchen: Names, Terms and Measures for the American Cook,* by Jane Garmey. New York: Kitchen Arts & Letters, 1994. (out of print)

*American Dietetic Association's Complete Food & Nutrition Guide,* by Roberta Larson Duyff. New York: John Wiley, 1998.

*Complete Guide to Home Canning, Preserving, and Freezing,* by the U.S. Department of Agriculture. 2nd revised ed. New York: Dover Publications, 1999. (The USDA revised home canning guidelines in December 1988. Verify that canning recipes in other sources are based on the revised USDA guidelines. In general, discard recipes dated prior to these guidelines.)

*Cooking A to Z: The Complete Culinary Reference Tool,* edited by Jane Horn. Santa Rosa, Calif.: Cole Publishing, 1998.

*Cookwise: The Hows and Whys of Successful Cooking,* by Shirley O. Corriher. New York: William Morrow, 1997.

*Dimensions, Tolerances, and Terminology for Home Cooking and Baking Utensils.* New York: American National Standards Institute, 1979. (out of print)

*Eggcyclopedia, Unabridged.* Park Ridge, Ill.: American Egg Board, 1999.

*Encyclopedia of American Food and Drink,* by John F. Mariani. New York: Lebhar-Friedman, 1999.

*Encyclopedia of Herbs, Spices and Flavorings,* by Elisabeth Lambert Ortiz. 1st American ed. New York: Dorling Kindersley, 1992.

*Food Lover's Tiptionary,* by Sharon Tyler Herbst. New York: Hearst Books, 1994.

*Great Food Almanac,* by Irena Chalmers. San Francisco: HarperCollins, 1994. (out of print)

*Handbook of Food Preparation,* by the Food and Nutrition section of the American Home Economics Association. 9th ed. Dubuque, Iowa: Kendall/Hun, 1993.

*Health Writer's Handbook,* by Barbara Gastel. Des Moines, Iowa: Iowa State University Press, 1997.

*International Dictionary of Food & Nutrition,* by Kenneth N. Anderson and Lois E. Anderson. New York: John Wiley, 1993.

*Kitchen Science,* by Howard Hillman. Revised ed. Boston: Houghton Mifflin, 1989.

*Larousse Gastronomique,* edited by Jenifer Harvey Lang. New York: Crown, 1988.

*La Varenne Pratique: The Complete Illustrated Guide to the Techniques, Ingredients and Tools of Classic Modern Cooking,* by Anne Willan. New York: Crown Publishers, 1989.

*Oxford Companion to Food,* by Allan Davidson. New York: Oxford University Press Inc., 1999.

*Resource Guide for Food Writers,* by Gary Allen, New York: Routledge, 1999.

*Substituting Ingredients: An A to Z Kitchen Reference,* by Becky Sue Epstein and Hilary Dole Klein. 3rd ed. Chester, Conn.: Globe Pequot Press, 1996.

*Uncommon Fruits & Vegetables: A Commonsense Guide,* by Elizabeth Schneider. New York: William Morrow, 1998.

*Webster's New World Dictionary of Culinary Arts,* by Steven Labensky, Gaye G. Ingram, and Sarah R. Labensky. 2nd ed. Englewood Cliffs, N.J.: Prentice-Hall, 1997.

## General Cookbooks

*The Best Recipe,* by the authors of *Cook's Illustrated* magazine. Brookline, Mass.: Boston Common Press, 1999.

*Betty Crocker's Cookbook.* New York: MacMillan, 1996.

*Essentials of Cooking,* by James Peterson. New York: Artisan, 2000.

*Fannie Farmer Cookbook,* by Marion Cunningham. 13th ed. New York: Alfred A. Knopf, 1996.

*How to Cook Everything,* by Mark Bittman. New York: Macmillan, 1998.

*Joy of Cooking,* by Irma S. Rombauer, Marion Rombauer Becker and Ethan Becker. New York: Scribner's, 1997.

*New York Times Cook Book,* by Craig Claiborne. New York: HarperCollins, 1990.

*Pillsbury Complete Cookbook.* New York: Clarkson Potter Publishers, 2000.

*Way to Cook,* by Julia Child. New York: Alfred A. Knopf, 1989.

## Specialty Books

*Art of Eating,* by M. F. K. Fisher. New York: IDG Worldwide, 1990.

*Ball Blue Book: Guide to Home Canning, Freezing, and Dehydration.* Volume 1. Muncie, Ind.: Alltrista Corporation, 1997.

*Barbecue Bible,* by Steven Raichlen. New York: Workman, 1998.

*Better Homes & Gardens: Grill It Right.* Des Moines, Iowa: Meredith Corporation, 1995.

*Better Homes and Gardens New Junior Cookbook,* by Jennifer Dorland Darling. Des Moines, Iowa: Meredith Books, 1997.

*Cake Bible,* by Rose Levy Beranbaum. New York: William Morrow, 1988.

*General Electric Microwave Guide and Cookbook.* New York: Random House, 1983.

*Good Housekeeping Illustrated Children's Cookbook,* by Marianne Zanzarella. New York: William Morrow & Co., 1997.

*Jewish Cooking in America,* by Joan Nathan. New York: Random House, 1998.

*Kids Cooking: Scrumptious Recipes for Cooks Ages 9 to 13,* by Susan Manlin Katzman. Alexandria, Va.: Time-Life Books, 1998.

*Microwave Cooking: 101 Essential Tips,* by Deni Bown. New York: DK Publishing, Inc., 1995.

*New American Heart Association Cookbook.* 6th ed. New York: Times Books, 1998.

*New Complete Book of Breads,* by Bernard Clayton. New York: Fireside, 1995.

*New Moosewood Cookbook,* by Mollie Katzen. Berkeley, Calif.: Ten Speed Press, 2000.

*Pie and Pastry Bible,* by Rose Levy Beranbaum. New York: Scribner's, 1998.

*Thrill of the Grill,* by Chris Schlesinger and John Willoughby. New York: William Morrow, 1990.

*Vegetarian Cooking for Everyone,* by Deborah Madison. New York: Broadway Books, 1997.

## International Cuisines

*Australian Food: In Celebration of the New Australian Cuisine,* by Alan Saunders. Berkley, Calif.: Ten Speed Press, 1999.

*Authentic Mexican: Regional Cooking from the Heart of Mexico,* by Rick Bayless. New York: William Morrow, 1987.

*Cooking of the Eastern Mediterranean,* by Paula Wolfert. New York: HarperCollins, 1994.

*Essentials of Classic Italian Cooking,* by Marcella Hazan. New York: Alfred A. Knopf, 1992.

*Essential Cuisines of Mexico,* by Diana Kennedy. New York: Clarkson Potter, 2000.

*Everybody Eats Well in Belgium Cookbook,* by Ruth Van Waerebeek-Gonzalez. New York: Workman, 1996.

*Food of Australia: Contemporary Recipes from Australia's Leading Chefs,* by Stephanie Alexander. Berkley, Calif.: Periplus Editions, 1999.

*German Cookery,* by Elizabeth Schuler. New York: Crown Publishers, 1988.

*Mastering the Art of French Cooking,* Volume I, by Julia Child, Louisette Berthole, and Simone Beck. New York: Alfred A. Knopf, 1961; Volume II, by Julia Child and Simone Beck. New York: Alfred A. Knopf, 1970.

*Modern Art of Chinese Cooking,* by Barbara Tropp. New York: Hearst Books. 1996.

*New German Cookbook,* by Jean Anderson and Hedy Wurz. New York: HarperCollins, 1993.

*New Zealand The Beautiful Cookbook,* edited by Tui Flower. Auckland, New Zealand: Shortland Publications, 1985. (out of print)

*Splendid Table: Recipes from Emilia-Romagna, The Heartland of Northern Italian Food,* by Lynne Rossetto Kasper. New York: William Morrow, 1992.

*Taste of India,* by Madhur Jaffrey. New York: IDG Worldwide, 1988.

*Taste of Quebec,* by Julian Armstrong. 2nd ed. Toronto: Macmillan of Canada, 2001.

*Two Hundred Years of New Zealand Food and Cookery,* by David Burton.

Wellington, New Zealand: A. H. Reed & A. W. Reed Ltd., 1982. (out of print)

## Large-Quantity Cookbooks

*Chef's Book of Formulas, Yields and Sizes,* by Arno Schmidt. 2nd ed. New York: John Wiley, 1995.

*Cooking for Fifty,* by Chet Holden. New York: John Wiley, 1993.

*Food for Fifty,* by Grace Shugart and Mary Molt. 10th ed. New York: Prentice Hall, 1996.

*Large Quantity Recipes,* by Margaret E. Tereel and Dorothea Headlund. 4th ed. New York: John Wiley, 1989.

*New Professional Chef,* by the Culinary Institute of America. 6th ed. New York: John Wiley, 1995.

*On Cooking (Trade Version): Techniques from Expert Chefs, Volume 1,* by Sarah R. Labensky, Alan M. Hause, Steven Labensky. 2nd ed. New York: Prentice-Hall, 1998.

*Professional Baking,* by Wayne Gisslen. 2nd ed. New York: John Wiley, 1993.

*Professional Cooking,* by Wayne Gisslen. 4th ed. New York: John Wiley, 1998.

*Professional Pastry Chef,* by Bo Friberg. 3rd ed. New York: John Wiley, 1996.

*Recipes for Large Numbers,* by Stephen Ashley and Sean Anderson. Melbourne: Hospitality Press, 1996.

## Food History

*Food: A Culinary History,* by Jean Louis Flandrin, Massimo Montanari and Albert Sonnenfeld. New York: Columbia University Press, 1999.

*Food in History,* by Reay Tannahill. New York: Crown Publishers, 1995.

*Great Cooks and Their Recipes: From Taillevent to Escoffier,* by Anne Willan. New York: Pavillion, 2000.

*Story of Corn,* by Betty Fussell. New York: North Point Press, 1999.

## Other Books on Recipe Writing

*Cardinal's Handbook of Recipe Development,* by Evelyn Hullah. Toronto: Cardinal Biologicals Ltd., 1984.

*Foodspell: A Guide to Commonly Used Food Terms,* published by the Association of Food Journalists, 38309 Genesee Lake Road, Oconomowoc, WI 53066. 2nd. ed., 1997.

*New Zealand Guild of Food Writers Handbook,* published by the New Zealand Guild of Food Writers, P.O. Box 74 262, Market Road, Auckland, New Zealand. 2nd ed., 1999.

*Recipes into Type,* by Joan Whitman and Dolores Simon. New York: HarperCollins, 1993. (out of print)

*Writing Cookbooks,* by Judith Comfort. Bellingham, Washington: Self-Counsel Press, 1997.

# Food Web Sites

There are thousands of food and recipe Web sites; here are a few key ones.

| | |
|---|---|
| **www.allrecipes.com** | Recipe database, menus, recipe exchange. |
| **www.culinary.net** | Consumer and large-quantity recipes, special information for food writers, photographs. |
| **www.e-licious.com** | Recipe database, menu planner, how-to video clips. |
| **www.epicurious.com** | Recipe database, links to magazines, other food information. |
| **www.foodfit.com** | Recipes and nutrition information. |
| **www.foodweb.com** | Recipes, newsletters, cooking schools, equipment. |
| **www.globalgourmet.com** | International recipes, cookbooks, food background information. |
| **www.kitchenlink.com** | Recipes, newsletters, diet information, newspaper food columns. |
| **www.sallys-place.com** | Food news, recipes, background information. |
| **www.slowfood.com** | Recipes, essays, product guides. |

## Beverages

**Australian Wine Bureau**
150 East 42nd Street, 34th Floor
New York, NY 10017
212-351-6785

**German Wine Information Bureau**
245 Fifth Avenue, Suite 2204
New York, NY 10016
212-896-3336
www.germanwineusa.org

**National Coffee Association**
15 Maiden Lane #1405
New York, NY 10038
212-766-4007
www.ncausa.org

**National Soft Drink Association**
1101 16th Street NW
Washington, DC 20036
202-463-6732
www.nsda.org

**Northern Ireland Food and Drink Association**
Interpoint, 20-24 York Street
Belfast BT 15 1AQ
Northern Ireland
44-28-90468360
www.nifda.co.uk

**Swiss Wine Exporters Association**
Avenue de l'Avant Poste
P.O. Box 1346
1001 Lausanne, Switzerland
41-21-3205083
www.swisswine.ch

**Tea Association of the USA, Inc.**
420 Lexington Avenue, Suite 825
New York, NY 10170
212-986-9415
www.teausa.com

**Vintners Quality Alliance-Canada**
110 Hannover Drive, Suite B205
St. Catharines, Ontario L2W 1A4
Canada
905-684-8070
www.inniskillin.com/vinifera/vqa.html

**Wine Institute of New Zealand Inc.**
P.O. Box 90276
Auckland Mail Centre
New Zealand
64-9-303-3527
www.nzwine.com

## Dairy, Margarine, and Eggs

**American Egg Board**
1460 Renaissance Drive, Suite 301
Park Ridge, IL 60068
847-296-7043
www.aeb.org

**Australian Dairy Corporation**
Locked Bag 104
Flinders Lane, Victoria 8009
Australia
61-3-9694-3777
www.dairycorp.com.au

**Canadian Egg Marketing Agency**
112 Kent Street, Suite 1501
Ottawa, Ontario K1P 5P2 Canada
613-238-2514
www.canadaegg.ca

**Dairy Farmers of Canada**
75 Albert Street, Suite 1101
Ottawa, Ontario K1P 5E7 Canada
613-236-997
www.dairyfarmers.org

**Dairy Management, Inc.**
(formerly United Dairy Industry
Association)
10255 West Higgins Road,
Suite 900
Rosemont, IL 60018
847-803-2000
www.dairyinfo.com

**The Margarine Association**
5775 Peachtree-Dunwoody Road,
Suite 500-G
Atlanta, GA 30342
404-252-3663
www.margarine.org

**National Yogurt Association**
2000 Corporate Ridge, Suite 1000
McLean, VA 22102
703-821-0770
www.affi.com

**Switzerland Cheese Marketing**
704 Executive Boulevard
Valley Cottage, NY 10989
914-268-2460 or 800-628-5226

**Wisconsin Milk Marketing Board**
8418 Excelsior Drive
Madison, WI 53717
608-836-8820
www.wmmb.org

# Fruits

**Apricot Producers of California**
2125 Wylie Drive, Suite 2A
Modesto, CA 95355
209-524-0801
www.apricotproducers.com

**California Avocado Commission**
1251 East Dyer Road, Suite 200
Santa Ana, CA 92705
714-558-6761
www.avocado.org

**California Cling Peach Association**
2300 River Plaza Drive, Suite 110
Sacramento, CA 95833
916-925-9131
www.calpeach.com

**California Date Commission**
P.O. Box 1736
Indio, CA 92202
760-347-4510
www.californiadates.org

**California Fig Advisory Board**
3425 North First Street, Suite 109
Fresno, CA 93726
559-224-3447
www.californiafigs.com

**California Kiwifruit Commission**
9845 Horn Road, Suite 160
Sacramento, CA 95827
916-362-7490
www.kiwifruit.org

**California Dried Plum Board**
5990 Stoneridge Drive, Suite 101
Pleasanton, CA 94588
925-734-0150
www.prunes.org

**California Raisin Marketing Board**
3445 North First Street, Suite 101
Fresno, CA 93726
559-248-0287
www.calraisins.org or
www.raisins.org

**California Strawberry Commission**
P.O. Box 269
Watsonville, CA 95077
831-724-1301
www.calstrawberry.com

**California Table Grape Commission**
392 Fallbrook Drive, Suite 101
Fresno, CA 93711
559-447-8350
www.tablegrape.com

**California Tree Fruit Agreement**
975 I Street, P.O. Box 968
Reedley, CA 93654
559-638-8260
www.caltreefruit.com

**Cherry Marketing Institute**
(tart cherries, maraschino
cherries)
P.O. Box 30285
Lansing, MI 48909
517-669-4264
www.cherrymkt.org

**Florida Department of Citrus**
1115 East Memorial Boulevard
Lakeland, FL 33801

941-499-2500
www.floridajuice.com

**International Banana Association**
727 N. Washington Street
Alexandria, VA 22314
703-836-5499

**National Watermelon Promotion Board**
P.O. Box 140065
Orlando, FL 32814
407-895-5100
www.watermelon.org

**New Zealand Kiwifruit (Enza/Zespri)**
2001 West Garfield
Pier 90 C-128, Building A500
Seattle, WA 98119
206-284-1705
www.zespri.com

**North American Blueberry Council**
4995 Golden Foot Hill Parkway,
Suite 2
El Dorado Hills, CA 95762
916-933-9399
www.blueberry.org

**Northwest Cherry Growers**
(fresh sweet cherries)
105 South 18th Street, Suite 205
Yakima, WA 98901
509-453-4837
www.nwcherries.com

**Ocean Spray Cranberries, Inc.**
1 Ocean Spray Drive
Lakeville-Middleboro, MA 02349
508-946-1000
www.oceanspray.com

**Oregon Raspberry and Blackberry Commission**
712 NW 4th Street
Corvallis, OR 97330
541-758-4043
www.oregon-berries.com

**Pacific Northwest Canned Pear Service**
P.O. Box 640388
San Francisco, CA 94164
415-673-5200
www.pnw-cannedpears.com

**Produce Marketing Association**
(see listing under "Vegetables")

**Sunkist Growers, Inc.**
(citrus)
14130 Riverside Drive
Sherman Oaks, CA 91423
818-986-4800
www.sunkist.com

**United Fresh Fruit and Vegetable Association**
(see listing under "Vegetables")

**U.S. Apple Association**
P.O. Box 1137
McLean, VA 22101
703-442-8850
www.usaapple.org

**Wild Blueberry Association of North America**
59 Cottage Street
Bar Harbor, ME 04609
207-288-2655
www.wildblueberries.com

# Meats

**American Lamb Council**
6911 South Yosemite Street
Englewood, CO 80112
303-771-3500
www.sheepusa.org

**American Meat Institute**
1700 North Moore Street,
Suite 1600
Arlington, VA 22209
703-841-2400
www.meatami.org

**Beef Information Centre of Canada**
2233 Argentia Road, Suite 100
Mississauga, Ontario L5N 2X7
Canada
905-821-4900
www.beefinfo.org

**Canadian Pork Council**
1101-75 Albert Street
Ottawa, Ontario K1P 5E7 Canada
613-236-9239
www.canpork.ca

**Meat and Live-Stock Australia**
750 Lexington Avenue, 17th Floor
New York, NY 10022
212-486-2405
www.australianbeef.com and
www.australianlamb.com

**National Bison Association**
4701 Marion Street, Suite 100
Denver, CO 80216
303-292-2833
www.nbabison.org

National Cattlemen's Beef
Association
5420 South Quebec Street
Englewood, CO 80111
303-694-0305
www.beef.org

National Country Ham Association
P.O. Box 948
Conover, NC 28613
800-820-4426
www.countryham.org

National Pork Producers Council
P.O. Box 10383
Des Moines, IA 50306
515-223-2600
www.nppc.org

New Zealand Beef and Lamb
Marketing Bureau
P.O. Box 33 648
Takapuna, Auckland 9
New Zealand
64-9-489-7119
www.beeflamb.co.nz

New Zealand Game Industry Board
P.O. Box 10702
Wellington, New Zealand
64-4-473-4500
www.nzvenison.com

New Zealand Pork
Level 4, 94 Dixon Street
(P.O. Box 4048)
Wellington, New Zealand
64-4-385-4229
www.pork.co.nz

Nuts

Almond Board of California
1150 Ninth Street, Suite 1500
Modesto, CA 95354
209-549-8262
www.almondsarein.com

Hazelnut Marketing Board
21595-A Dolores Way NE
Aurora, OR 97002
503-678-6823 or 800-503-NUTS
www.oregonhazelnuts.org

National Pecan Shellers Association
5775 Peachtree-Dunwoody Road
Atlanta, GA 30342
404-252-3663
www.ilovepecans.org

Peanut Advisory Board
50 Hurt Plaza, Suite 1220
Atlanta, GA 30303
770-998-7311
www.peanutbutterlovers.com

Walnut Marketing Board
1540 River Park Drive, Suite 203
Sacramento, CA 95815
916-646-3807
www.walnuts.org

Pasta, Rice, and
Grains

National Barley Foods Council
5901 Phinney Avenue North,
Suite 110
Seattle, WA 98103
206-706-5988

**National Pasta Association**
2101 Wilson Boulevard, Suite 920
Arlington, VA 22201
703-841-0818
www.ilovepasta.org

**USA Rice Federation**
P.O. Box 740123
Houston, TX 77274
713-270-6699
www.usarice.com

**U.S. Wild Rice**
1306 West County Road F, #109
St. Paul, MN 55112
651-638-1955

**Wheat Foods Council**
10841 South Parker Road #105
Parker, CO 80134
303-840-8787
www.wheatfoods.org

## Poultry

**American Emu Association**
HC66 Box 367A
Kooskia, ID 83539
208-983-2737

**Canadian Turkey Marketing Agency**
969 Derry Road East, Unit 102
Mississauga, Ontario L5T 2J7
Canada
905-564-3100
www.canturkey.ca

**Duckling Council**
P.O. Box 1783
Des Plaines, IL 60017
847-228-7117
www.duckling.org

**National Chicken Council**
128 North Pitt Street, 2nd Floor
Alexandria, VA 22314
703-684-1766
www.eatchicken.com

**National Turkey Federation**
1225 New York Avenue NW,
Suite 400
Washington, DC 20005
202-898-0100
www.eatturkey.com

**New Zealand Poultry Industry Association**
1st Floor, 96D Carlton Gore Road
Auckland, New Zealand
64-9-520-4300

## Sauces, Seasonings, and Oils

**American Spice Trade Association**
560 Sylvan Avenue
Englewood Cliffs, NJ 07632
201-568-2163

**Association for Dressings & Sauces**
5775 Peachtree-Dunwoody Road,
Suite 500-G
Atlanta, GA 30342
404-252-3663
www.dressings-sauces.org

**Canola Information Service**
Box 1645
Lloydminster, Saskatchewan
S9V 1K6 Canada
306-387-6610
www.canolainfo.org

**Horseradish Information Council**
5775 Peachtree-Dunwoody Road,
Suite 500-G
Atlanta, GA 30342
404-252-3663
www.horseradish.org

**International Olive Oil Council**
921 SW 16th Street
Portland, OR 97205
503-221-0480

**Salt Institute**
700 North Fairfax, Suite 600
Alexandria VA 22314
703-549-4648
www.saltinstitute.org

**The Vinegar Institute**
5775 Peachtree-Dunwoody Road,
Suite 500-G
Atlanta, GA 30342
404-252-3663
www.vinegar.org

## Seafood and Fish

**Alaska Seafood Marketing Institute**
311 North Franklin, Room 200
Juneau, AK 99801
907-465-5560
www.alaskaseafood.org

**Halibut Association of North America**
2319 North 45th Street
Seattle, WA 98102
206-325-3413

**Maine Lobster Promotion Council**
382 Harlow Street
Bangor, ME 04401
207-947-2966
www.mainelobsterpromo.com

**National Fisheries Institute**
1901 North Fort Myer Drive,
Suite 700
Arlington, VA 22209
703-524-8881
www.nfi.org

**New England Fisheries Development Association**
197 Eighth Street, Suite 600A
Charlestown, MA 02129
www.fishfacts.com

**Surimi Seafood Education Center**
1901 North Fort Myer Drive,
Suite 700
Arlington, VA 22209
703-524-8881
www.nfi.org

## Snacks and Sweets

**Chocolate Manufacturers' Association**
7900 Westpark Drive, Suite A-320
McLean, VA 22102
703-790-5011
www.candyusa.org

**National Honey Board**
390 Lashley Street
Longmont, CO 80501
303-776-2337
www.honey.com

**Popcorn Institute**
401 North Michigan Avenue,
Suite 2200
Chicago, IL 60611
312-644-6610
www.popcorn.org

**Sugar Association, Inc.**
1101 15th Street NW, Suite 600
Washington, DC 20005
202-785-1122
www.sugar.org

## Vegetables

**Belgian Endive Marketing Board**
Kempenarestraat 64
2869 Sint Kateligne Waver
Belgium
32-15554694
www.belgianendive.org

**California Artichoke Advisory Board**
P.O. Box 747
Castroville, CA 95012
831-633-4411
www.artichokes.org

**California Asparagus Commission**
4565 Quail Lakes Drive, Suite A-1
Stockton, CA 95207
209-474-7581
www.calasparagus.com

**California Olive Committee**
1903 North Fine Street, Suite 102
Fresno, CA 93727
559-456-9096
www.calolive.org

**California Tomato Commission**
1625 East Shaw Avenue, Suite 122
Fresno, CA 93710
559-230-0116
www.tomato.org

**Florida Tomato Committee**
P.O. Box 140635
Orlando, FL 32814
407-894-3071
www.FloridaTomatoes.org

**Idaho Bean Commission**
P.O. Box 2556
Boise, ID 83701
208-334-3520
www.state.id.us/bean

**Michigan Asparagus Advisory Board**
P.O. Box 900
De Witt, MI 48820
517-669-4250
www.asparagus.org

**Michigan Bean Commission**
1031 South U.S. 27
St. Johns, MI 48879
517-224-1361
www.michiganbean.org

**Mushroom Council**
11875 Dublin Boulevard,
Suite D262
Dublin, CA 94568
925-556-5970
www.mushroomcouncil.com

**National Onion Association**
822 Seventh Street, Suite 510
Greeley, CO 80631
970-353-5895
www.onions-usa.org

**National Potato Promotion Board**
7555 East Hampden Avenue,
Suite 412
Denver, CO 80231
303-873-2331
www.potatohelp.com

**New Zealand Vegetable and Potato Growers Federation Inc.**
P.O. Box 10232
Wellington, New Zealand
64-4-472-3795
www.vegetables.co.nz

**North Carolina Sweet Potato Commission**
1327 North Brightleaf Boulevard, H
Smithfield, NC 27577
919-989-7323
www.ncsweetpotatoes.com

**Produce Marketing Association**
P.O. Box 6036
Newark, DE 19714
302-738-7100
www.pma.com

**United Fresh Fruit and Vegetable Association**
727 North Washington Street
Alexandria, VA 22314
703-836-3410
www.uffva.org

**USA Dry Pea & Lentil Council**
5071 Highway 8 West
Moscow, ID 83843
208-882-3023
www.pea-lentil.com

# Other Food-Related Organizations

**American Center for Wine, Food and the Arts**
1700 Soscol Avenue, Suite 1
Napa, CA 94559
707-257-3606
www.theamericancenter.org

**American Diabetes Association**
1701 North Beauregard Street
Alexandria, VA 22311
703-299-2087
www.diabetes.org

**American Institute of Baking**
1213 Bakers Way, P.O. Box 3999
Manhattan, KS 66505-3999
www.aibonline.org

**American Frozen Food Institute**
2000 Corporate Ridge, Suite 1000
McLean, VA 22102
703-821-0770
www.affi.com

**American National Standards Institute**
11 West 42nd Street
New York, NY 10036
212-642-4900
www.ansi.org

**Bread Machine Industry Association**
P.O. Box 1832
Milwaukee, WI 53201
800-471-0828
www.breadmachine.org

**Canned Food Alliance–Steel Packaging Council**
1101 17th Street NW, Suite 1300
Washington, DC 20036
202-452-7135
www.steel.org

**Food Marketing Institute**
(supermarket industry)
655 Fifteenth Street NW, Suite 700
Washington, DC 20005
202-452-8444
www.fmi.org

**Institute of Food Technologists**
221 North LaSalle Street,
Suite 300
Chicago, IL 60601
312-782-8424
www.ift.org

**International Cookbook Revue**
Lagasca 27-1-E
Madrid 28001, Spain
34-91-575-9350
www.connoisseur.se

**International Food Information Council Foundation**
1100 Connecticut Avenue NW,
Suite 430
Washington, DC 20036
202-296-6540
www.ificinfo.health.org

**Mycological Society of America**
P.O. Box 1897
Lawrence, KS 66044
www.msafungi.com

**National Association for the Specialty Food Trade**
(Fancy Food Shows)
120 Wall Street, 27th Floor
New York, NY 10005
212-482-6440
www.fancyfoodshows.com or www.specialty-foods.com

**National Restaurant Association**
1200 17th Street NW
Washington, DC 20036
202-331-5900
www.restaurant.org

**North American Mycological Association**
Joe Miller, Executive Secretary
101 Lynn Brooke Place
Charleston, WV 25312
304-744-1654
www.namyco.org

**Oldways Preservation and Exchange Trust**
266 Beacon Street
Boston, MA 02116
617-421-5500
www.oldwayspt.org

**Organic Trade Association**
74 Fairview Street
Greenfield, MA 01302
413-774-7511
www.ota.com

**Slow Food USA**
P.O. Box 1737
New York, NY 10021
877-756-9366
www.slowfood.com

# U.S. Government Agencies

**USDA Consumer Information Center**
Pueblo, CO 81009
719-948-4000
www.pueblo.gsa.gov

**Food and Drug Administration**
Office of Consumer Affairs and Information
5600 Fisher Lane, Room 16-85
Rockville, MD 20857
301-827-4420 or 888-INFOFDA
www.fda.gov

**Food and Nutrition Information Center**
National Agricultural Library, Room 304
Department of Agriculture
10301 Baltimore Avenue

Beltsville, MD 20705
301-504-5719
www.nal.usda.gov/fnic

**Superintendent of Documents**
U.S. Government Printing Office
P.O. Box 371954
Pittsburgh, PA 15250
202-512-1800
www.gpo.gov

**USDA Meat and Poultry Hotline**
Food Safety and Inspection Service
1400 Independence Avenue SW, Room 2925
Washington, DC 20250
800-535-4555
www.fsis.usda.gov

# International Governmental or Promotional Food Agencies

**Australia New Zealand Food Authority**
P.O. Box 7186
Canberra MC ACT 2610
Australia
61-2-6271-2620
www.anzfa.gov.au

**Australia New Zealand Food Authority**
P.O. Box 10559
The Terrace
Wellington 6036, New Zealand
64-4-473-9942
www.anzfa.govt.nz

**Austrian Trade Commission**
150 East 52nd Street, 32nd Floor
New York, NY 10022
212-421-5250
www.austriantrade.org

**Bord Bia—Irish Food Board**
Clanwilliam Court
Lower Mount Street
Dublin 2, Ireland
353-1-668-5155
www.bordbia.com or
www.foodisland.com

**Canadian Food Inspection Agency**
Communications Office
59 Camelot Drive
Nepean, Ontario K1A 0Y9 Canada
613-225-2342
www.cfia-acia.agr.ca

**Food & Wine from France**
215 Park Avenue South,
Suite 1600
New York, NY 10003
212-477-9800

**Food from Britain (North America)**
1037 East Putnam Avenue
Riverside, CT 06878
203-698-9000
www.ffbna.com

**Food from Sweden**
Box 5513
Storgatan 19
11485 Stockholm, Sweden
46-8-783-86-88
www.foodfromsweden.org

**Foods from Spain**
405 Lexington Avenue, 44th Floor
New York, NY 10174
212-661-2787

**German Agricultural Marketing Board-CMA**
P.O. Box 3239
Alexandria, VA 22302
703-931-2300
www.cmanorthamerica.org

**Greek Food and Wine Institute**
825 Eighth Avenue
New York, NY 10019
212-474-5588

**Italian Trade Commission**
499 Park Avenue
New York, NY 10022
212-980-1500
www.naturalmenteitaliano.com

**Ministry of Agriculture, Fisheries and Food**
Nobel House, 17 Smith Square
London SW 1P 3JR, England
20-7238-3000
www.maff.gov.uk

**New Zealand Trade Development Board**
12400 Wilshire Boulevard #1220
Los Angeles, CA 90025
310-707-5065
www.discovernz.com

**Quebec Trade Office**
20 Park Plaza, 4th Floor
Boston, MA 02116
617-948-2190
www.quebectrade.qc.ca

Tasting Australia
P.O. Box 274
Subiaco 6904, Western Australia
61-8-9388-8877
www.tasting-australia.com.au

Welsh Development Agency Food Directorate
Cardiff Business Technology Centre
Senghennydd Road
Cardiff CF24 4AY, Wales
29-2082-8982

## Professional Associations

American Association of Family and Consumer Sciences
1555 King Street
Alexandria, VA 22314
703-706-4600
www.aafcs.org

American Culinary Federation
P.O. Box 3466
St. Augustine, FL 32085
904-824-4468
www.acfchefs.org

American Dietetic Association
216 West Jackson Boulevard, Suite 800
Chicago, IL 60606
312-899-0040
www.eatright.org

American Institute of Wine and Food
304 West Liberty Street, Suite 201
Louisville, KY 40202
502-992-1022
www.aiwf.org

American School Food Service Association
700 South Washington Street, Suite 300
Alexandria, VA 22314
703-739-3900
www.asfsa.org

American Society of Journalists and Authors
1501 Broadway, Suite 302
New York, NY 10036
212-997-0947
www.asja.org

Association of Food Journalists
38309 Genesee Lake Road
Oconomowoc, WI 53066
414-965-3251
www.afjonline.com

Canadian Association of Journalists
St. Patrick's Building
Carleton University
1125 Colonel By Drive
Ottawa, Ontario K1S 5B6 Canada
613-526-8061
www.eagle.ca/caj/

**Circle of Wine Writers**
c/o Nicholas Faith, Treasurer
2 Cardozo Road
London N7 9RL, England
20-7609-5748
www.winedine.co.uk/radford/
cww.htm

**Consumer Science Business Professionals**
P.O. Box 4444
Pasco, WA 99302
509-547-5538
www.consumerexpert.com

**Food Media Club Australia**
745 Darling Street
Rozelle, Sydney, NSW 2039
Australia
61-2-9555-6039

**Foodservice Consultants Society International**
304 West Liberty Street, Suite 201
Louisville, KY 40202
502-583-3783
www.fcsi.org

**International Association of Culinary Professionals**
304 West Liberty Street, Suite 201
Louisville, KY 40202
502-581-9786
www.iacp.org

**International Foodservice Editorial Council**
P.O. Box 491
Hyde Park, NY 12538
914-229-6973
www.ifec-is-us.com

**International Inflight Food Service Association**
304 West Liberty Street, Suite 201
Louisville, KY 40202
502-583-3783
www.inflight.org

**Irish Food Writers Guild**
c/o Biddy White Lennon
Monckswood, Tinnehinch
Enniskerry, County Wicklow
Ireland
353-1-286-3853

**James Beard Foundation**
167 West 12th Street
New York, NY 10011
212-675-4984 or 800-36-BEARD
www.jamesbeard.org

**Les Dames d'Escoffier International**
P.O. Box 2103
Reston, VA 20195
703-716-5913

**National Association of College and University Food Services**
1405 South Harrison Road,
Suite 305
East Lansing, MI 48824
517-332-2494
www.nacufs.org

**National Writers Union**
113 University Place, 6th Floor
New York, NY 10003
212-254-0279
www.nwu.org

**New Zealand Guild of Food Writers**
P.O. Box 74 262
Market Road
Auckland, New Zealand

**Periodical Writers Association of Canada**
54 Wolseley Street, Suite 203
Toronto, Ontario, Canada
416-504-1645
www.pwac.ca

**Public Relations Society of America**
Food and Beverage Section
33 Irving Place
New York, NY 10003
212-995-2230
www.prsa.org

**Research Chefs Association**
304 West Liberty Street, Suite 201
Louisville, KY 40202
502-992-0438
www.researchchef.org

**Retail Bakers Association**
14239 Park Center Drive
Laurel, MD 20707
301-725-2149
www.rbanet.com

**Society for Food Service Management**
304 West Liberty Street, Suite 201
Louisville, KY 40202
502-583-3783
www.sfm-online.org

**United Kingdom Guild of Food Writers**
48 Crabtree Lane
London SW6 6LW, England
20-7610-1180
www.gfw.co.uk

**Women Chefs and Restaurateurs**
304 West Liberty Street, Suite 201
Louisville, KY 40202
502-581-0300
www.chefnet.com/wcr

**Writers Union of Canada**
24 Ryerson Avenue
Toronto, Ontario M5T 2P3
Canada
416-703-8982
www.writersunion.ca/

# Food Seminars and Courses

Classes on food and recipe writing are sometimes offered at adult education programs, community colleges, and cooperative extension centers, as well as by professional associations. Check your local news outlets for information about such classes.

The following schools, colleges, and symposiums provide degree or non-degree programs on different aspects of food writing, editing, styling, and photography.

**Boston University**
Special Programs
808 Commonwealth Avenue
Boston, MA 02215
617-353-9852
www.bu.edu

**California Culinary Academy**
625 Polk Street
San Francisco, CA 94102
415-292-8280

**Culinary Institute of America**
433 Albany Post Road
Hyde Park, NY 12538
914-451-1286 or 800-888-7850
www.ciachef.edu

**Culinary Institute of America at Greystone**
2555 Main Street
St. Helena, CA 94574
707-967-0600 or 800-333-9242
www.ciachef.edu

**Food on Film ®**
(food styling and food photography seminar)
Twin Cities Home Economists in Business
c/o Nancy Iverson
7227 West Fish Lake Road
Maple Grove, MN 55311
612-420-4552

**Johnson & Wales University**
1 Washington Avenue
Providence, RI 02905
401-598-1858
www.jwu.edu

**Mississippi University for Women**
Culinary Arts Institute
Box W-1639
Shattuck Hall
Columbus, MS 39701
877-462-8439 ext. 7472
www.muw.edu/interdisc

**New York University**
Department of Nutrition and Food Studies
35 West 4th Street, 10th Floor
New York, NY 10012
212-998-5580
www.nyu.edu

**New School University**
66 West 12th Street
New York, NY 10011
212-255-4141
www.nsu.newschool.edu

**Oxford Symposium on Food & Cookery**
Jane E. Levi, Organiser
101 Millennium Tower
65 Hopton Street
London SE1 9JL, England
44-7768-891-021
www.members.tripod.com/rdeh

**Symposium for Professional Food Writers at The Greenbrier**
The Greenbrier
300 West Main Street
White Sulphur Spring, WV 24986
304-536-7892
www.greenbrier.com

THE STYLE MANUALS AND GUIDES listed here are proprietary material shared by the companies for this book. They are not available to the public, hence there is no listing of author or date of publication.

*Author Guidelines,* Williams-Sonoma Kitchen Library.

*The Betty Crocker Stylebook,* General Mills Inc.

*Consumer Service Recipe Style Manual,* The Pillsbury Company.

*Cookbook Guidelines,* Simon & Schuster.

*Kraft General Foods Recipe Style Manual,* Kraft General Foods.

*Recipe Editing Rules for Jerome Foods, Inc.*, The Turkey Store.

*Recipe Guidelines*, Chronicle Books.

*Recipe Guidelines for Contributors*, Food & Wine.

*Recipe Style*, Chicago Tribune.

*Recipe Write-Up Procedure*, Heinz Consumer Test Kitchens.

*Southern Living Recipe Editing Style Book*, Southern Living.

*Style Guide*, Better Homes & Gardens.

*Style Guide*, Canadian Living.

*Style Guidelines for Woman's Day Food Department*, Woman's Day.

*Style Manual*, The Wimmer Companies.

*Writer Guidelines*, Country Home.

In addition to the books listed here, some of the books listed in Chapter Fourteen, "Resources," were consulted for information.

# A

inexact amounts and, 71
for large-quantity recipes, 113, 126
metric, *see* Metric system
multiple, 8, 19
for pan sizes, 263
recipe testing and, 113, 114
of temperature, *see* Temperature
Meats, 75–76
doneness tests for, 75
food safety and, 128
organizations promoting, 283–284
purchasing information for, 245
recipe testing and, 119–120
Meter, 193
Method, *see* Preparation instructions
Metric system, 191–201
adapting U.S. recipes to, 193–195
conversion charts for, 197–200
conversion formulas for, 194–195
in dual-measurement recipes,
191–192, 196
information source for, 197
terminology for, 193, 195–196
Microwave recipes
style sheet for, 94–96
testing, 124–125
Milk, 150
purchasing information for, 236
Milliliter, 193, 195, 197
Millimeter, 195
Misspelled words, 165–179
Mixers, 76
Mixing procedures, recipe testing
and, 121
Mold sizes, 264
Muffin pan sizes, 265
Mushrooms, 77, 151–152, 182

## N

Names of recipes, *see* Recipe titles
Notes
at end of recipe, 24

headnotes, 10, 14, 22, 116
Numbers
fractions, 64–65, 77
in ingredient lists, 16–17, 77–78
spelling out, 77–78
for steps in preparation, 22
Nut(s), 34, 78
organizations promoting, 284
purchasing information for,
249–250
toasting, 18, 78
Nutrition analysis, 203–208
Nutrition information, 9, 24–25

## O

Oils
organizations promoting, 285, 286
purchasing information for, 237
vegetable, 74, 91, 160–161, 237
Olives, 153
Omelet pan size, 267
Onions, 153–154
*Optional/if desired,* 71
Optional ingredients, 17, 71
Orange juice/peel, 78
*Organic,* 79
Oven cooking, *see* Baked goods;
Baking utensils; Roasting
Oven temperature, 79, 82, 122
metric-U.S. conversion chart for,
198
*Overnight,* 79

## P

Package directions, 80, 115
Package sizes, metric-U.S. conversion
chart for, 200
Pan sizes, 263–267
of baking pans, 122, 126, 264, 265,
266, 267

mixing procedures and, 121
for oven cooking, 121–122
for pasta, rice, grains, and breads,
118–119
for professional or large-quantity
recipes, 112–113, 125–127
for stove-top cooking, 122–123
target audience and, 109–110
tracking sheet for, 113, 133
worksheet for, 111, 131–132
Recipe titles, 15
consumer preferences regarding, 7
Recipe users
beginning, testing recipes for, 127
culinary illiteracy among, 5–6
experience of, 3–4
importance of knowing, 3–4,
109–110
recipe format preferences of, 7–9
Record keeping, for recipe testing,
111–112, 113, 131–133
Rectangular baking pan sizes, 265
Red pepper, 83
Reference books
basic, 273
on canning, 130
on food history, 278
on foods and beverages, 274–275
general cookbooks as, 275–276
on international cuisines, 277–278
large-quantity cookbooks as, 278
on recipe writing, 278–279
recommendations for, 271–272
specialty books as, 276–277
on writing and style, 273–274
Refrigeration, food safety and,
128–129
Remaining ingredients, 83–84
Rereading, 28–29
*Reserve/reserving/reserved*, 84–85, 87
Rice, 156
organizations promoting, 285
recipe testing and, 118–119

Roasting
pan sizes for, 122, 265
testing recipes for, 121–122
Room temperature, 85
Round baking pan sizes, 265

# S
Safety
with eggs, 59–60
of marinades, 123–124
with microwave cooking, 95–96
with plants, 59, 129
recipes for children and, 127
recipe testing and, 128–130
Salad oil, *see* Vegetable oil
Salt, 86, 157
Sample recipes, 96–107
for children, 104–105
for large quantities, 105–107
Sauce(s), 86
organizations promoting, 285
Saucepan/saucepot sizes, 86, 123,
266
Scoop sizes, 268
Seafood, *see also* Fish
food safety and, 128
organizations promoting, 286
recipe testing and, 119–120
Seasonings, *see also* Herbs; Spices;
*specific seasonings*
organizations promoting, 285, 286
Secondary recipes, 21
Seminars, 294–295
Sentence structure, 25–26
Servings, *see* Yield
*Set aside*, 84, 87
Shellfish, 62–63, *see also* Seafood
doneness tests for, 63
food safety and, 129
purchasing information for,
238–239
Shortening, vegetable, 91–92

U.S. Department of Agriculture,
Food and Nutrition
Information Center of,
204–205
U.S. government agencies, 204–205,
290
Utensils, *see* Equipment

## V

Variations, 24
Vegetable(s)
organizations promoting, 287–288
purchasing information for,
254–261
recipe testing and, 118
Vegetable oil, 91, 160–161
purchasing information for, 237
Vegetable oil spread, 74
Vegetable shortening, 43, 91–92
purchasing information for, 237
Vinegar, 49, 161
Volume measurements, metric-U.S.
conversion chart for, 197

## W

Water, 92
Web sites
on food and recipes, 279
recipes for, 217, 226–229
Weight measurements, metric-U.S.
conversion chart for, 198
Wheat, 162
Wine(s), 92–93
capitalization of, 93
curdling due to, 56
Worksheet, for recipe testing, 111,

131–132
Writing style, 4–5, 13–29
consumer preferences regarding,
7–9
for divided ingredients, 20–21
grammar and punctuation in,
25–28
for headnotes, 14
for ingredient lists, 15–17
manuals and guides for, 24,
297–298
for measurements, 19–20
for notes at ends of recipes, 24
for nutrition information, 24–25
personal, 10–11
for preparation instructions, 17–19,
21–24
for recipe names, 15
reference books on, 273–274
for remaining ingredients, 83
for reserved ingredients, 84
for secondary recipes, 21
style sheets and, 5, 6–7
for variations, 24
for yield, 24

## Y

Yeast, 93, 163, 245
Yield
for large-quantity recipes, 127
specification of, 9, 24, 36, 52,
93–94, 114

## Z

Zest, 163

# About the Authors

BARBARA GIBBS OSTMANN is a food writer with more than 25 years experience in newspaper, magazine, and cookbook writing and editing. Since 1993 she has written a weekly food feature for the *New York Times* Regional Newspaper Group. She was food editor of the *St. Louis Post-Dispatch,* in St. Louis, Missouri, from 1975 to 1990, and food columnist for the *Post-Dispatch* magazine in 1991 and 1992. She was an assistant professor and the coordinator of the Agricultural Journalism program at the University of Missouri-Columbia from 1991 to 1993.

Ostmann is a past president of the Association of Food Journalists (formerly Newspaper Food Editors and Writers Association), past chair of the Food Writing and Publishing Section of the International Association of Culinary Professionals, and founding president of the St. Louis Culinary Society.

Ostmann received the first Columbia College Professional Achievement Award in 1988; and the first Joseph Pulitzer Jr. Fellowship in 1989. She is listed in several editions of *Who's Who* and is a member of Les Dames d'Escoffier. Ostmann has won numerous writing awards, including Vesta Awards for excellence in reporting news about food, Golden Carnation Awards for nutrition writing, the Association of Food Journalists awards for food feature writing, and the National Federation of Press Women awards for food and travel writing.

Ostmann has a bachelor of journalism and master of arts in journalism from the University of Missouri-Columbia.

In addition to the 11 cookbooks Ostmann has coedited with Jane L. Baker, she compiled and edited *The Best Recipes Cookbook* for the *St. Louis Post-Dispatch* and has contributed to several cookbooks.

J ANE L. BAKER is a home economist with more than 30 years experience in food writing, editing, and recipe development. She currently is marketing director for the Cherry Marketing Institute (CMI), a national promotion organization for cherries. At CMI, Baker develops promotions and publicity for cherries; she is responsible for creating, writing, and editing cherry recipes for consumers and food service operators.

Prior to joining CMI in 1989, Baker was food editor of the *Phoenix Gazette*, in Phoenix, Arizona, for 14 years. She also was a staff home economist in the test kitchens at Borden, Inc., where she helped develop a recipe-writing manual for the company, and a publicity writer for the H. J. Heinz Co. Baker has a bachelor of science degree in commercial foods with a minor in journalism from Ohio University, Athens, Ohio.

Baker is a past president of the Association of Food Journalists (formerly Newspaper Food Editors and Writers Association) and past chair of the Arizona and Michigan Home Economists in Business. Baker received the 1993 Michigan Business Home Economist of the Year Award. As food editor, she received numerous honors, including Golden Carnation Awards for excellence in reporting nutrition news, Vesta Awards for outstanding food reporting, and the Arizona Dietetic Association Recognition Award.

She is a member of the International Association of Culinary Professionals, the Public Relations Society of America, the International Foodservice Editorial Council, and the American School Food Service Association.

In addition to the 11 cookbooks she has co-edited with Barbara Gibbs Ostmann, Baker wrote a syndicated newspaper series on children's cooking in the 1980s.